JAMES FLETCHER-WATSON'S

Watercolour Secrets

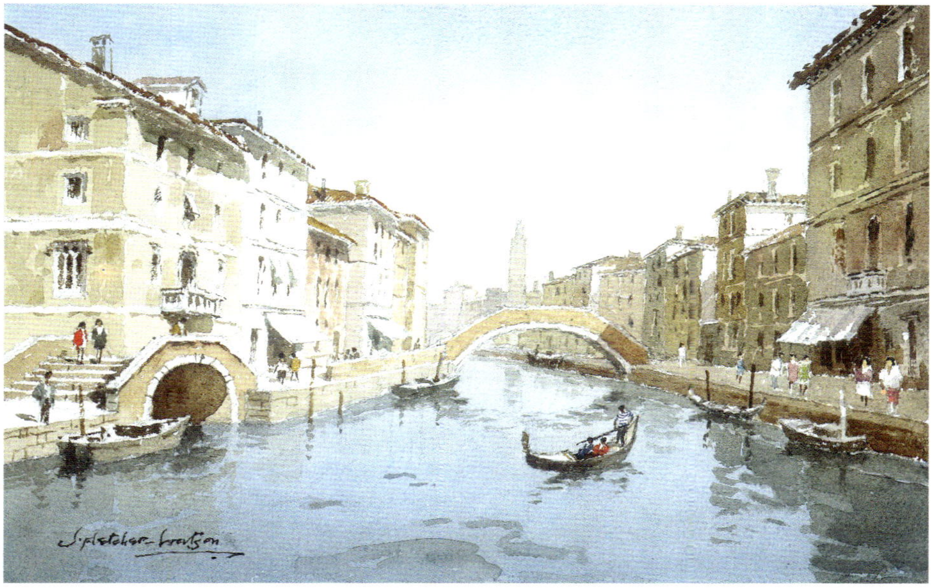

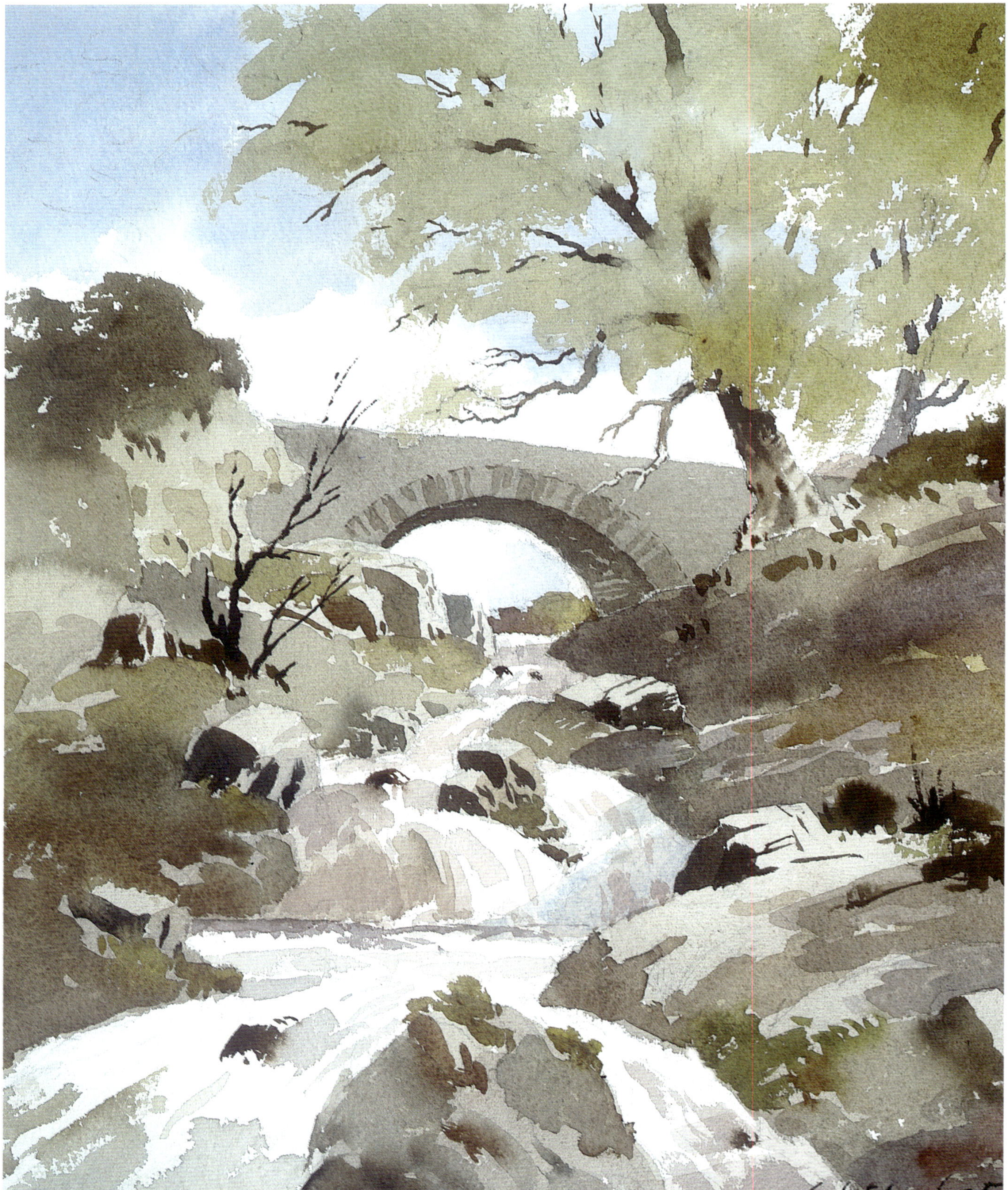

JAMES FLETCHER-WATSON'S

Watercolour Secrets

B T Batsford Limited, London

First Published as *The Secret of Watercolour* in 1997

This revised edition first published in 2002
Reprinted 2003

Illustrations by James Fletcher-Watson

ISBN 0 7134 8757 7

A CIP catalogue record for this book is available from the British Library.

Typeset in Bembo
Printed by Kyodo in Singapore
for the publishers

B T Batsford
The Chrysalis Building
Bramley Road
London W10 6SP
www.batsford.com

A member of **Chrysalis** Books plc

Distributed in the United States and Canada by Sterling Publishing Co.,
387 Park Avenue South, New York, NY 10016, U.S.A.

CONTENTS

Dedicated to my dear wife, Gill,
whose unfailing help and encouragement is a tremendous
support to me in all my endeavours.

INTRODUCTION

In this new book you will find I have introduced quite a number of new pictures, which have not been exhibited or published before. This has given me the opportunity to introduce some new subjects and different techniques. I am continually meeting people who have just taken up watercolour painting and who are in need of practical guidance. This book, *Watercolour Secrets* will, I hope, give them the help which they require to improve their skills. It will also, I hope, be of use to more advanced painters who need encouragement to add to the quality of their sketches and pictures.

Some people feel that watercolour is very difficult, but it is often the case that they have not given enough thought to the subject before they start. Painting is a constant challenge to produce the perfect picture, and studying composition, as described in Chapter 2, is the basis of all good landscapes. The great masters like Turner, Cotman, De Wint and Bonington showed us the way and it is right that we should follow in their footsteps, not copying but receiving inspiration from them. Constable was another genius and, although essentially an oil painter, he was one of the greatest interpreters of the landscape with his simplified treatment of trees, skies, water reflections and distant views.

My aim is to carry on the torch, encouraging today's painters to express the beauty of the landscape simply and effectively. I hope this book will inspire many people to paint with enthusiasm and achieve successful works in watercolour. It is a very lovely medium to use, especially if you can master the technique of creating transparent washes, one of the hallmarks of a good watercolour.

Chapter 1

EQUIPMENT

In this chapter, I will outline the various watercolour painting materials it is advisable to have. Whether you are an outdoor landscape painter, an indoor still life painter, or someone unable to paint out-of-doors because of ill health, you will still require certain basic items, such as paints, a selection of brushes, some pencils and paper. If you are a newcomer to painting, it is very easy to go into an art supply shop and buy the wrong type of equipment or perhaps some unnecessarily expensive items that you do not really require. Even worse, a well-meaning aunt may give you a present of a large paintbox containing entirely the wrong selection of colours!

There is also the question of where best to do your painting. A lot of people have time to paint only in the evenings or at weekends and the kitchen table might be the only suitable place for painting. I found this problem when I first started out and I know what a nuisance it is having to clear up after each painting session.

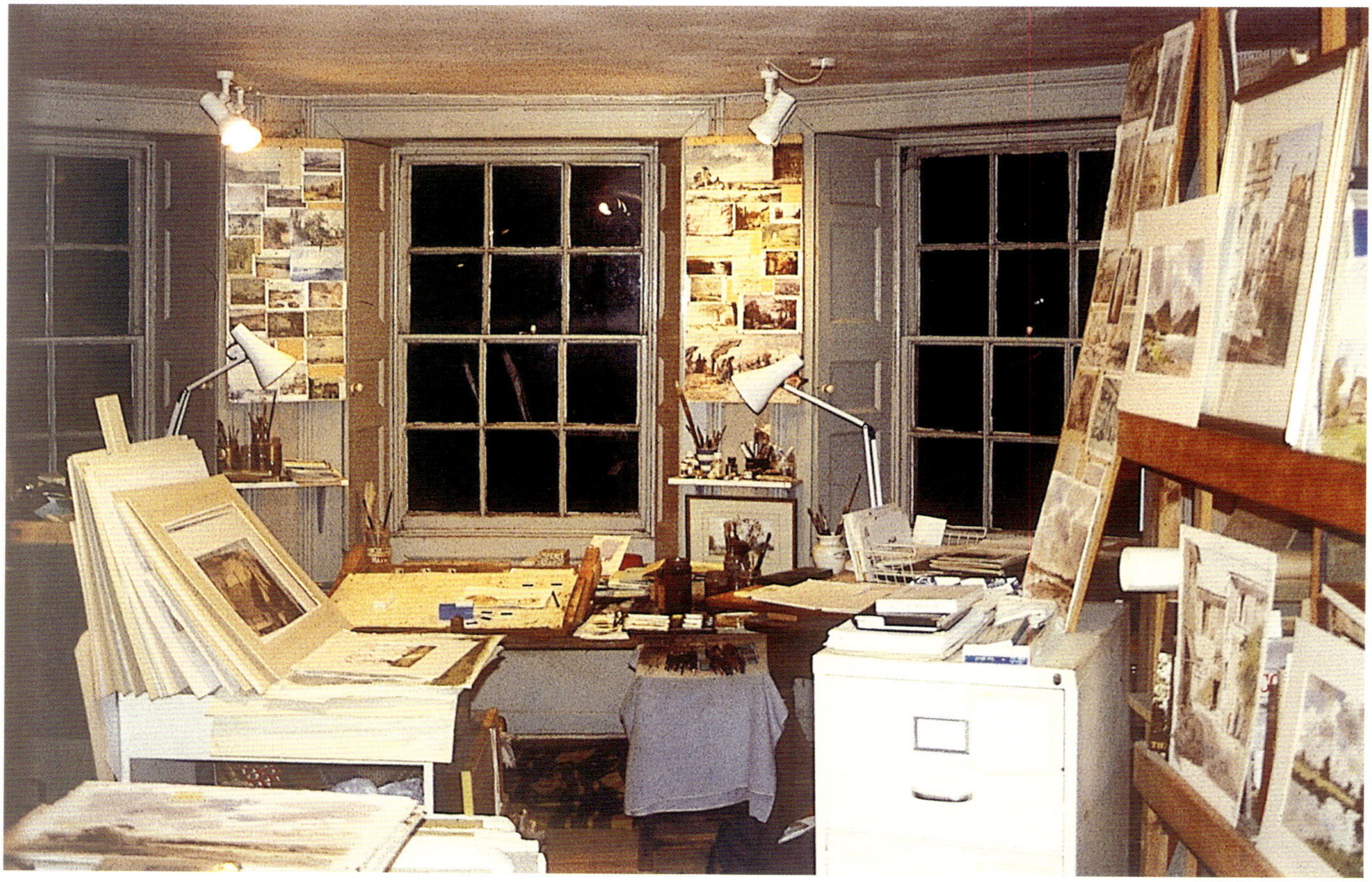

Figure 1
The Studio showing north-facing windows and additional artificial lights.

Of course you should ideally have a room you can devote to painting. **Figure 1** shows a general view of my studio, which has three large windows facing north. This is preferable, as you do not want sunlight and shadows lying across your painting board or easel. You will notice two anglepoise lamps, which are fitted with daylight bulbs. These, combined with the four ceiling lights, which are not daylight, give me an extremely good artificial light to work under. It is a great advantage to be able to continue painting after dark.

Figure 2 shows my paintbox, brushes and water jars on the right side of my work-table, where they are always ready for immediate use. Before I actually start painting, my first act is to soften up all the watercolours in their pans with a stiff oil painter's brush that had been held under the hot tap. This is a very useful tip, as colours have a nasty habit of going hard when not used for a day or two, and it is very bad for good sable brushes to work on a hard colour that has not been softened.

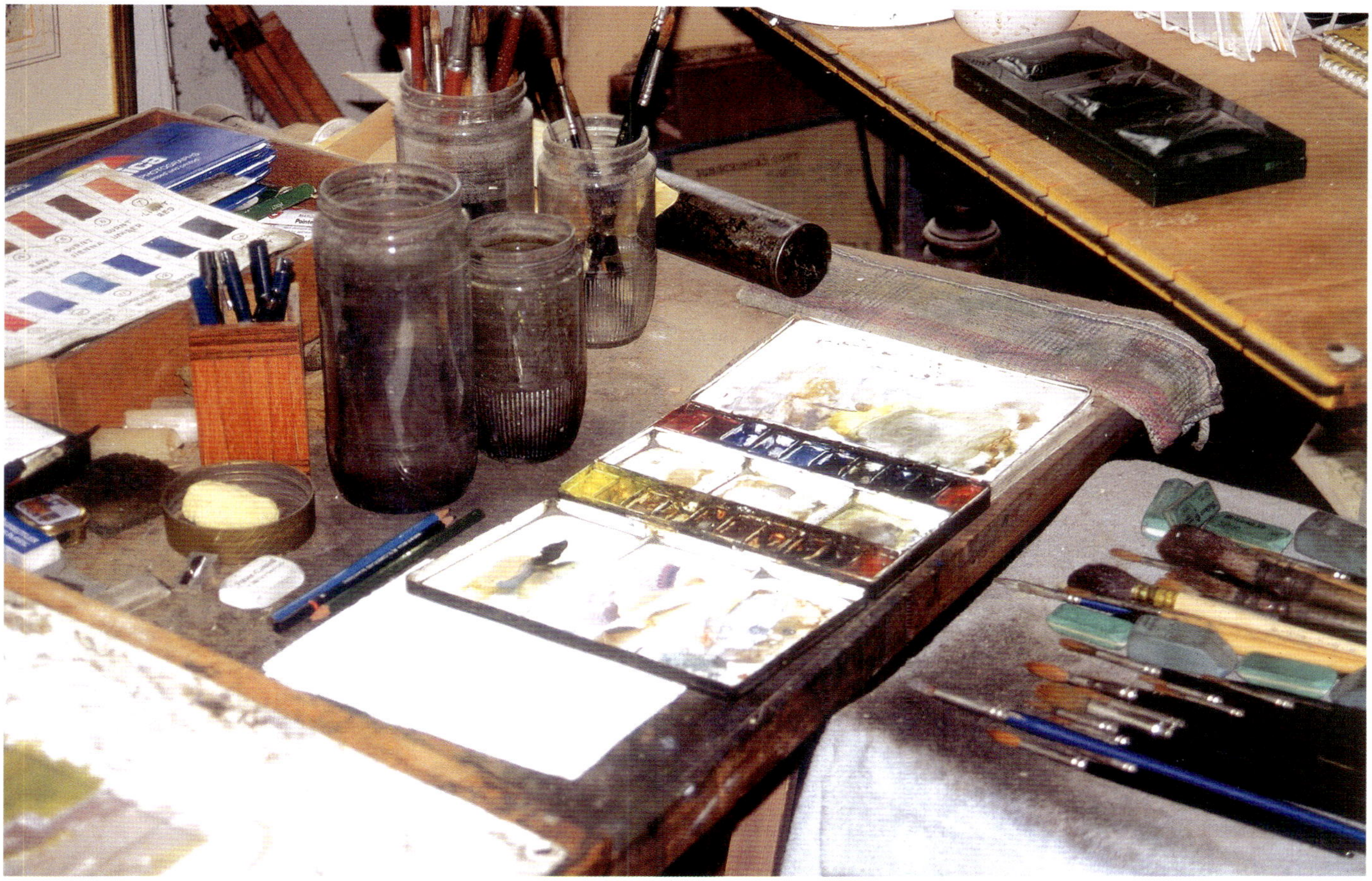

Figure 2
My paint box with mixing dishes.

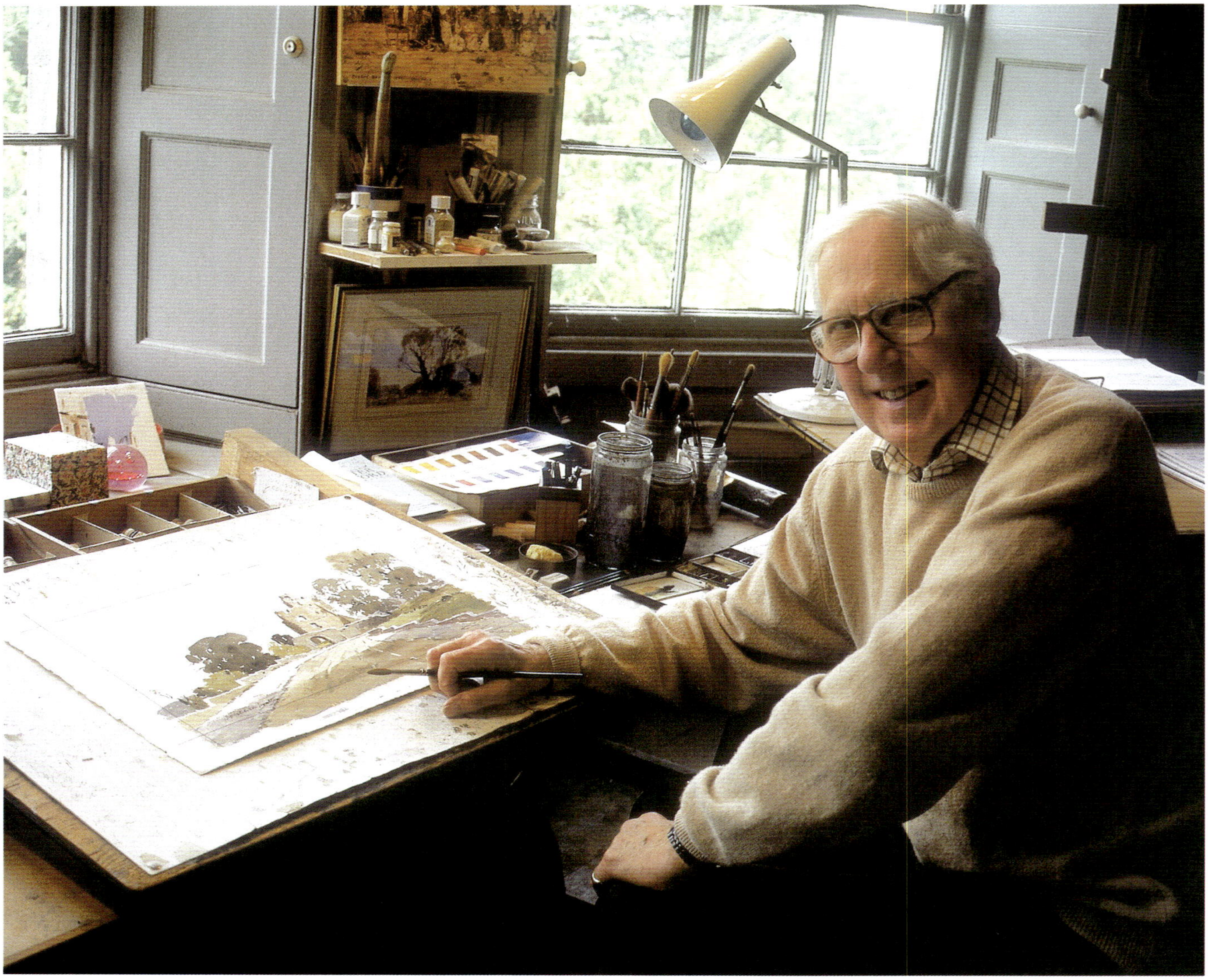

Figure 3
At work in my studio.

Figure 3 shows me at work at my large board in the studio window. This board is resting at a slight angle and is an ideal height for painting when sitting on a chair.

The view from the window takes in a bit of garden and plenty of trees and fields with Cotswold hills in the distance, and a wide expanse of sky. Although I know the view well, I still find it to be a continuous inspiration, for it reflects the changing colours of spring, summer, autumn and winter, and is especially useful for observing changing skyscapes. When painting in the studio, I often find that the view of the sky from the window is an ideal subject.

As regards the actual range of materials the watercolour painter needs, I have dealt with this at some length in my previous books, but I would like to mention them once again briefly here.

PENCILS

HB, B and 2B are sufficient for drawing a subject that is to become a watercolour picture, while 4B, 5B and 6B are useful for doing pencil drawings in a sketchbook, to be referred to at a later date when making a watercolour. Throughout the book, you will see various examples of such sketches.

ERASER

Good makes are the Factis or Faber-Castell pencil erasers, which stay flexible longer than most types and are available in art shops.

BRUSHES

Numbers 1, 3, 5, 7 and 10 will give you all the brushes you require for any size of picture. Sable brushes are best, but are expensive. Synthetic brushes made by most art firms are quite adequate. I also have a No. 8 squirrel mop brush at hand as well, which is useful for doing a loose watercolour sketch or painting skies or trees.

Figure 4
Preparatory sketch showing use of 4B and 6B pencils.

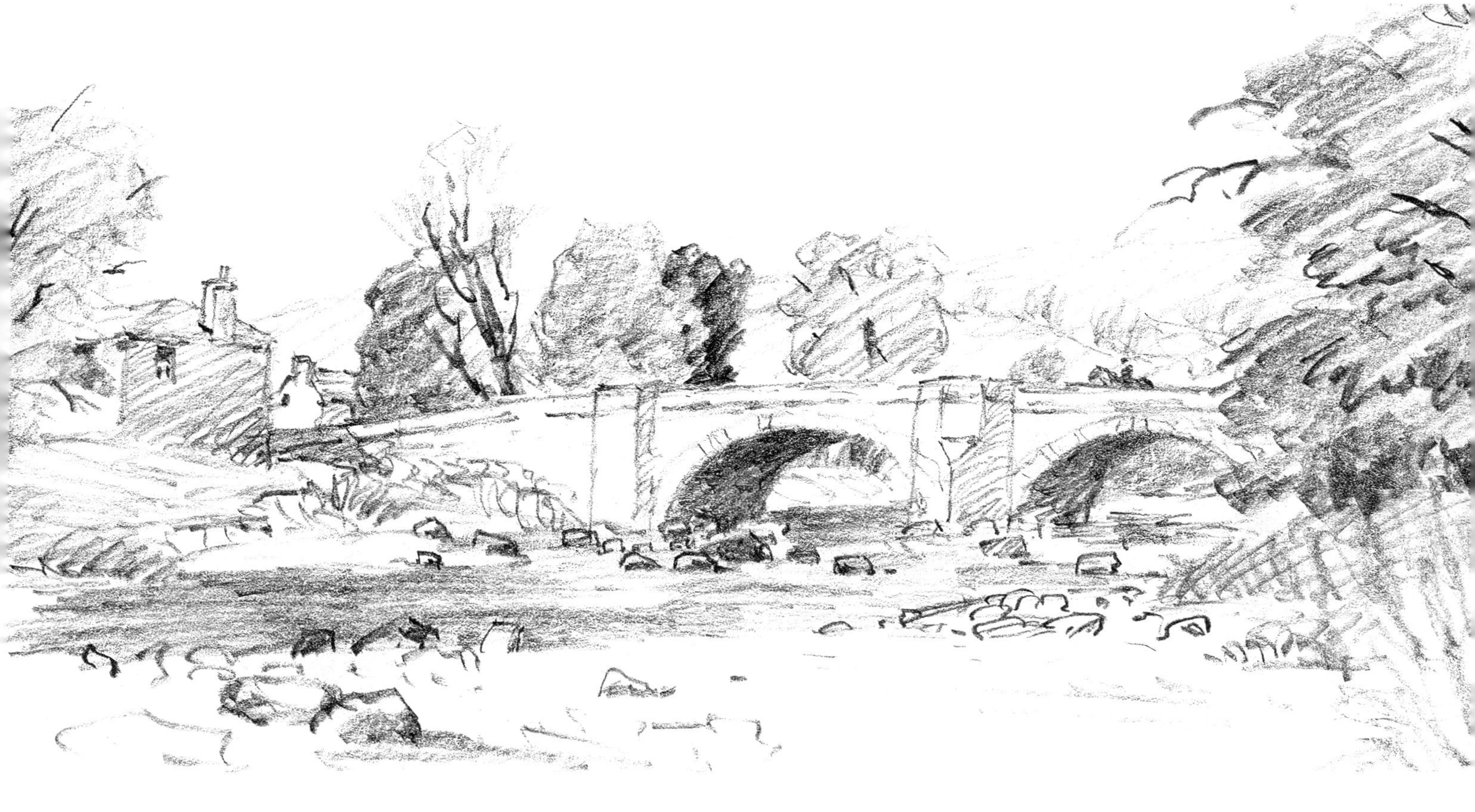

PAINTS

I tend to use tubes of colour to replenish my pans as the colour gets used up. My list of 14 colours is given below.

1. Cadmium Lemon
2. Cadmium Yellow
3. Raw Sienna
4. Raw Umber
5. Burnt Sienna
6. Burnt Umber
7. Light Red
8. Indian Red
9. Rose Madder
10. Cobalt Blue
11. Cerulean Blue
12. French Ultramarine
13. Winsor Blue
14. Payne's Gray

There are several brands of watercolour paint and you can take your choice. I have always preferred Winsor & Newton colours. This company has recently introduced a number of new colours, but the colours mentioned in this book remain part of its standard list.

PAINT BOX

I like using the old style of box that holds individual pans and has ample mixing palettes in the folding lid. Various sizes are available, but I find the bigger the better (see **figure 2**).

PAPER

A great many types are sold in all good art shops. My favourite makes are Winsor & Newton watercolour paper, Whatman paper, Saunders-Waterford, and Bockingford papers. I recommend the latter for a beginner, as it is the least expensive and can be obtained in single large sheets or in book form. All the papers mentioned here are made in different weights (thicknesses) and have different textures ('Rough' or 'NOT' – i.e., smooth). You must experiment yourself and discover which you like best. I use all the above depending on the subject and effect I aim to achieve.

SKETCHBOOKS

Daler books of cartridge paper are the ones I like best and are ideal for lead-pencil sketching. They come in all sizes from very small to quite large.

CHAIR OR STOOL

I find a chair or stool ideal for outdoor painting. Many makes are available – I prefer a comfortable one with a back as I will often work in this way for several hours at a time. I also like a low chair so that I can reach my paints on the ground by my side.

DRAWING BOARD

A piece of very stiff cardboard is good for clipping your paper to with large paper clips. This is lighter than a wooden board and easier to carry – quite a consideration when you are loaded up with your outdoor sketching gear!

EASEL

There are many types of easel on the market and it is important to select one that is not too heavy to carry when it is folded. It is a very personal choice and can be quite an expensive investment so choose carefully. I tend not to use my easel very often.

WATER

A large glass or plastic jar with a watertight screw top is ideal as a container for water.

ADDITIONAL ITEMS

A small sponge is used for cleaning your palette or wiping out paint on your picture. A brush case for protecting your brushes is also useful. Mine is a tube with a removable top at the open end. Blotting paper is important for emergencies during painting, while you will find a penknife very handy for sharpening pencils and for scratching out during the painting process. Finally, a canvas carrying bag for holding all your equipment is helpful.

Figure 5
Colour chart.

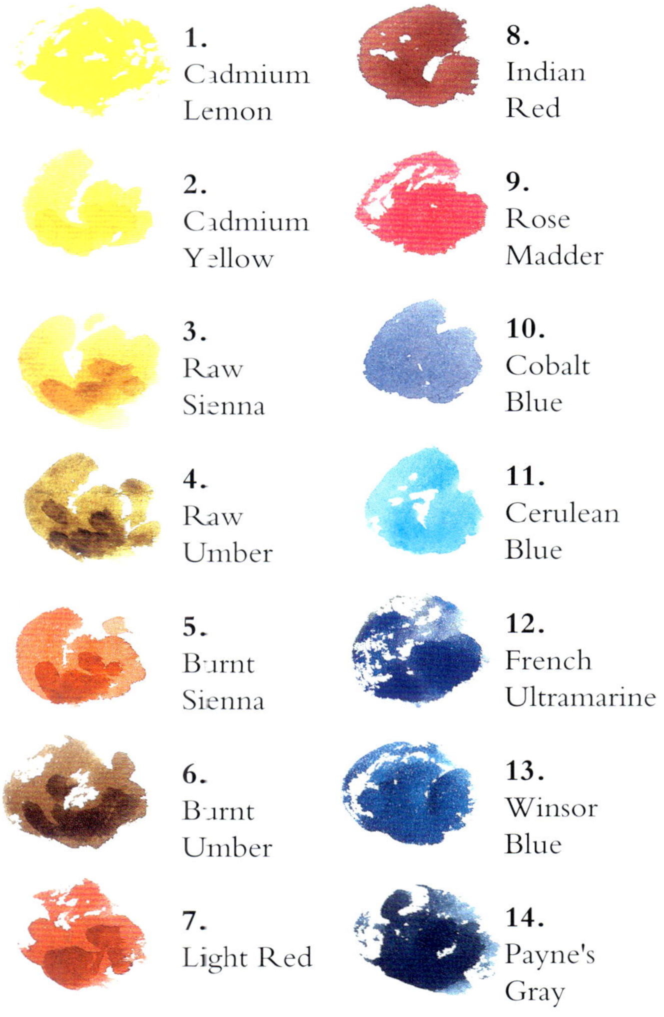

Chapter 2

COMPOSITION

I am starting off with this chapter on composition because it is the first thing you should consider when choosing a landscape, townscape or even a still life subject. My motto is always – if a subject will not make a good composition, then don't paint it!

Let us now take a look at **figure 6**, *Seathwaite, Cumbria.* This picture shows a simple and satisfactory composition of a mountain scene in the Lake District with a small white farmhouse as the centre of interest.

The diagram in **figure 6a** shows you the main points I considered before painting the picture. The farmhouse (1) itself could have been in any position, but I chose to have it just over one-third from the right side. The high mountain (2) on the left acted as a counterbalance to the farmhouse and was a strong feature because of its height and strength of tone. When planning the picture, I purposely arranged the main patch of blue sky (3), to be in the top right position to give a further counterbalance of less strength but still of importance. You always have the freedom to adjust a cloudy sky to suit your purpose, rather than slavishly copying it.

Figure 6
Seathwaite, Cumbria, England. 324 × 476mm (12¾ x 18¾in)

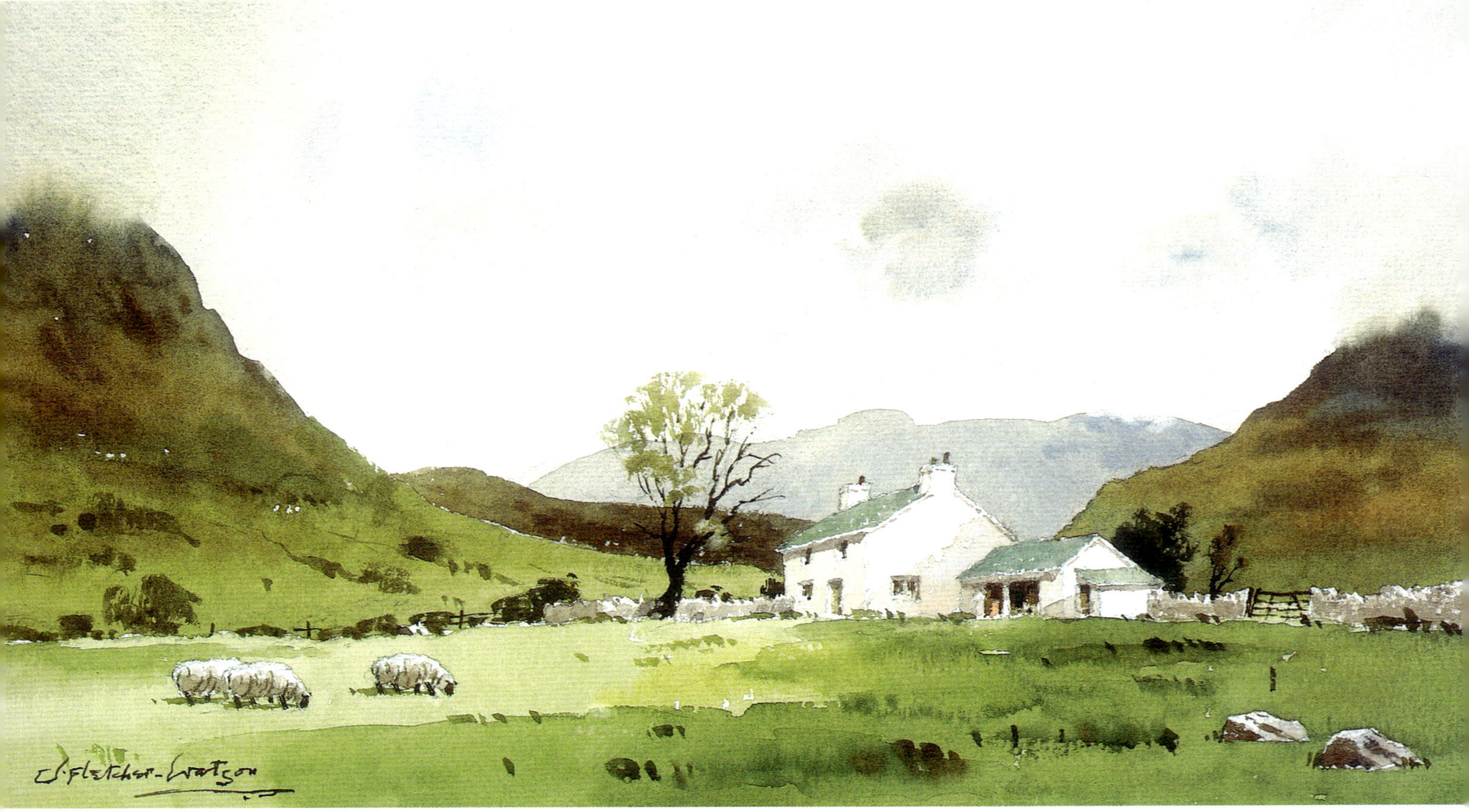

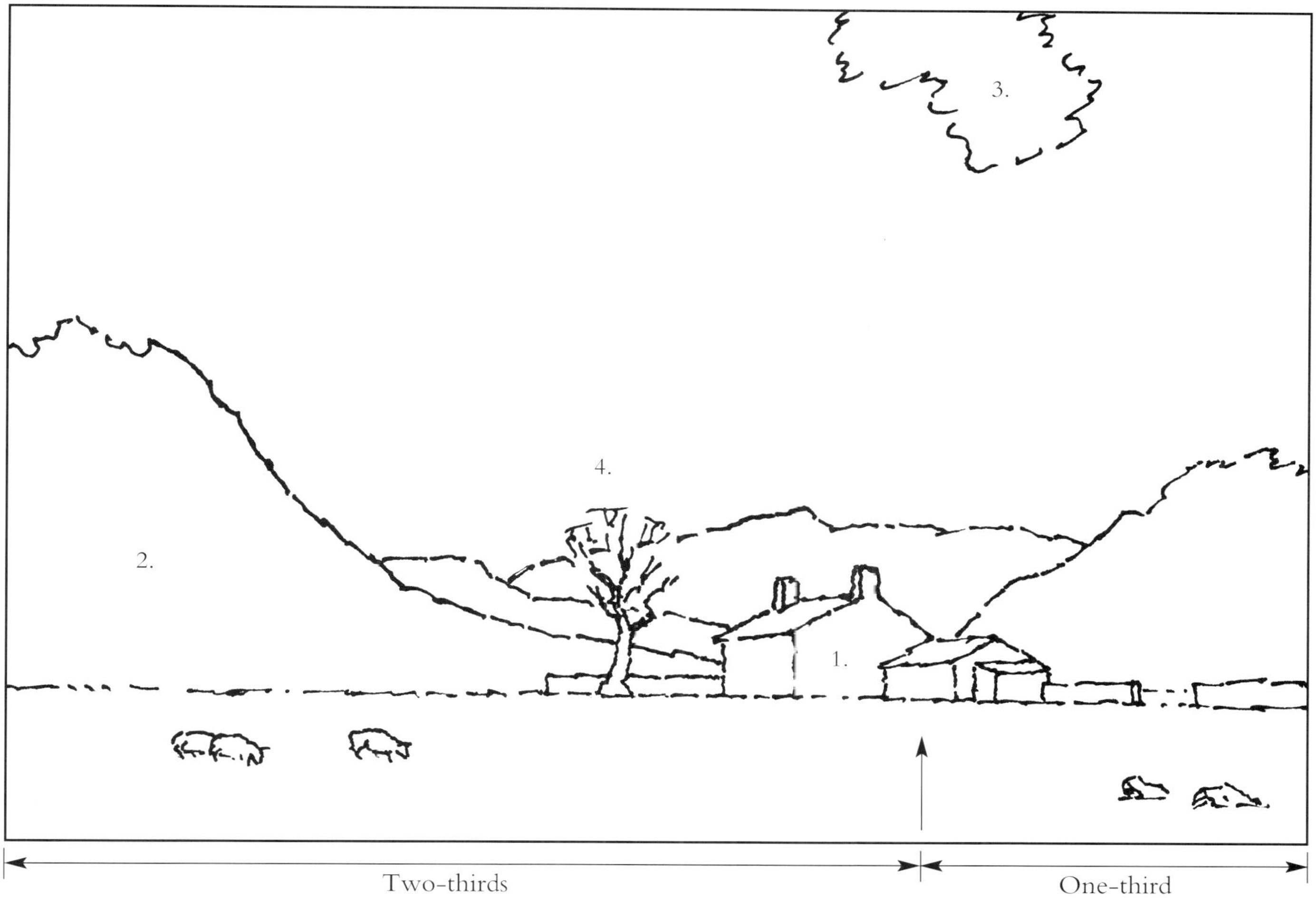

Figure 6a
Compositional Sketch.

Another dominant feature is the tree (4). This is just to the left of centre and gives a useful vertical feature, contrasting well with the horizontal and sloping lines of the fields and hills.

Looking in more detail at **figure 6**, other elements of the composition are the three sheep on the left and the two rocks in the right foreground. Neither of these actually featured in the picture when I painted it on the spot, but there were rocks and sheep visible elsewhere in the landscape. Artist's licence plays a part in landscape painting and it may be used, within reason. Note the distant mountains, which are painted blue-grey. They are a tremendous help in giving the picture the third dimension of distance. Finally, the thin stretch of low hill seen in the centre and going behind and to the left of the house is of great importance. It has a very dark cloud shadow on it, which gives punctuation to the whole picture. Also, the foreground cloud shadow on the grass helps to give depth and perspective to the overall composition.

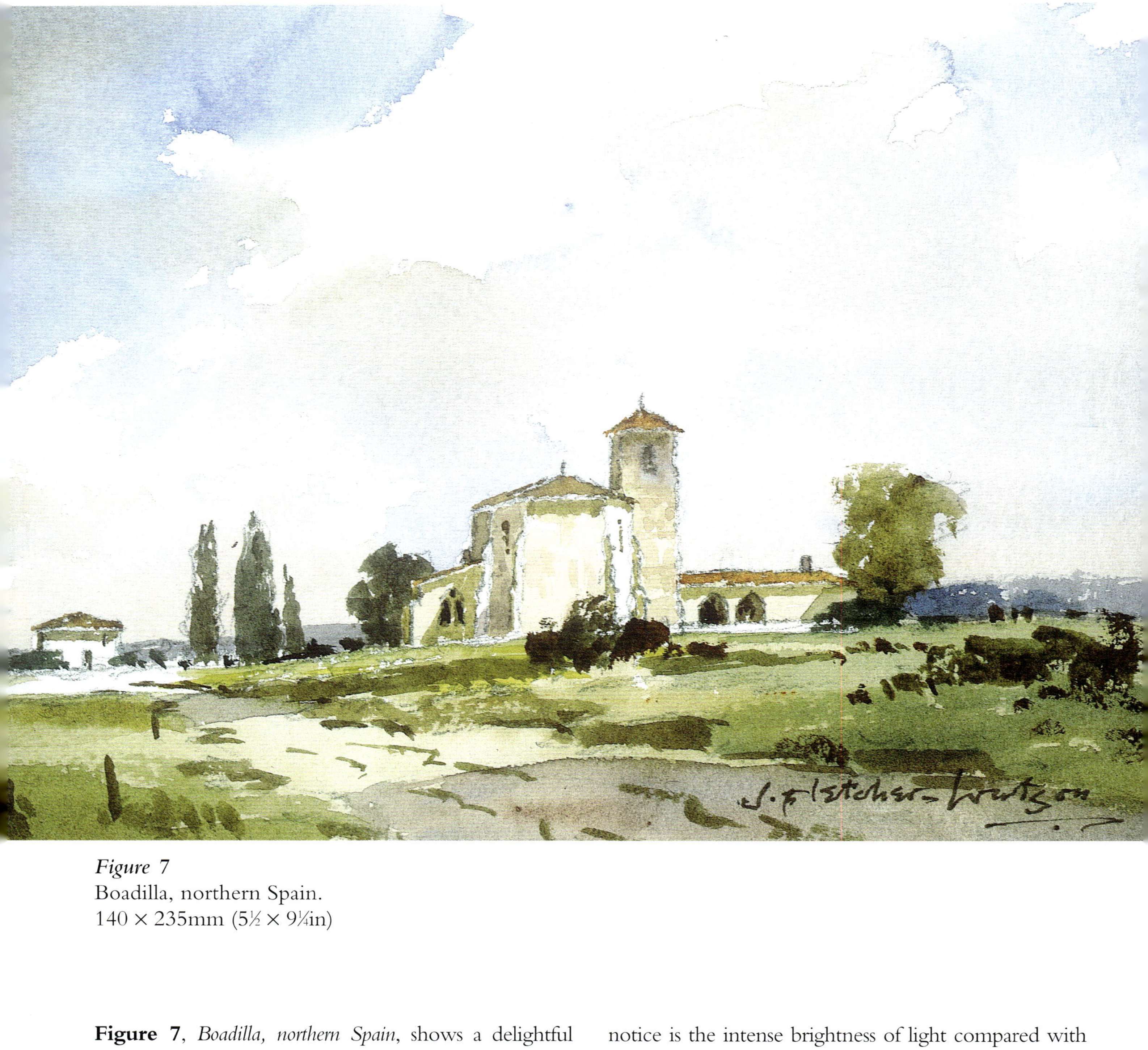

Figure 7
Boadilla, northern Spain.
140 × 235mm (5½ × 9¼in)

Figure 7, *Boadilla, northern Spain*, shows a delightful small village with a large church, which my wife and I came across during a recent painting trip. This is rather a different example of composition. The first thing you notice is the intense brightness of light compared with the last picture of the Lake District. The hot Spanish sun was glaring down on the scene, causing strong shadows to be cast on the buildings and ground.

If you look now at **figure 8**, you will see I have shown in a diagrammatic sketch the striking *vertical* forms that contrast well with the equally pronounced *horizontal* lines.

The main *verticals* are the body of the church and the tower, the two cypress trees to the left and the large tree on the right. The horizontals are the distant line of blue hills running the full width of the picture, the cloister building on the right side of the church, the various cloud shadows lying across the landscape, and the edges of the road, which are almost *horizontal* and carry the eye into the picture, also giving a useful perspective. The sky echoes the perspective of the road with sweeping grey and white clouds and some strong patches of blue.

Tone values are an important part of composition and here we have the strong dark green of the cypress trees, the tree behind the left-hand wing of the church and the low shrubs immediately in front of the church. These dark items help to intensify the sunlight and generally give a crisp quality to the composition.

Figure 8
Compositional sketch.

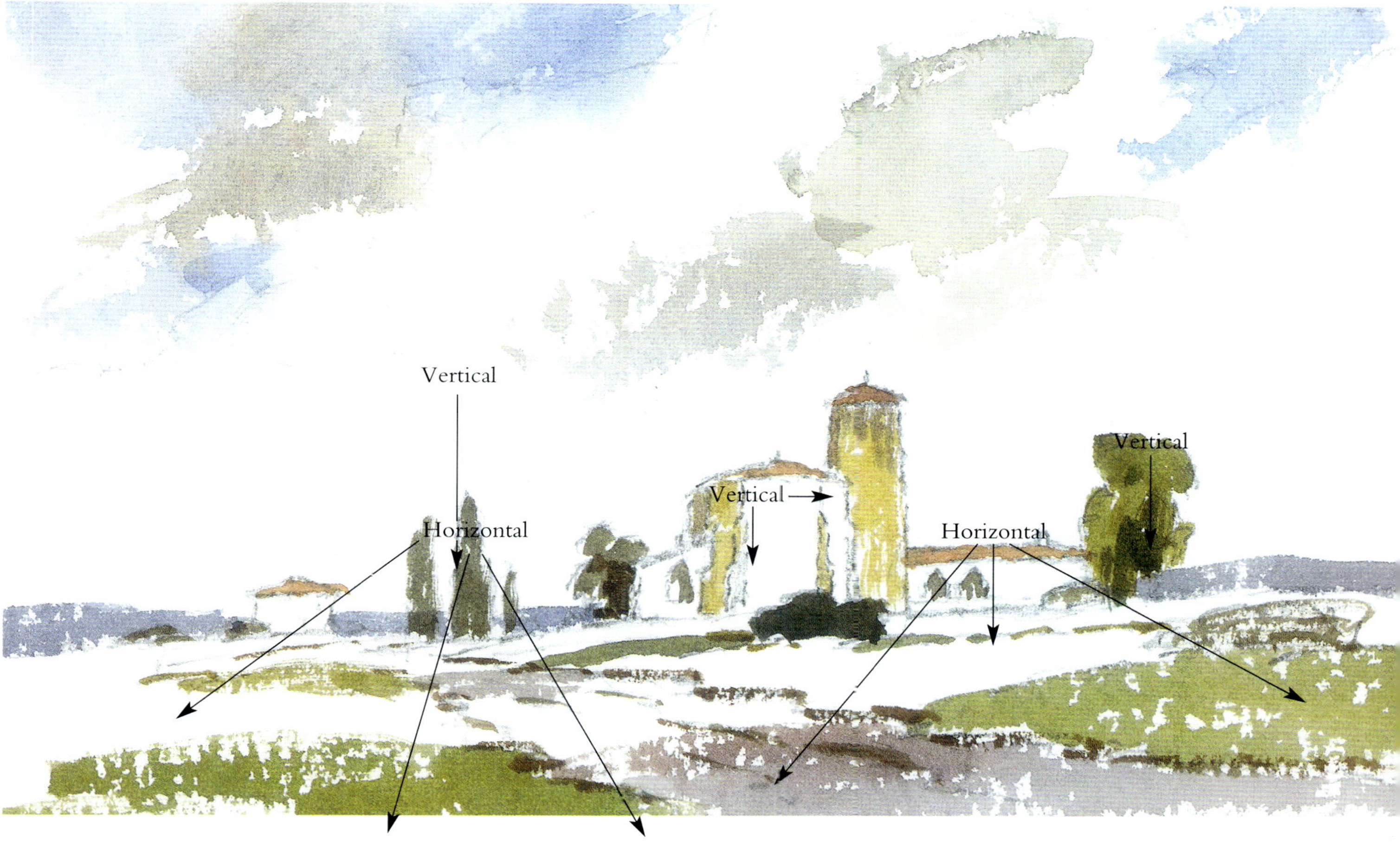

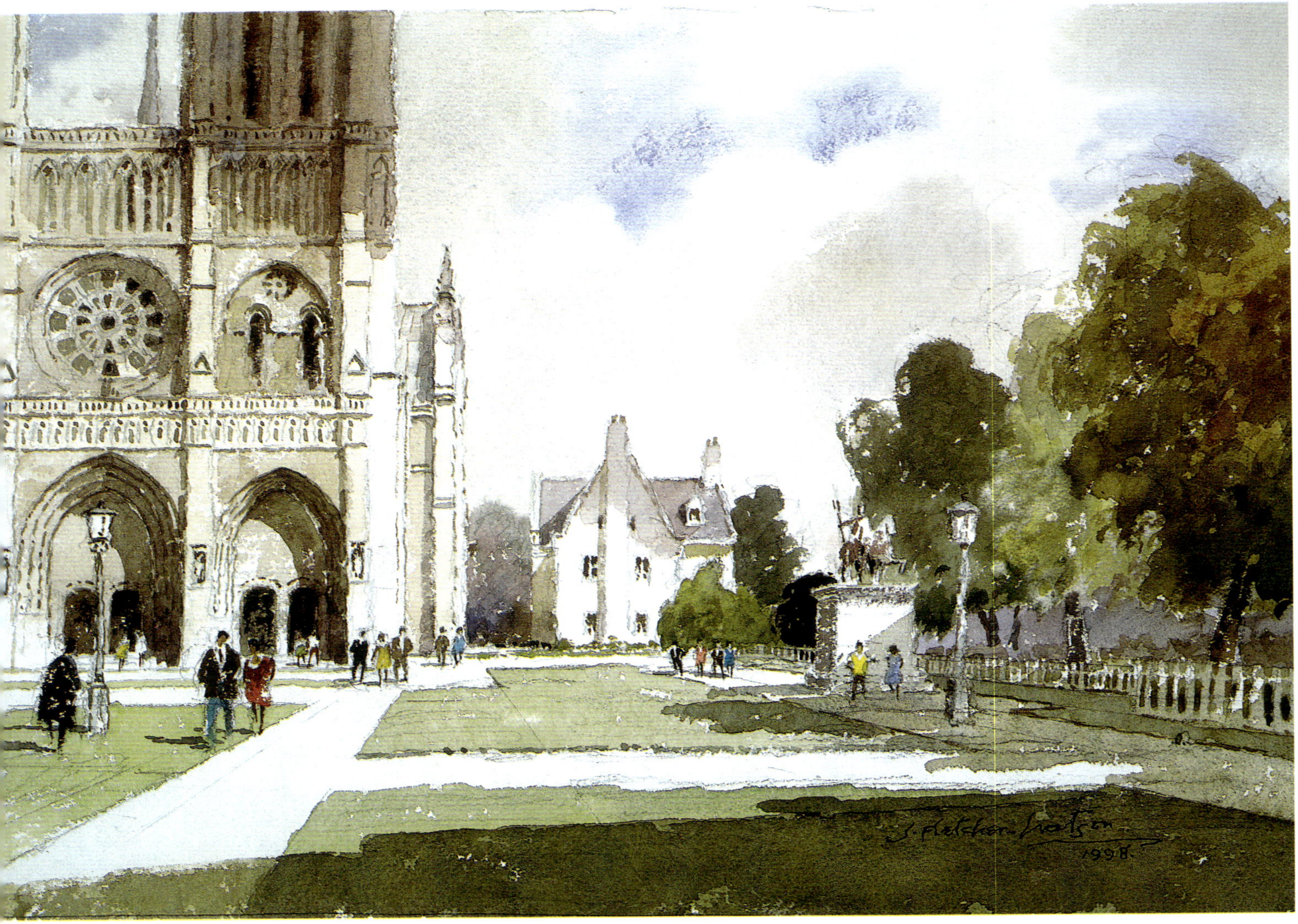

Figure 9
Notre Dame Cathedral, Paris.
362 × 311mm (14½ × 12¼in)

For a mainly architectural subject, I have chosen a west end view of *Notre Dame Cathedral, Paris* (**figure 9**). This composition is slightly unusual in that I have shown only half of the cathedral west end, as I also wanted to include the presbytery house and equestrian statue on the right with attractive trees. It is not always possible to show only half of an important building, as this could be detrimental to a good architectural subject. In this case however it has allowed me to make a more detailed close-up view of the cathedral and I feel that the composition has been successful. You will observe the interesting cloud shadows on the right-hand tower of the cathedral, and also very useful shadows in the foreground from the tall trees on the right.

The Market Square, Pollensa (**figure 10**) is another composition made interesting because the cathedral, with its tall tower, is not absolutely dominating the subject. Rather it is simply playing a part in the composition of the whole picture, which includes old buildings round the square and a beautiful tree on the right. The central steps and figures also play an important part in creating depth and balance while the umbrellas add a few spots of bright colour to contrast with the more subtle tones of the buildings behind.

Figure 10
The Market Square, Pollensa, Majorca.
318 × 476mm (12½ × 18¾in)

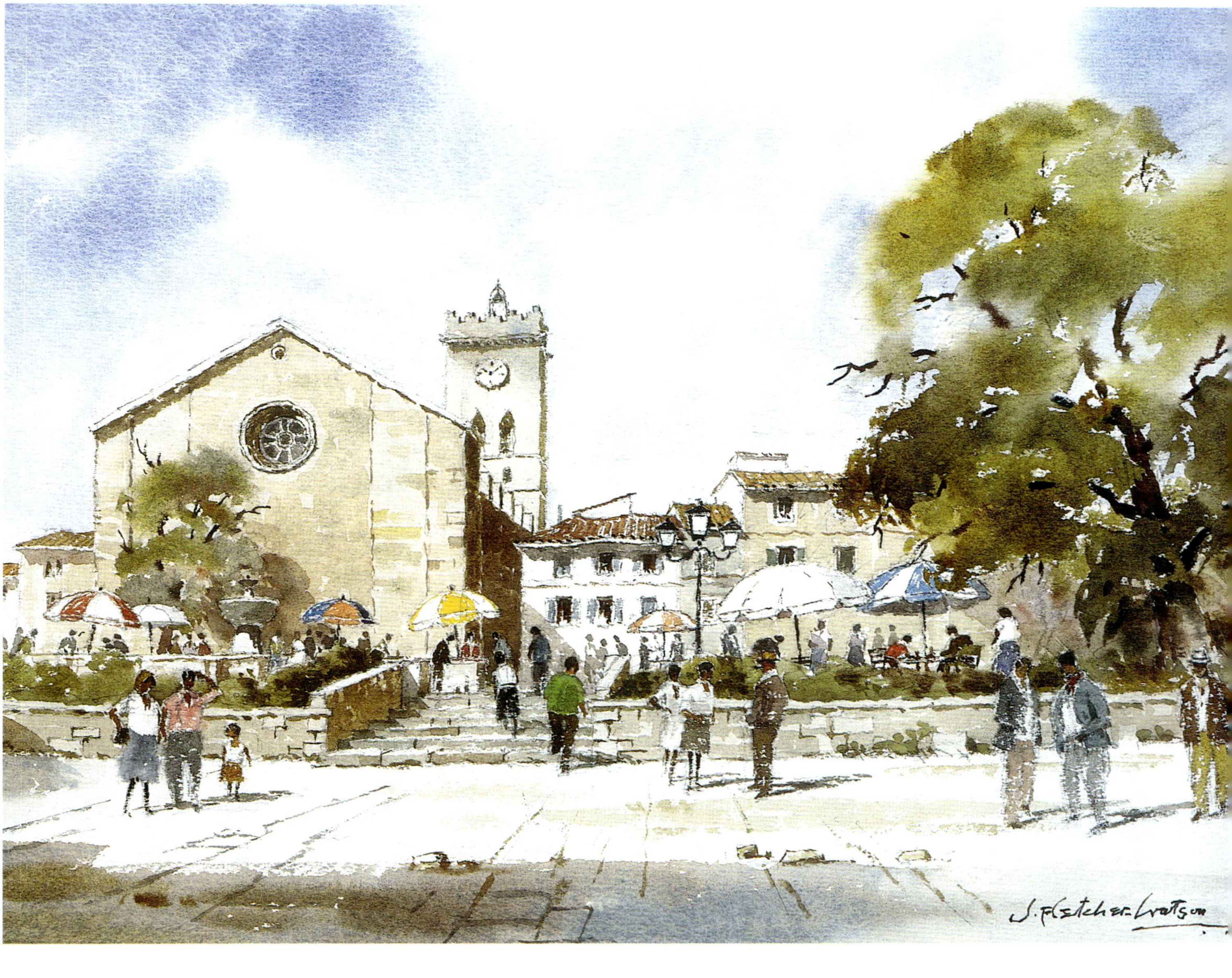

This *Cotswold Barn* (**figure 11**) is a favourite subject, within walking distance of my home. It makes a well-balanced composition, with the barn as the central focus. The loosely painted clouds racing across the sky and the trees leaning to the right depict a windy day.

I made a sketch of the subject while on a walk and completed the painting later in the studio. I limited the colour range to just four colours: Raw Sienna, Cobalt Blue, Burnt Umber and French Ultramarine. Note that I outlined the building using a very small brush and brown paint, not a pencil. Try this method and you will find it gives your painting a certain looseness, which is always a desirable element in watercolour painting.

Figure 11
Cotswold Barn, England.
235 × 362mm (9½ × 14¼in)

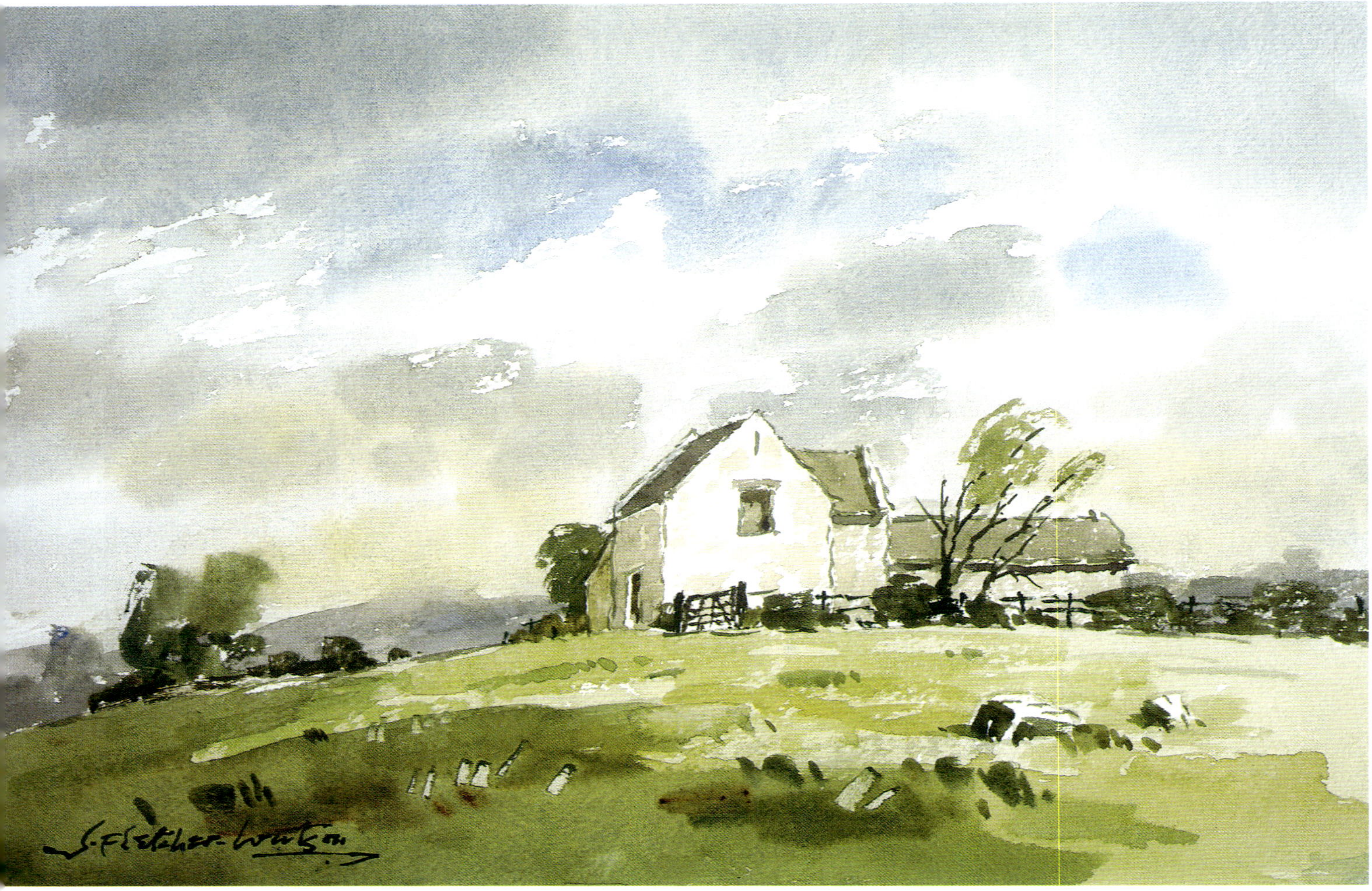

I shall be referring to composition many times throughout this book, as it is such a vital ingredient for a picture. I hope, thought, that I have made clear the main points to look for when selecting and creating a good composition. It is all about balance, positioning features, tone values and colour quality. I think the whole essence of composition will gradually dawn on you as you go through the book; it is not something that can be defined in just a few words.

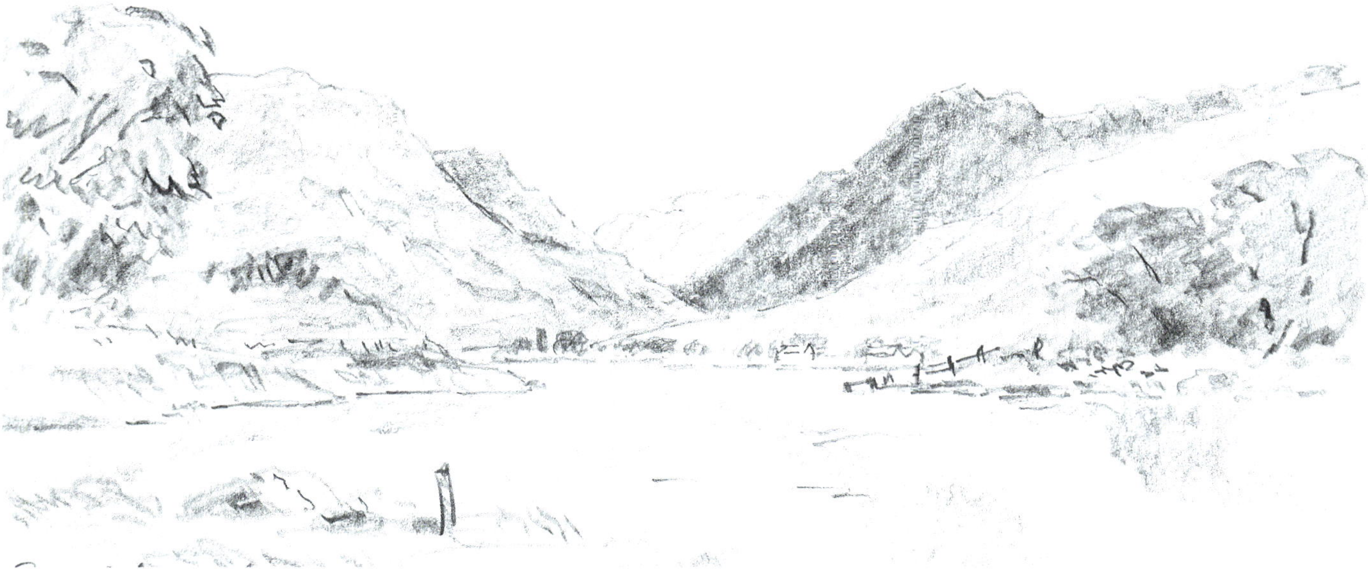

TIPS AND TECHNIQUES

- Composition should be the first thing to think about when you are planning a painting
- Consider the linear movement in a painting, such as the use of a path leading the eye into the picture. Remember to balance the vertical and horizontal to give an overall harmony
- Distant elements in a landscape, such as mountains or a castle, will give an important impression of depth to the picture
- It is important to achieve a balance between light and dark tones
- Carefully plan the colour elements in a painting at the composition stage – different colour combinations can dramatically change the mood of a painting
- Remember that you can use some artist's licence to strengthen the composition of an observed landscape

Chapter 3

SKIES

Sunny skies; cloudy skies; evening and early morning skies; cloud shadows and storm clouds

The sky is one of the most important elements for the landscape painter to consider since it can set the whole tone and character of the picture. For this reason it is therefore essential to study the techniques for painting different types of sky. In Britain, we are fortunate in having an enormous variety of weather conditions and so do not need to travel very far to find varying sky examples. Constable once wrote, 'The sky is the source of light in Nature, and governs everything.' We must not forget this.

Let us start with a bright sunny day with blue sky and no clouds as shown in **figure 12**. The first thing is to know how to lay a controlled wash on the paper. For this exercise. we will not bother about the subject of the landscape.

With your paper laid flat on your sketching board, damp the paper all over with clear water and a fairly large brush (No. 8 or No. 10). When this is half dry, tilt the board to slope towards you and start painting at the top with your large brush and a fairly strong mixture of Cobalt Blue. Drag the brush from one side to the other with steady strokes, gradually working down the paper and making the blue application weaker by adding a little water in your palette. By the time you reach the bottom of the sheet, your brush should have almost no colour on it at all.

Figure 12
Sunny day with clear sky.

Figure 13
Early morning sky.

Now we will try an early morning sky as shown in **figure 13**. Damp the paper with clear water as before and start painting at the top with Cobalt Blue, weakening the blue mixture as you paint. When you get a third of the way down, wash out your brush. Then use a weak mixture of Raw Sienna to start with, getting a little stronger as you near the bottom. The very last bit should be weak again. Early morning skies can vary: for instance, there could be a slight mist hanging in the air, which would cause the yellow colour to vary in tone. You will need to look carefully at the sky before you start this delicate wash.

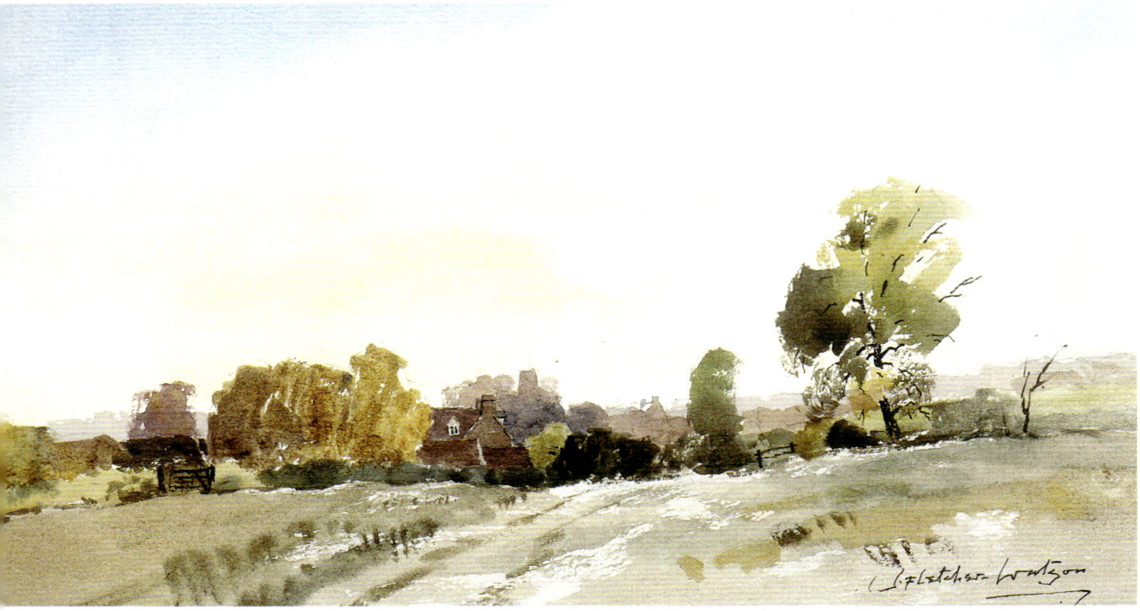

Figure 14
Autumn trees, Windrush, England.
260 × 470mm
(10½ × 18½in)

Figure 15
Evening sky.

Figure 14, *Autumn trees, Windrush*, illustrates this type of misty morning sky. In this instance, the area of blue at the top is very pale.

In **figure 15** we see that the low area of sky near the horizon is pink, the sun having just sunk down below it. Go through the same process as for a morning sky, but stop the yellow wash two-thirds of the way down and change to a weak mixture of Light Red. For all these cloudless skies, you can vary the shade of blue, yellow and pink used.

Turner was passionately fond of evening sunset skies as well as early morning ones. He was often out painting before breakfast to catch the light.

Now we will look at some cloudy skies, which I must admit are my favourite type.

Figure 16 shows a fairly typical skyscape with broken clouds allowing the blue sky to show through a number of gaps.

The painting procedure is first to damp the paper. When it is half dry, float in grey clouds with a No. 10 brush using a mixture of French Ultramarine and Burnt Umber. Start right at the top of the paper and work gradually downwards, leaving white unpainted gaps as you go. The secret of a good cloudy sky is to make the grey areas large near the top and smaller as you go down, and the white gaps the same, from large to small. The reason for this is to give perspective in the sky in the same way as you have perspective on the land – for example, trees appear smaller as they become more distant. The clouds should also become less dark as they get further away, and I sometimes introduce a touch of Raw Sienna into the lower clouds. Now for the pockets of blue sky seen in between the grey clouds. Starting at the top with a No. 8 brush and a fairly strong mixture of French Ultramarine, first paint a moderately large area of blue in one or two places, taking care to form interesting white cloud shapes as you apply the blue paint. As you come lower down, make the blue areas slightly smaller and sometimes a long thin shape. They should also definitely be a weaker tone of blue.

At the lowest point, the blue areas should be made very thin and painted a different tone of blue, either Cobalt Blue or Cerulean Blue, or even a very watered-down Winsor Blue. At this stage, I usually find it necessary to reinforce the grey clouds with some slightly darker over-painting on some of the cloud areas.

Having given you the general principle of painting a cloudy sky, I must add that there are, of course, many variations of cloud and sky arrangements. Sometimes you get a big area of blue sky near the horizon and the clouds are only high up over your head. At other times, the whole sky will be grey cloud with no blue sky at all. But do not despise it – a grey day in the country can be attractive and mysterious.

Figure 16
Cloudy sky.

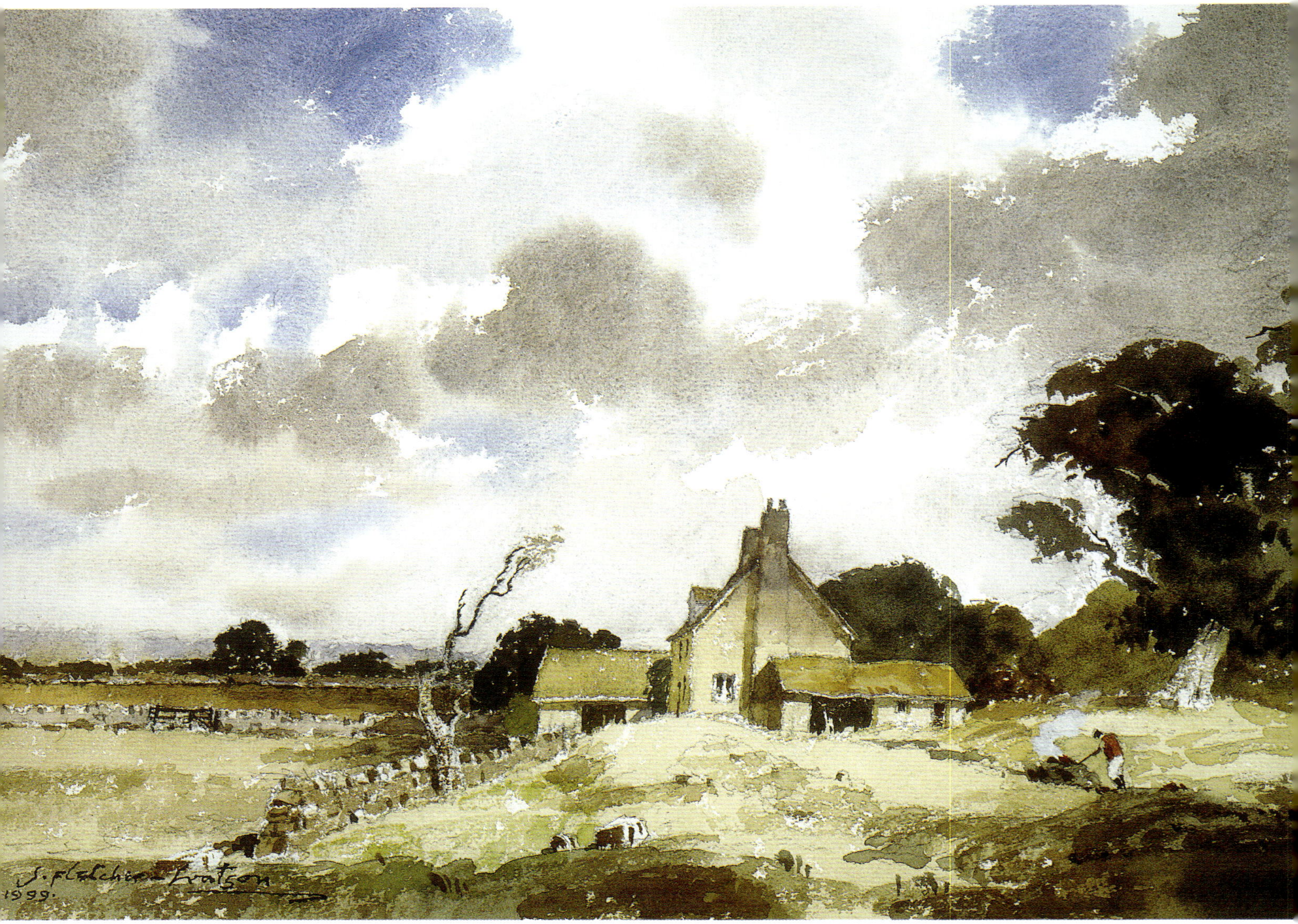

Figure 17
Cotswold Farm, England.
318 × 476mm (12½ × 18¾in)

This simple subject, *Cotswold Farm* (**figure 17**) with outbuildings, is greatly enhanced by the riotous sky of white clouds, grey clouds and a patch or two of blue. There is clearly a lot of movement from wind as the clouds are blown from left to right. You will note the central leafless tree bending to the right in the strong wind. The cloud shadow on the gable end of the building and on the chimneys is most effective.

Another farmhouse, this time in Cumbria (**figure 18**), is painted in a perfect setting of mountains and trees, with rocks and cows in the foreground. As for the painting on the facing page, I have used a mixture of French Ultramarine and Burnt Umber for the grey clouds, with important areas of white between them, and French Ultramarine for the dark blue. Without the composition of various cloud shapes, this picture would not be half as interesting, so I beg my readers to pay particular attention to a cloudy day for a landscape.

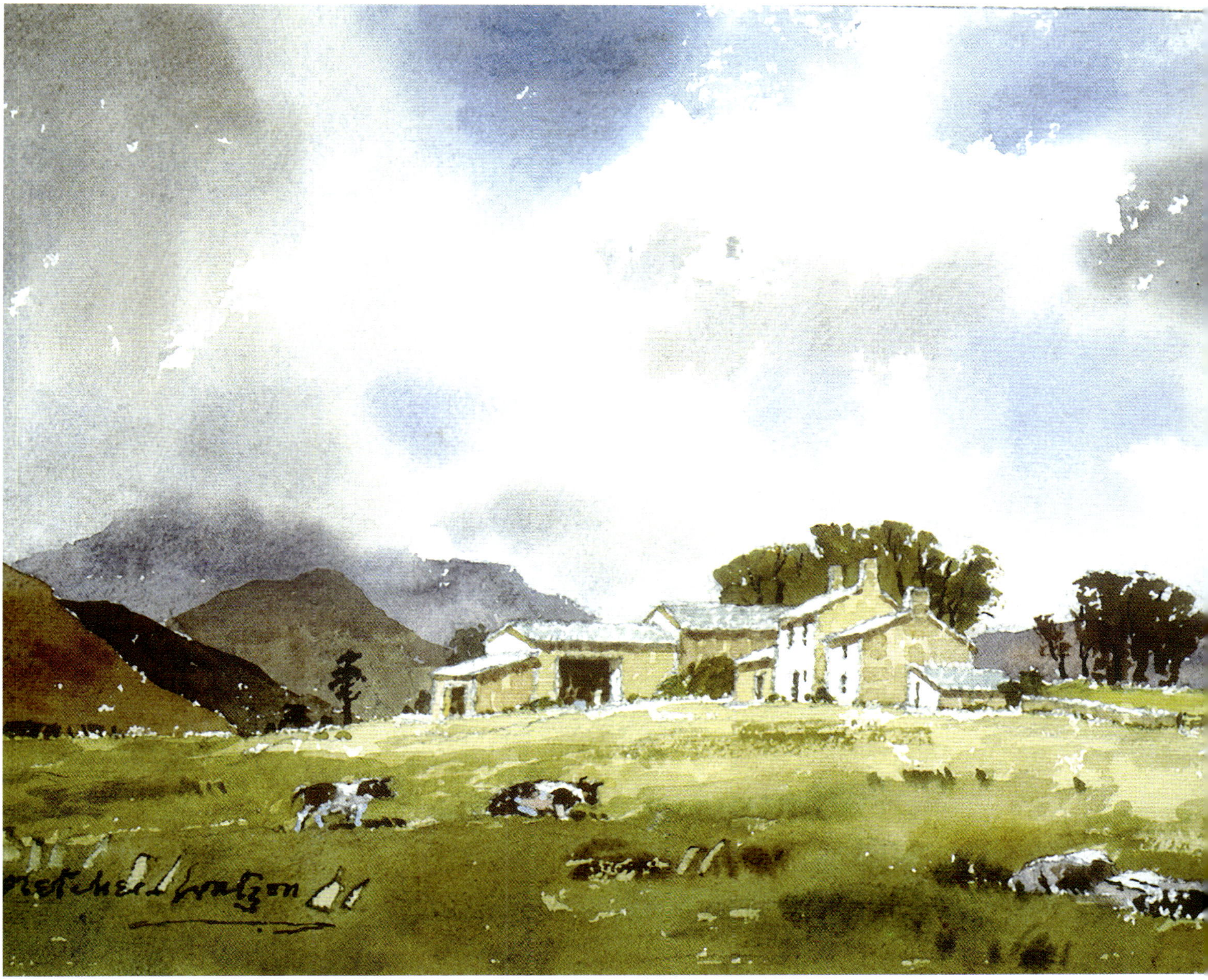

Figure 18
Farm in Cumbria, England. 235 × 362mm (9½ × 14¼in)

Figure 19 is a pleasing example of low clouds actually creeping over mountain tops. I will describe how this is done below.

Having sketched in your mountain scene lightly with a pencil, paint the complete skyscape right down over the mountains to water level and allow this to dry completely. Then start painting the mountains one by one from the bottom upwards, keeping your paper in a horizontal position. When you get near the top of the mountain, take another small brush (No. 6) and, using clear water, paint over the top area of the mountain, including slightly above it. Do not use too much water. Now continue with the mountain, using the first brush and a darker colour. Paint upwards into the damp area in a way that will give an interesting cloud shape. The secret of success is not to have a very wet brush full of colour, but to make it rather a dry mixture so that the colour does not run out of control. When you have experimented with this on a rough piece of paper, you will see what I mean.

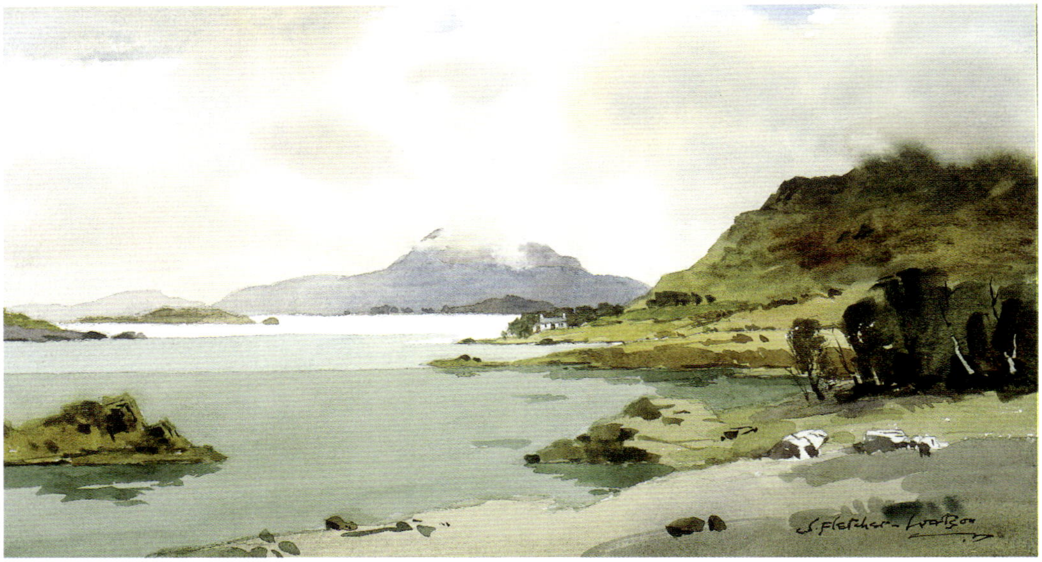

Figure 19
Low cloud over mountains.
318 × 476mm (9½ × 14¼in)

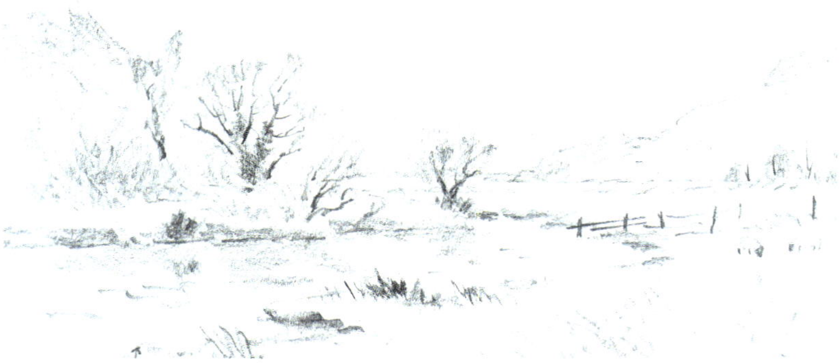

This painting of *Deia, Majorca* (**figure 20**) is a very good example of how to show a hot day when the sky is all blue, except for a few small white puffy clouds. For this type of sky, the first task must be to paint the whole sky area with clear water. Then, as the wash dries off, start painting the whole sky from the top downwards with a blue colour, carefully leaving various white clouds unpainted.

Figure 20
Deia, Majorca.
318 × 476mm (12½ × 18¾in)

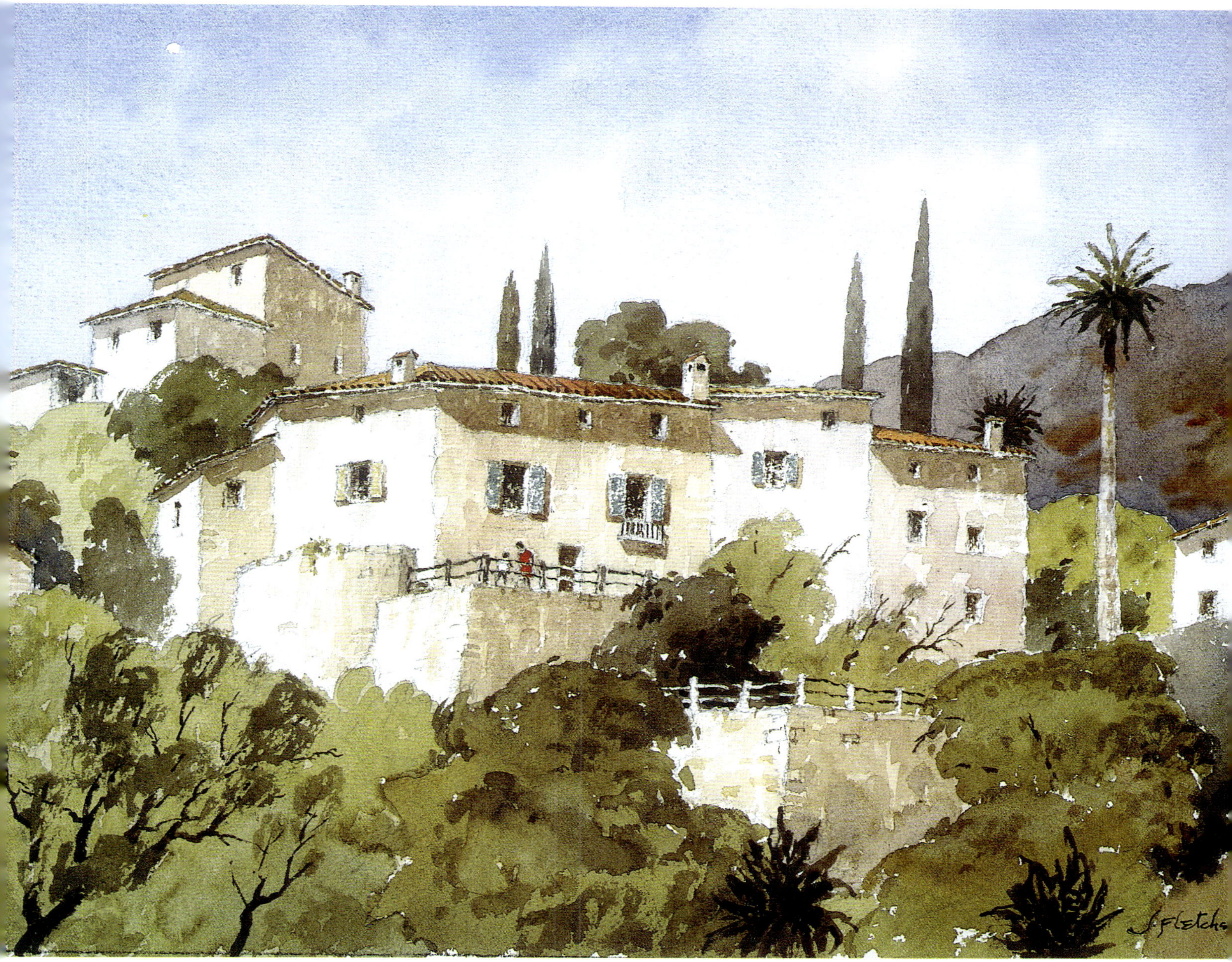

Figure 21, *Morston Marshes, Norfolk*, shows another type of cloudy sky painted entirely with different strengths of Payne's Gray and a small touch of Raw Sienna in the right-hand clouds. The big dark clouds on the left side are moving across the landscape with vertical streaks of rain indicated. The whole sky area was kept damp so that the clouds had soft edges. It was all painted quickly so as to complete it before it was able to dry and cause hard edges. There are glimpses of sunlight on the land, caused by narrow breaks in the cloud which cannot be seen from the viewpoint at ground level.

I do not intend to show any more sky pictures in this chapter, although there is still a variety of skyscapes I could describe. In the ensuing chapters, a number of alternative skies can be seen in landscape pictures that depict other subjects, including trees, country buildings, mountains, water and even snow.

Figure 21
Morston Marshes, Norfolk, England.
318 × 476mm (12½ × 18¾in)

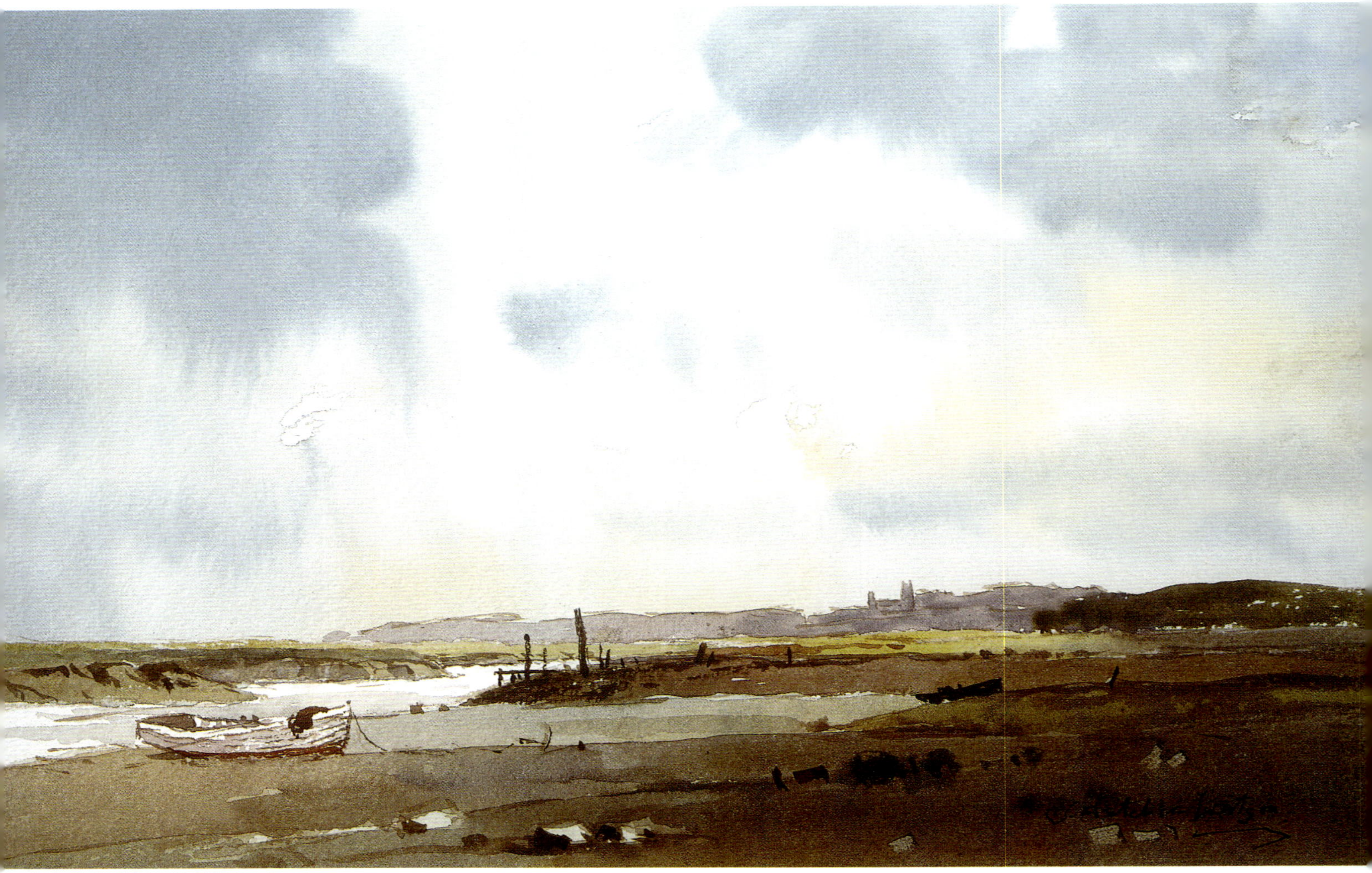

TIPS AND TECHNIQUES

- When painting a grey, cloudy sky, you can increase the impression of perspective by making the grey cloud areas and the white gaps decrease in size from the top of the page
- A blue sky always gets fainter towards the horizon, so make sure you achieve the same effect in your painting
- Grey storm clouds can be reinforced by over-painting them in a darker colour
- Do not use too much water when painting skies, or the mixture may get out of control
- Low clouds will increase the impact of an atmospheric mountain scene

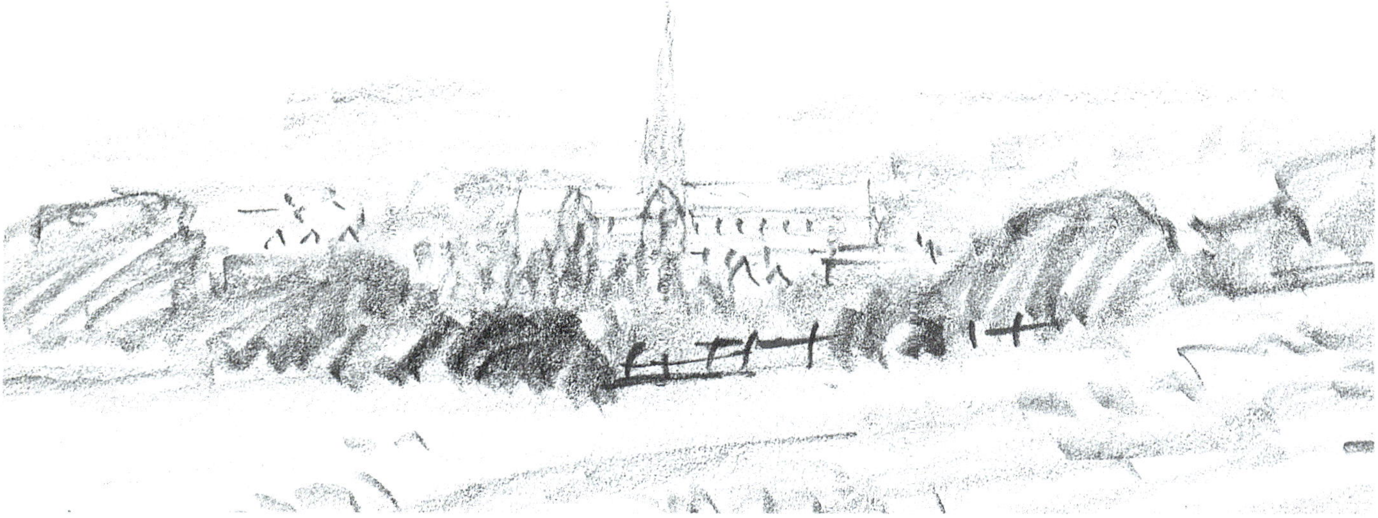

Chapter 4

TREES

Winter trees; summer trees; autumn trees, trees with buildings; trees on country roads

In my years of teaching, trees have often proved troublesome to students. Even experienced painters sometimes find it difficult to paint trees convincingly. I can sympathize with this, but assure you that, with plenty of practice, you will eventually find that you can paint even the most challenging tree subjects. It is very much a matter of how you look at trees and what type of brush you use, as well as what type of paper.

Look now at **figure 22**, *Winter ash tree*, and you will see that the main feature is the tree in the foreground. A few yellow autumn leaves linger on, which lend interest. It is a good thing to learn a little about the anatomy of trees as seen in winter before painting a summer tree.

I am not going to describe the painting of this picture in full detail, as I want to concentrate on the

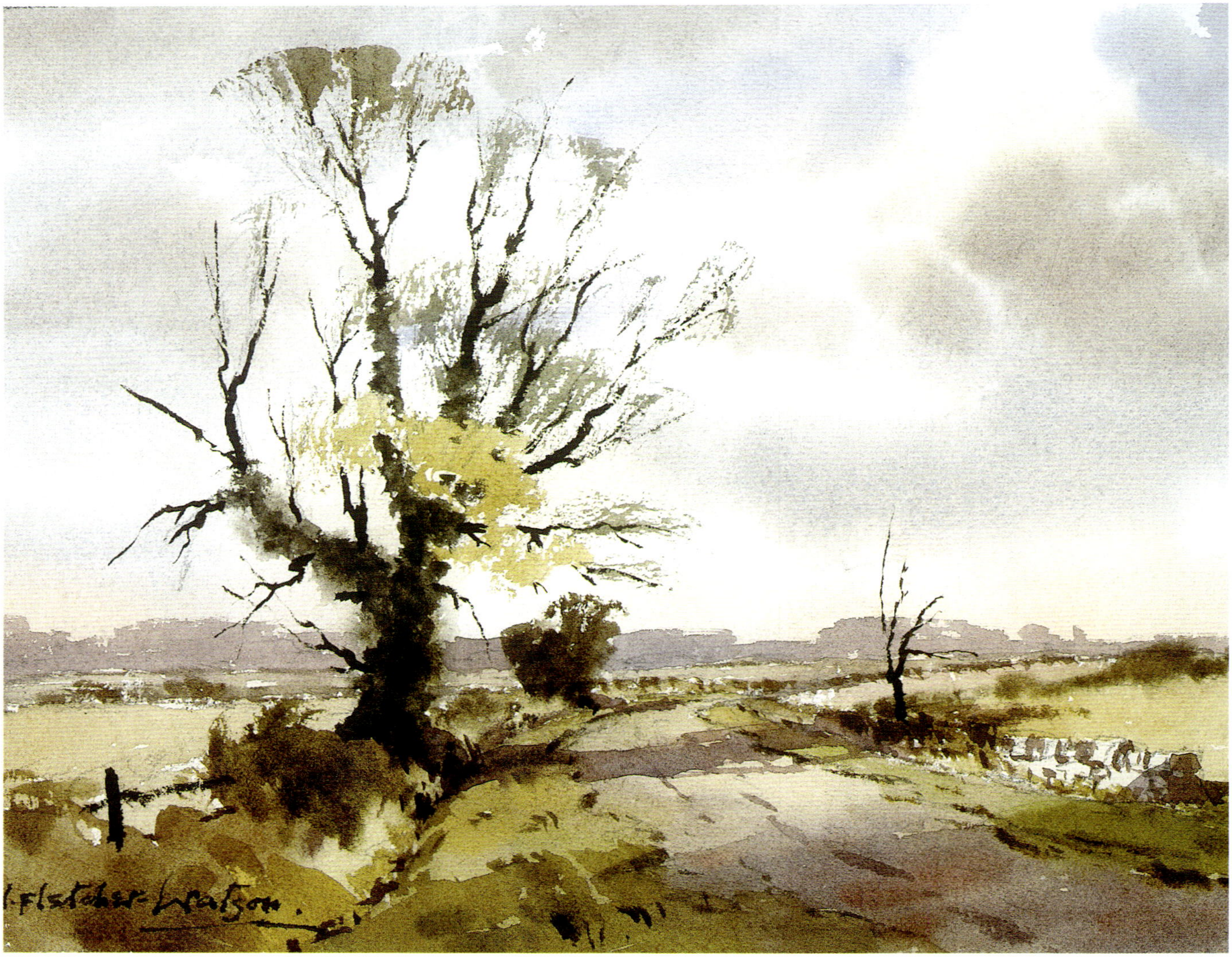

Figure 22
Winter ash tree. 235 × 362mm (9½ × 14¼in)

tree. Briefly, the method was as follows. First I pencilled in the road and fencing, a bit of stone wall on the right and the distant horizon line. Then the grey, cloudy sky was painted and the tree was also tackled at this early stage. Next followed the yellow grass verges and yellow fields, and finally the distant belt of grey-blue trees, the cloud shadow in the foreground and the tree shadow across the road.

Figure 23 shows the bare bones of the tree painted straight onto a white sheet of paper. I used Whatman paper 140lb rough. Use good-quality paper even for practice. I first drew with a 2B pencil the trunk and branches and also the central shape of yellow leaf foliage.

I then mixed Burnt Umber and Payne's Gray and started painting the main trunk from the bottom upwards, using a No. 5 brush. The lower trunk and branches were covered with ivy creeper and I suggested this by making the edges rough and blobby. I had also damped the trunk area with clear water prior to starting to obtain a slightly blurred effect. I changed to a No. 3 brush for the upper branches, some of which were very thin. Then I painted round the yellow foliage area.

Figure 23 shows how I have sketched in the outline of the road and the distance purely to indicate the composition of the picture. Looking again at **figure 22**, you can see that at the extremities of a winter tree the branches become extremely thin; they are just twigs and you should not attempt to paint them individually. They are best painted with a medium size brush (No. 5) and a rather dry mix of Burnt Umber and Payne's Gray. Use the side of the brush, not the point, and stroke it downwards on the paper, getting a little fan-shaped area of paint conforming to the treetop outline. This is known as dragged brushwork.

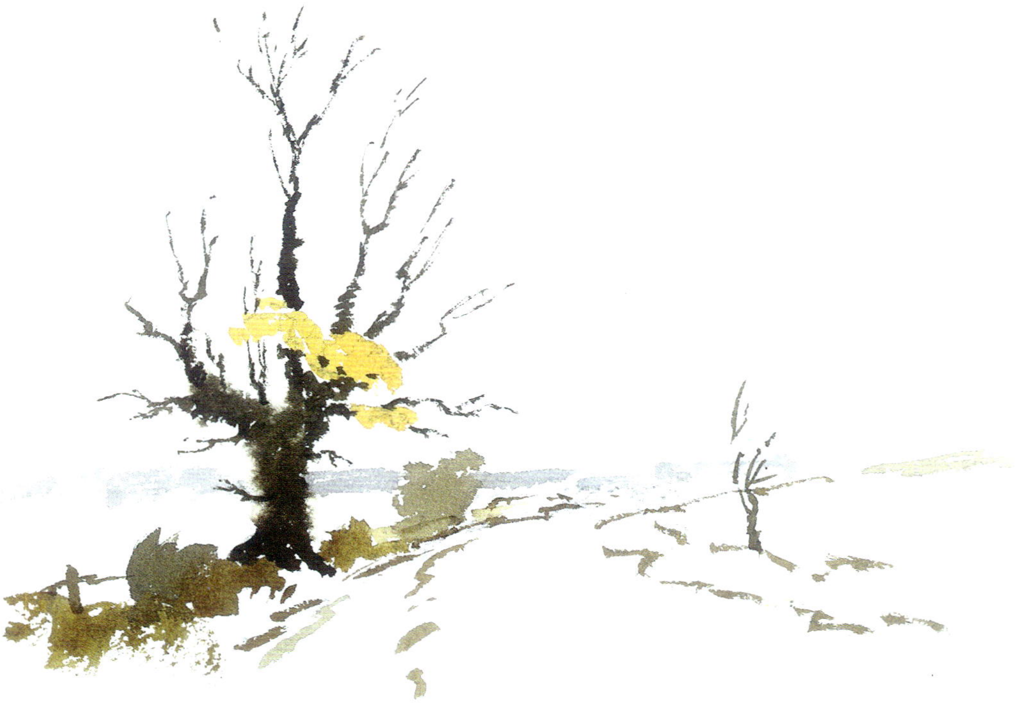

Figure 23
Winter ash tree, stage one.

Figure 24, *Country Lane*, is a rather small picture showing another tree with a field gate and farm track. It is – I hope you agree – a charming subject and yet it is only a portrait of an old tree! Don't overlook this type of scene when on your country walk looking for a subject. Of course, an interesting cloudy sky and some vague distance help to make a better picture. This particular tree also has ivy on its trunk and main branches, but it has more twigs at the extremities than the one in **figure 22**. Use the same method and paint these twig areas with dry brushwork. Note that the trunk and main branches are really very thick. You often see paintings of trees with the trunks much too thin. This is a sure sign they have been painted by an inexperienced artist, so don't fall into this trap yourself.

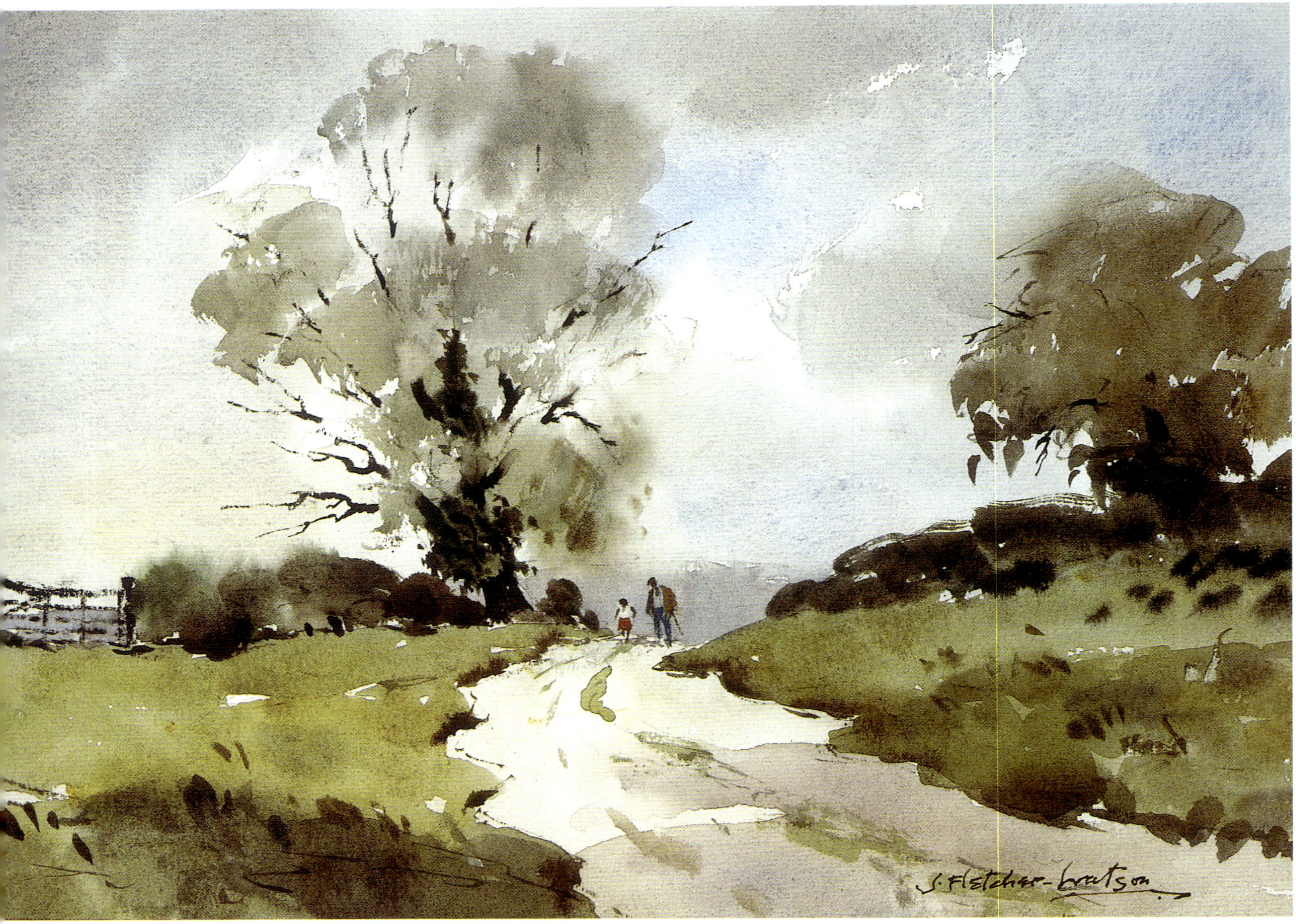

Figure 24
Country Lane.
152 × 253mm (6 × 9¼in)

Figure 25, *Leaning tree, autumn*, is another small sketch showing some autumn leaves already blown away to reveal bare branches. See how attractive and poetical a leaning tree can be. Don't miss painting a tree like this if you spot one – it is better than fifty upright trees!

First of all, I drew the line of the hedge, the tree trunk and a branch or two lightly in pencil. Then I painted the sky. When this was dry I used a No. 8 brush and washed in the tree foliage, using Raw Sienna and Payne's Gray for the top lighter areas, and Burnt Umber and Payne's Gray for the lower darker areas of foliage (**figure 26**). The great thing is to be bold with your foliage brushwork, using the brush sideways and dragging it quickly across the paper. It may look a mess at first, but when you put in the trunk and branches everything comes to life splendidly. Note that the bottom of the trunk is a lighter tone where it bends forward into the ground and catches the light.

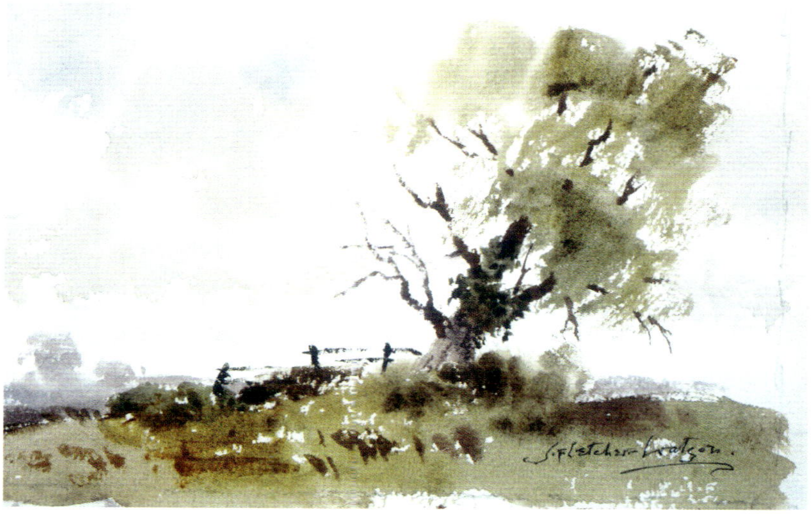

Figure 25
Leaning tree, autumn.
152 × 235mm (6½ × 9¼in)

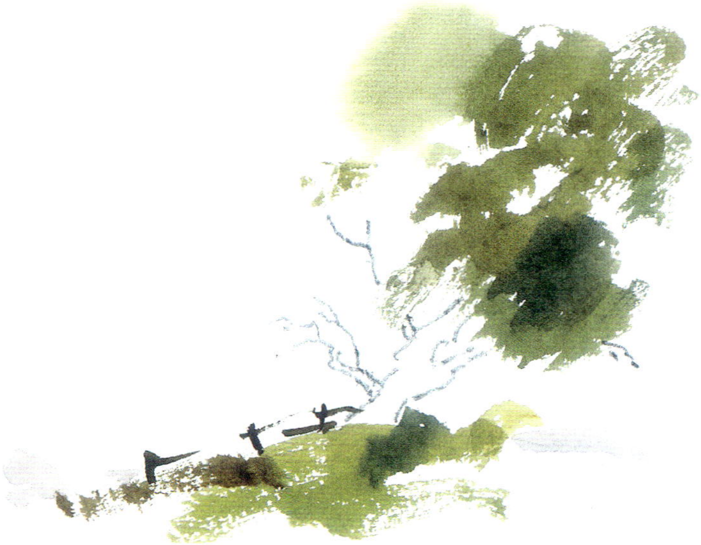

Figure 26
Leaning tree, stage one.

Figure 27a
Summer tree, stage one.

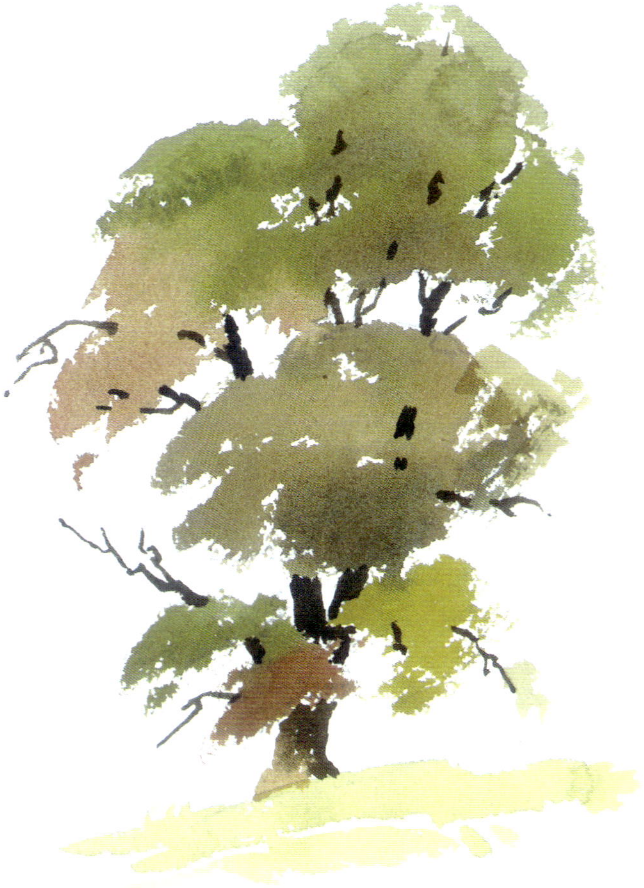

Figure 27b
Summer tree, stage two.

We will now look at a tree in full summer leaf. **Figure 27a** shows the first stage of painting, after I had first lightly pencilled in the trunk and main stems. I used a mixture of Raw Sienna and French Ultramarine on a No. 8 brush for the green foliage, with a dash of Indian Red here and there to give variety of tone. In **figure 27b**, you can see the effect of adding the trunk and branches, preferably while the foliage wash is still damp so that the branches merge slightly. No. 6 and No. 3 brushes were used for the trunk and branches, with a mixture of Burnt Umber and Payne's Gray.

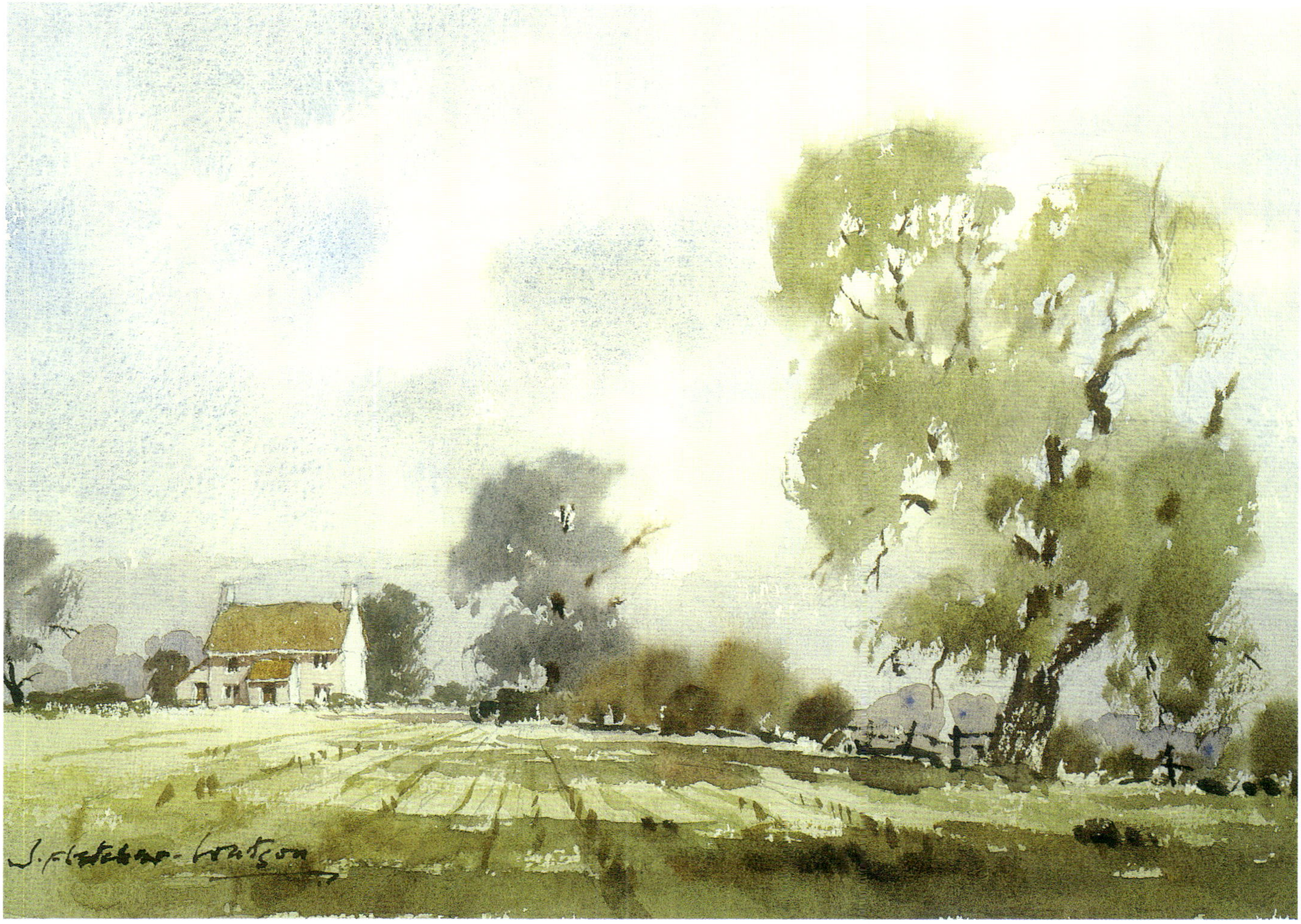

Figure 28
Cotswold stubble field, England.
317 × 476mm (12½ × 18¾in)

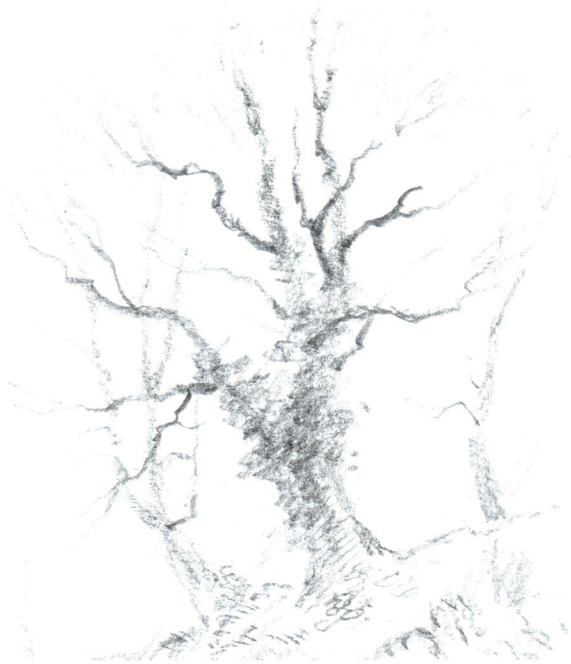

Figure 28, *Cotswold stubble field*, shows a finished picture of the stubble field and a very fine ash tree on the right, which is of just the same type as that shown in **figure 27**.

You will note this tree is leaning to the right which adds character, and it is casting a meaningful shadow across the stubble field. The adjoining field hedge and post and rails are attractive features in the general composition.

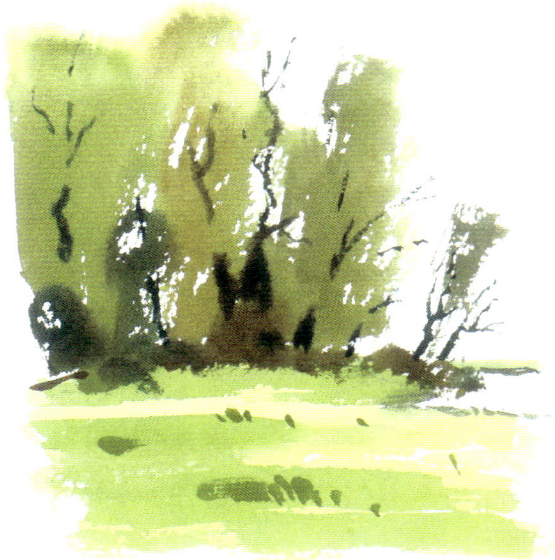

Figure 29a
Small wood near a lake.

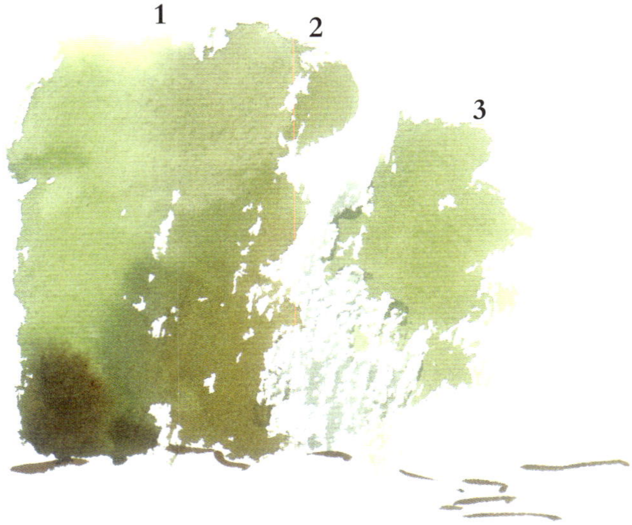

Figure 29b
Building up a group of trees.

So far, we have been dealing with individual trees; let us now look at trees collectively. **Figure 29a** shows the edge of a small wood near a lake. I was using Whatman paper (medium rough 140lb) and I used a pencil to draw a slightly curved ground line indicating a small rise. No other pencil work was necessary.

I started painting with a No. 8 brush (see **29b 1**) with a green mixture of Cadmium Yellow, Winsor Blue and Burnt Umber. I damped the area at the treetop with clear water, then I dragged the brush, which was well loaded with colour, sideways and downwards in a quick stroke. Using the brush sideways, I could give a fairly flat top to this left-hand tree. I stopped the brush at the ground line and added a little more Burnt Umber to the mixture. I then painted the next tree (**29b 2**) with a fairly stiff mixture (not too much water), and with a quick downward stroke allowed the paper to breathe through the wash, showing glimpses of sky. I then floated in a darkish green area at the bottom of the first two trees (**29b 1** and **2**) while they were still damp, adding a strong touch of Winsor Blue to the mixture for this.

Then I started painting the third tree (**29b 3**), slightly varying the colour by adding more Cadmium Yellow. I have stopped halfway down in order to show you clearly how the downward wash was applied. A couple of brushstrokes were all I used and only two more brushstrokes would be required to finish it.

Finally, I put in the small sapling on the right (this is not shown in **figure 29b**). Looking now at **figure 29a**, you can see how I hastily painted small dark washes at the base of all the trees, using the same three colours. This was done while the first washes were still damp. Up to this stage, the whole process had taken about five minutes.

It was important to put in the tree trunks and branches before the work was all dry. I quickly mixed Burnt Umber and Payne's Gray and with a No. 3 brush painted in the dark trunks and upper branches of all the trees. By keeping everything damp, a softer result was achieved, which is more suitable for a tree subject than the hard edges that are more acceptable when painting buildings, for example.

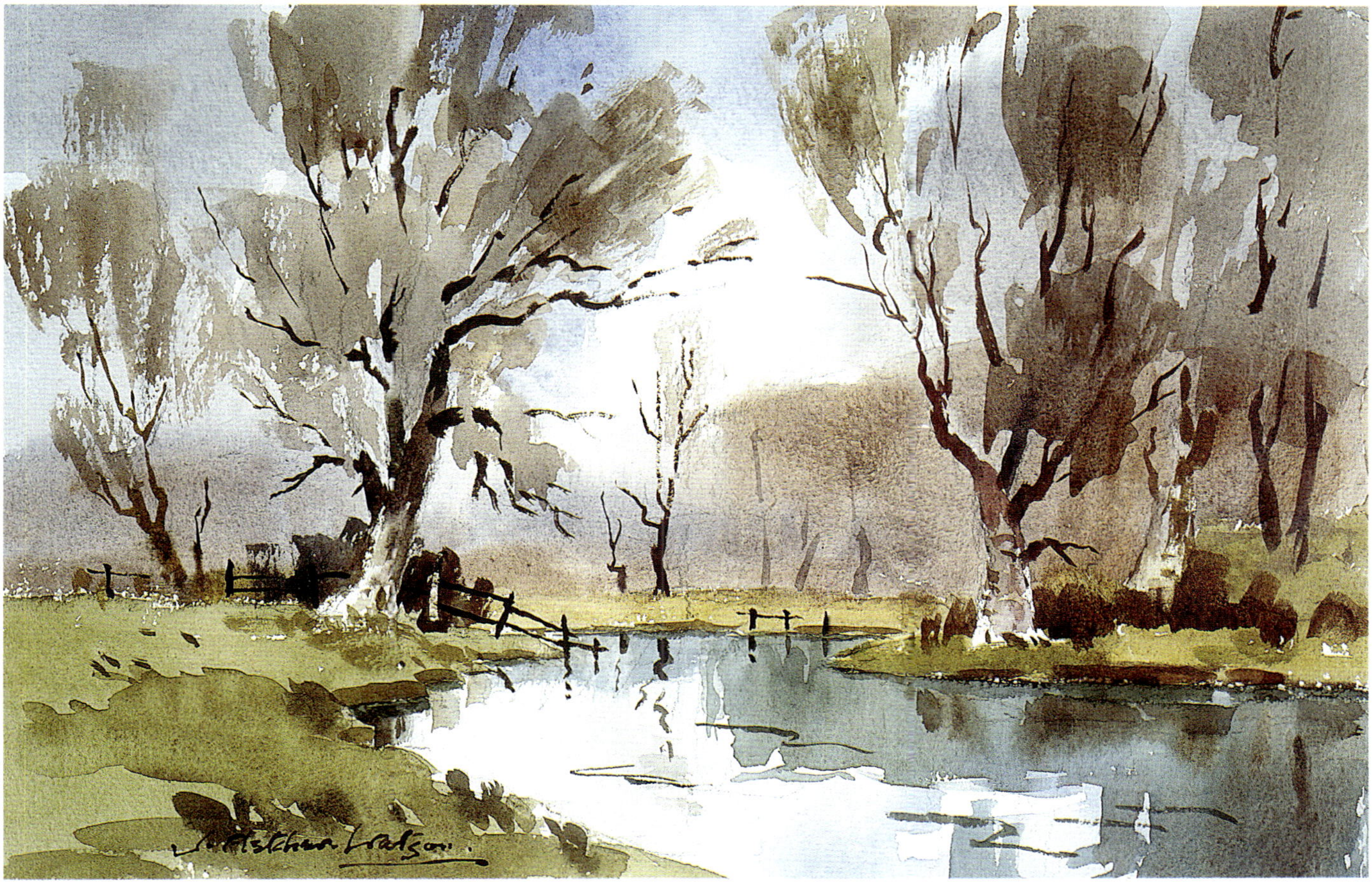

Figure 30
Stream through a wood. 235 × 362mm (9½ × 14¼in)

Lastly, the foreground grass went in; the first wash was a mixture of Cadmium Yellow and Winsor Blue. The darker green shadow wash simply had Burnt Umber added. This second stage of painting darker foliage, tree trunks and foreground took roughly another ten minutes.

Another type of tree subject is shown in **figure 30**, *Stream through a wood.* This is a tributary of the Windrush River quite near where I live and is a delightful little scene. Here it is illustrated in late autumn, when the leaves were beginning to come off the trees, making the branches more visible. The distant part of the wood is a good example of how to paint background trees. It consists of a mixture of French Ultramarine and Light Red with a touch of Raw Sienna. I had damped the sky area with clear water so that the background trees would merge and give the necessary impression of distance.

The large willow trees in the foreground were a mixture of Raw Umber and Cobalt Blue. The tree trunk and branches were the usual Burnt Umber and Payne's Gray and were painted while the foliage was still damp in the same way as **figure 29**. Note that the base of the trunks in **figure 30** was left light.

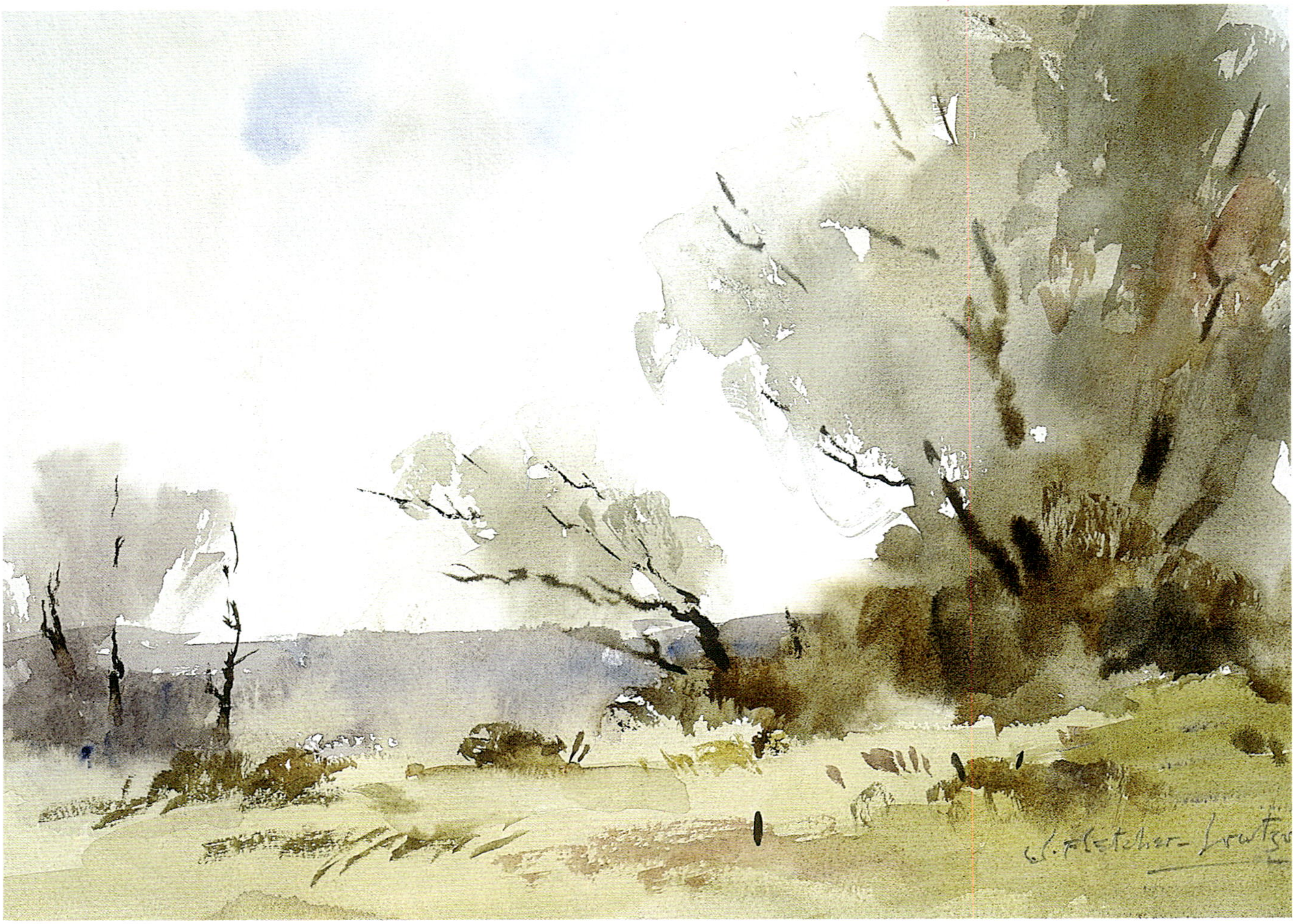

Figure 31
Old willow trees. 235 × 362mm (9½ × 14¼in)

A different type of treescape is shown in **figure 31**, *Old Willow Trees*. This was painted on a grey cloudy day with a little mist, and makes a poetical composition; the leaning tree in the centre is of great artistic value. Being autumn, the general colouring of rough grass and trees is a dull grey-yellow, obtained with French Ultramarine, Light Red and Raw Sienna. The far distant line of woods uses only French Ultramarine and Light Red, giving a perfect blue-grey distance. The only other colour used in this picture was Burnt Umber for the branches and odd sticks in the ground, which makes a total of four colours. The sky consisted of a mixture of French Ultramarine and Burnt Umber for the cloud area, and the small touches of blue sky were painted with French Ultramarine.

I have chosen this picture of *Norwich Cathedral* (**figure 32**) because, although a mainly architectural subject, it owes a great deal to the presence of the trees on the left. Without these trees, it would not be nearly as interesting. The fact that these are mainly bare winter trees means that they do not obscure the building but allow the architecture to show through.

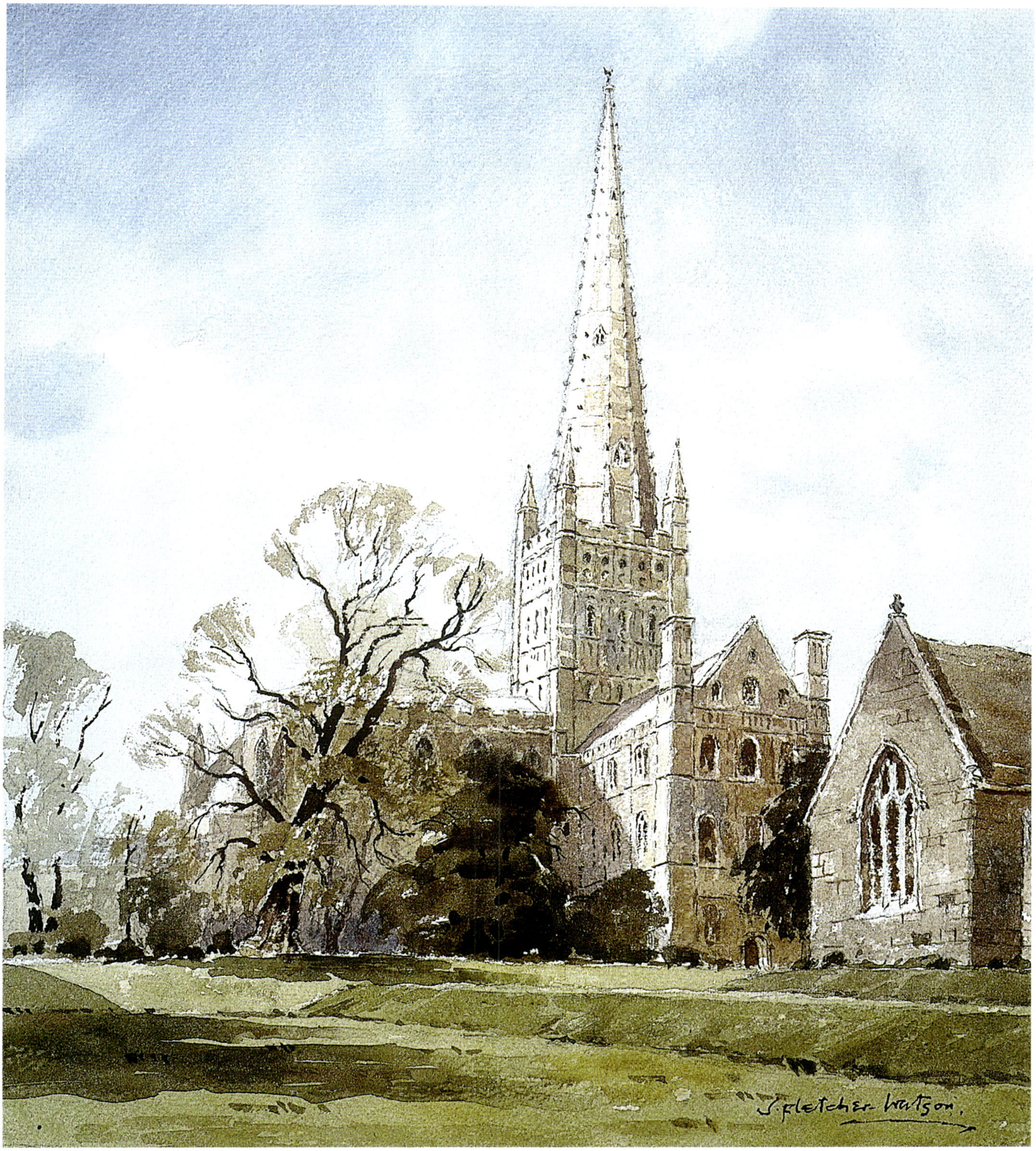

Figure 32
Norwich Cathedral, Norfolk, England.
362 × 311mm (14½ × 12¼in)

This charming composition of *Winter trees and water* (**figure 33**) is an example of nature at her best without the interference of man. Nobody would have ever thought of positioning those trees in this way if they were planting out a wood. The small amount of post and rail fencing is a very important feature of this picture. The general colour scheme of this winter subject is an object lesson, with the green-grey grass banks, the brown tree trunks and the distant grey-blue hills.

Many people might have overlooked this subject of a *Mountain Path, Majorca* (**figure 34**). Its potential as a picture to paint is not immediately obvious, but after standing looking at it for a moment or two, I realized that it was a perfect gem! The cypress tree is a wonderfully strong vertical feature, contrasting with rugged mountains and lighter-coloured, smaller trees, while the small gate in the wall suggests another exciting view beyond. The whole composition really was irresistible.

Figure 33
Winter tree and water.
318 × 476mm (12½ × 18¾in)

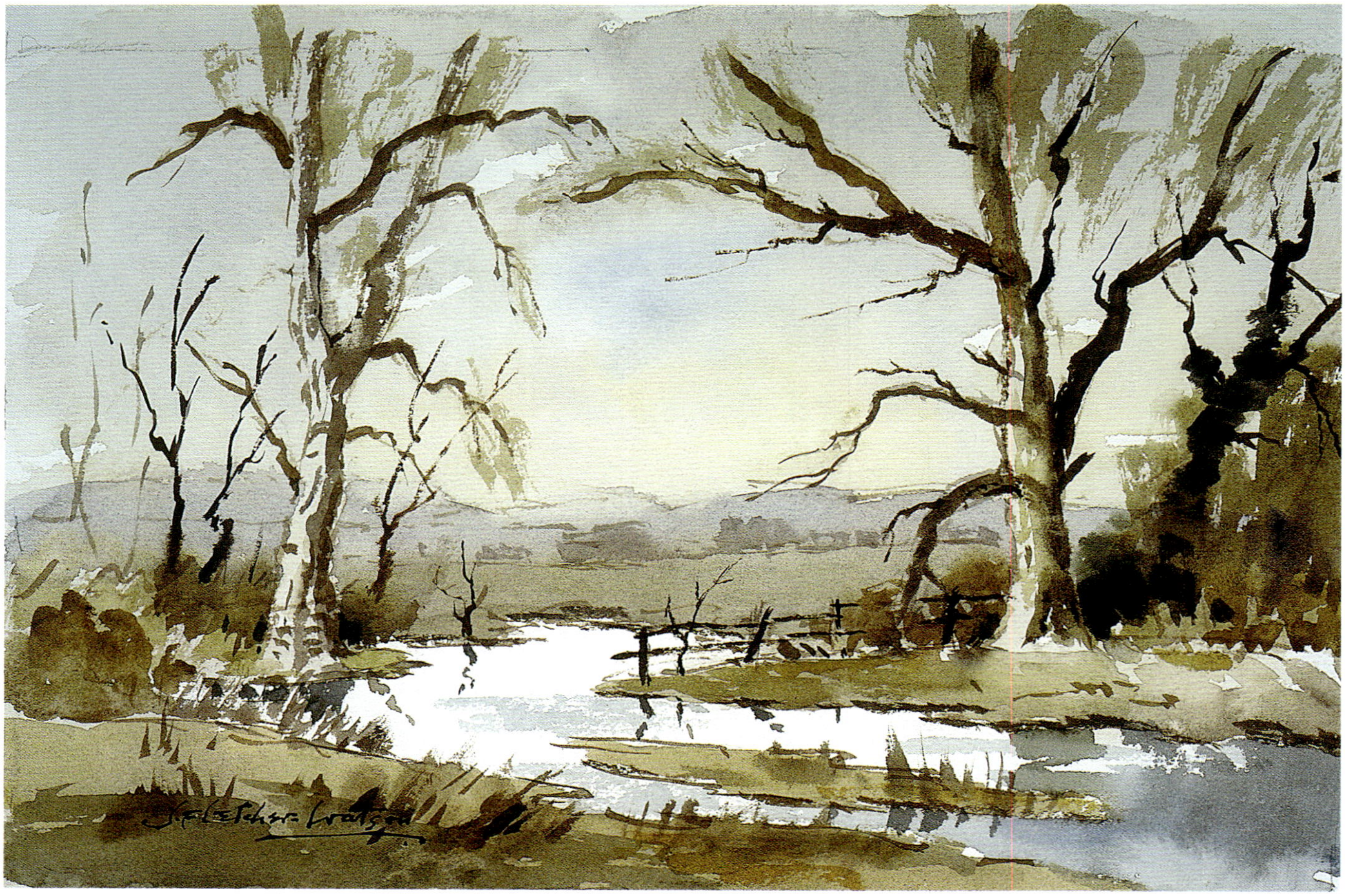

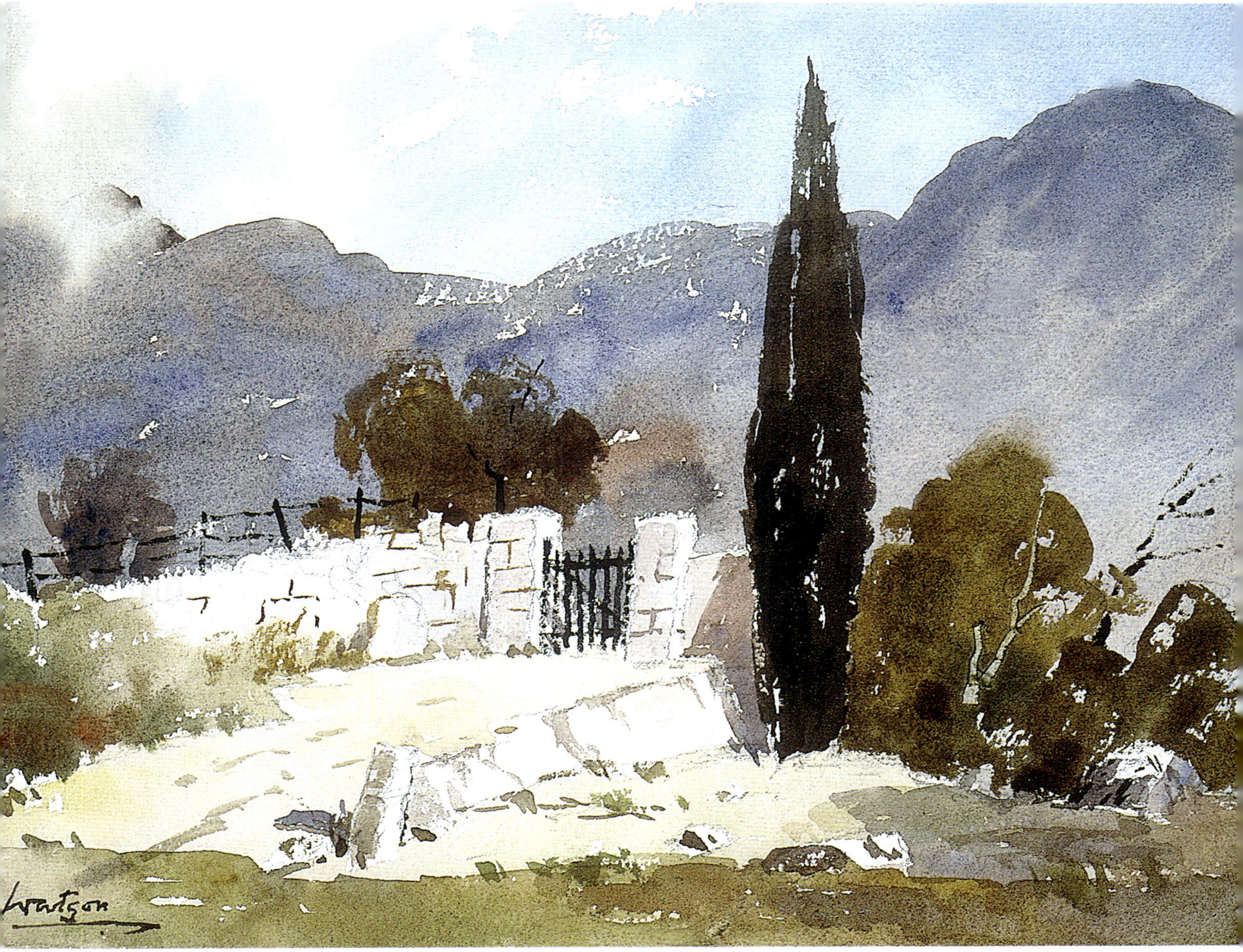

Figure 34
Mountain path, Majorca.
235 × 362mm (9½ × 14¼in)

Before leaving this chapter, I must just show you two examples of trees with buildings. There are some buildings that depend very largely on the presence of trees to make them into attractive compositions for the painter, as you will see in the following examples.

The only problem with this subject, *Dedham cottages* (**figure 35**), was that I was sitting in the middle of a public footpath to paint it, but I stuck to it with dogged determination and sat there for at least two hours!

You will notice what a splendid part the many trees play in this composition, especially the trees behind the buildings. You should always watch out for this type of well-balanced subject. The colour mix I used for the roofs consisted of Burnt Umber and a touch of Cobalt Blue, while the trees are a very varied selection of Burnt Umber, Winsor Blue and Cadmium Yellow.

Figure 36, *Windrush village*, seen from across the fields, is a nice view of cottages strung out in a line

Figure 35
Dedham cottages, England.
235 × 362mm (9½ × 14¼in)

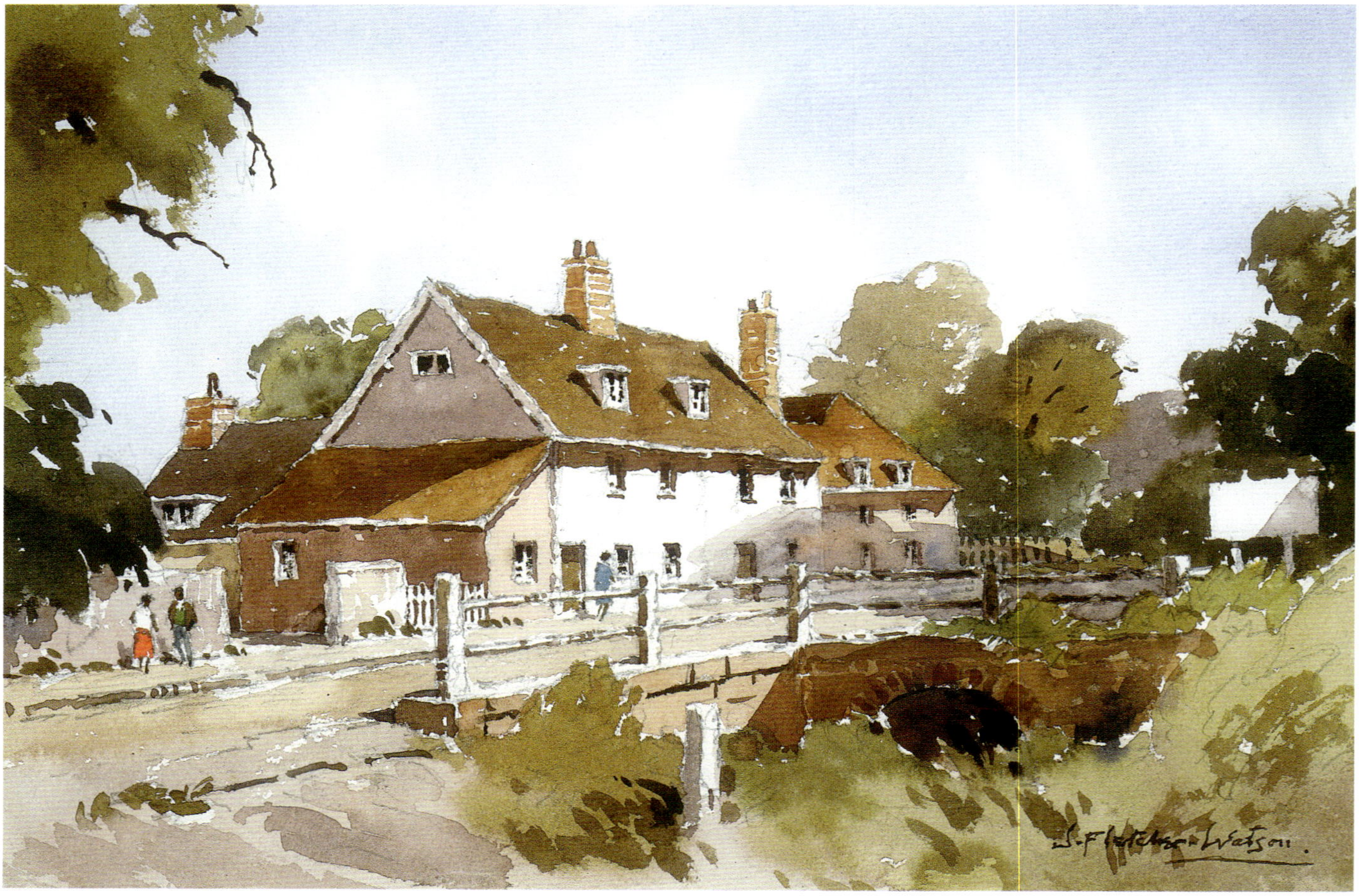

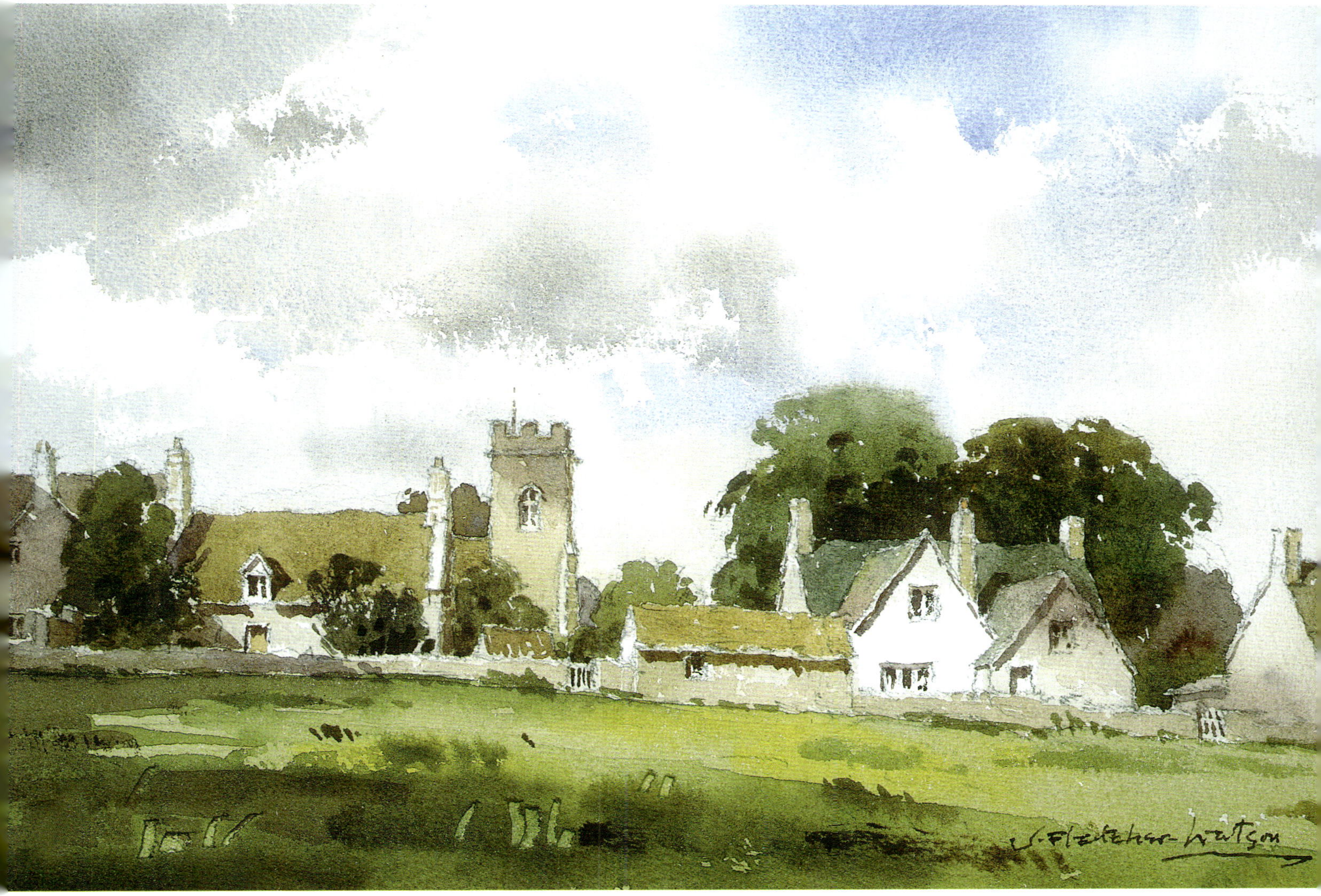

Figure 36
Windrush village, England.
235 × 362mm (9½ × 14¼in)

with the church tower in the middle giving a focal point. On the right, there is a tall group of lime trees forming an invaluable background to emphasize two of the cottages. This was painted in high summer, when trees can be really dark, and how splendidly they make the buildings and chimneys stand out. There is also part of a tree showing to the left of the tower, which has the same effect, and some low tree-tops to the right of the tower giving emphasis to the low brown-roofed outbuilding. The small tree and shrub are useful features, breaking up the elevations of the left-hand cottages. These trees give tremendous strength and character to the view, which would be far less interesting without them. My colours for all the trees were mixtures of Cadmium Yellow, Winsor Blue and Burnt Umber.

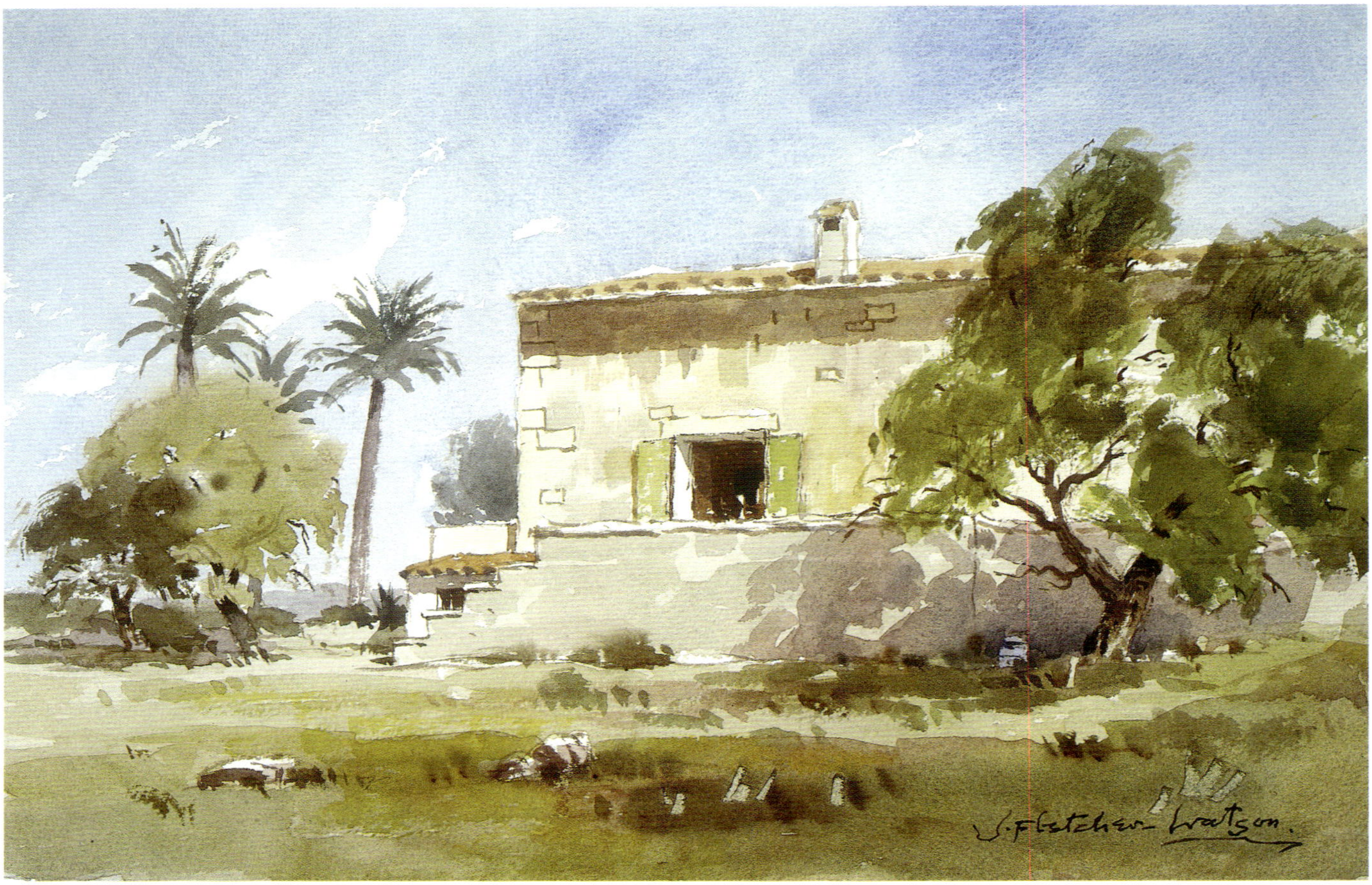

Figure 37
A Majorcan farmhouse.
235 × 362mm (9½ × 14¼in)

Lastly we have **figure 37**, *A Majorcan farmhouse*, which was painted on the spot in May. The tree on the right is an ancient olive, which was casting a lovely shadow on the adjoining wall. This tree, together with the two palm trees on the left, made an excellent composition. Note also the small grey tree peeping round the corner of the house, which helped to give contrast to the stonework. This is a very simple subject that would be quite without interest had it not been for the trees.

I hope I have given you some useful examples to enable you to paint some good tree studies and to gain a knowledge of the techniques required for forming a good tree landscape.

Of course, if you are going to get really interested in trees, you should study the different types closely. For instance, the big tree on the right in **figure 28** on page 37 is an ash tree, which is always a very graceful tree type. **Figure 31** on page 40 shows willow trees, which have a distinctive blue-green colour. The large trees in **figure 36** on page 45 are limes. An oak tree tends to be rather square in shape owing to individual branches growing at right angles to each other. In the autumn, trees turn very different colours; for example, the leaves of an autumn beech tree are a glorious yellow-red.

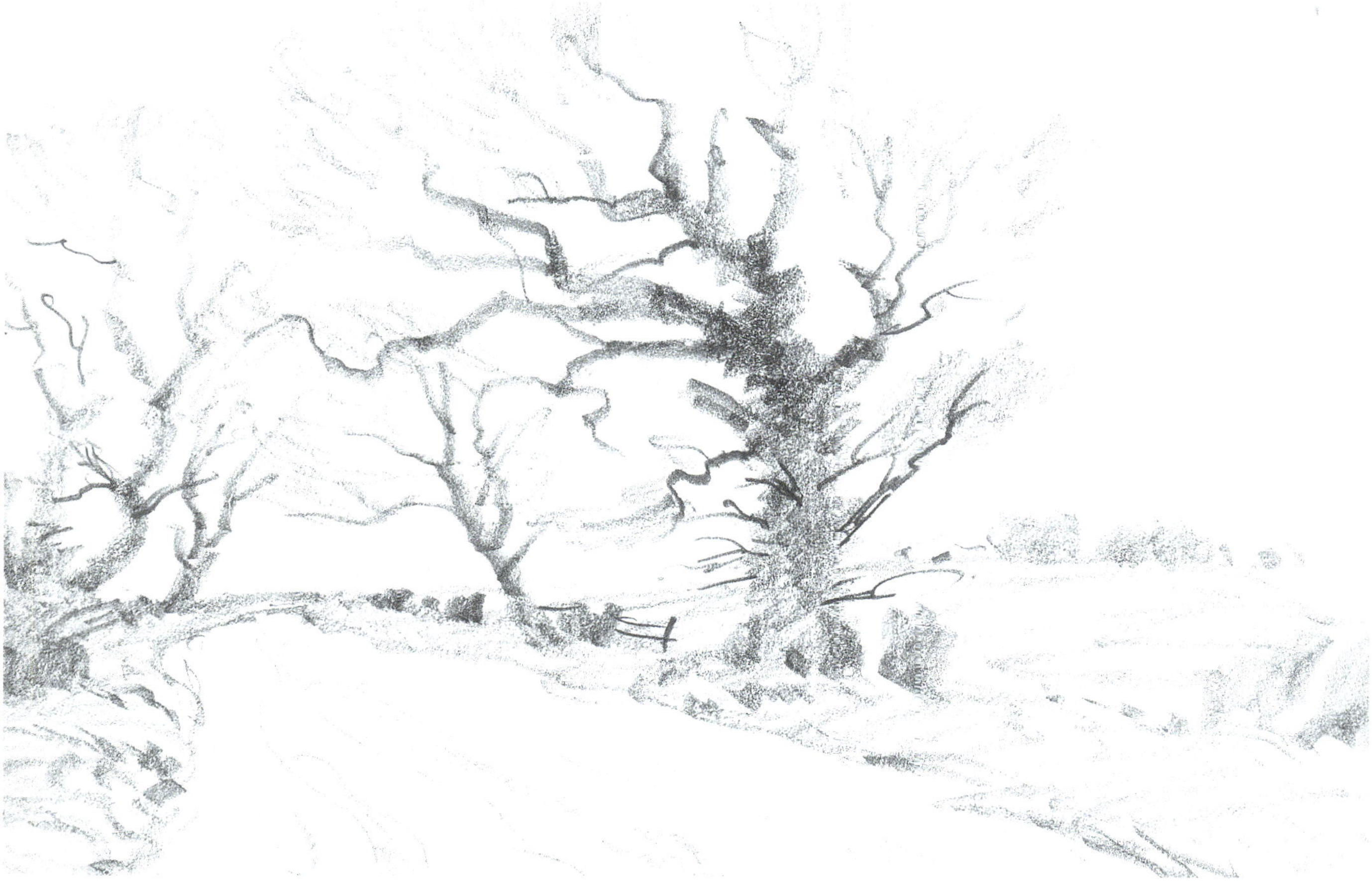

TIPS AND TECHNIQUES

- Familiarize yourself with the anatomy of the different species of trees (seen in winter) before painting them covered with foliage
- Don't attempt to paint twigs individually – use a medium-size brush with a dry mix of Burnt Umber and Payne's Gray
- Dragged brushwork can effectively suggest the delicacy of treetop outlines
- Use careful observation to avoid underestimating the weight and width of the trunk and branches of a tree
- Use bold brushwork for foliage, using the brush sideways and dragging it quickly across the paper
- Add the trunk and branches while the foliage wash is still damp. This will integrate the branches effectively with the colour of the foliage

Chapter 5

COUNTRY BUILDINGS

Welsh farm cottage; Norfolk water mill; Northumbrian castles; Suffolk farm buildings

By country buildings, I am referring here to buildings in the British Isles, which are not quite the same as those in, for example, America, France or Australia. That said, the principles governing the painting of such buildings are fairly similar the world over. I am constantly fascinated by the marvellous variety of world architecture, from tenth-century castles and medieval Tuscan hilltop villages to the gracious houses and churches of eighteenth-century New England.

The small, simple dwelling in its lovely setting shown in **figure 38** was chosen mainly for its superb composition. I placed the group of buildings slightly to the right of centre, and the sloping ground made an attractive feature. The farm track leads the eye into the picture, and the thin leaning trees on the right give a lovely foil to the horizontal blue mountain range behind them. I used Saunders-Waterford paper, which has a slightly rough surface and is a light cream colour.

I decided not to use any pencil, but to draw with a very small brush and a mixture of Burnt Umber and Payne's Gray. With this method, you cannot afford to make any mistakes! The final picture benefits by having a loose, simple clarity. If you are a beginner, I recommend using a pencil.

Having completed the drawing of the cottage, trees and road, I painted the sky using mixtures of French Ultramarine and Burnt Umber, and Cobalt Blue for the two patches of blue sky. These washes were carried over the mountain areas down to the ground, carefully painting round the cottage outline.

Figure 39 shows the next stage. I completed all the buildings as follows. The roofs were Cerulean Blue and Light Red, giving a good greenish-grey Welsh slate colour. The stone walls followed, using Cobalt Blue, Light Red and Raw Sienna with plenty of water for a light tone. When dry, a slightly darker tone was applied to give a stone texture. Then the windows and lean-to shed openings were painted with Burnt Umber and a touch of French Ultramarine. When these were dry, a much darker mixture was painted on parts of the shed openings and on the thin line of the porch door. Then came the trees showing behind the buildings, which were painted using Burnt Umber and Winsor Blue, and finally the shadows under the eaves of all the buildings with Cobalt Blue, Light Red and a touch of Raw Sienna. The dark background trees were painted last of all.

To complete the whole picture (**figure 38**), I painted the distant mountains with French Ultramarine and Light Red, the grass areas with Cobalt Blue and Raw Sienna, and the ground shadows with a stronger mixture of the same colours. The foreground tree foliage was painted with a mixture of Raw Sienna and French Ultramarine, while the strong foreground shadow across the track consisted of a mix of French Ultramarine, Light Red and a touch of Raw Sienna. The rocks featured shadows of the same mixture but in a darker tone.

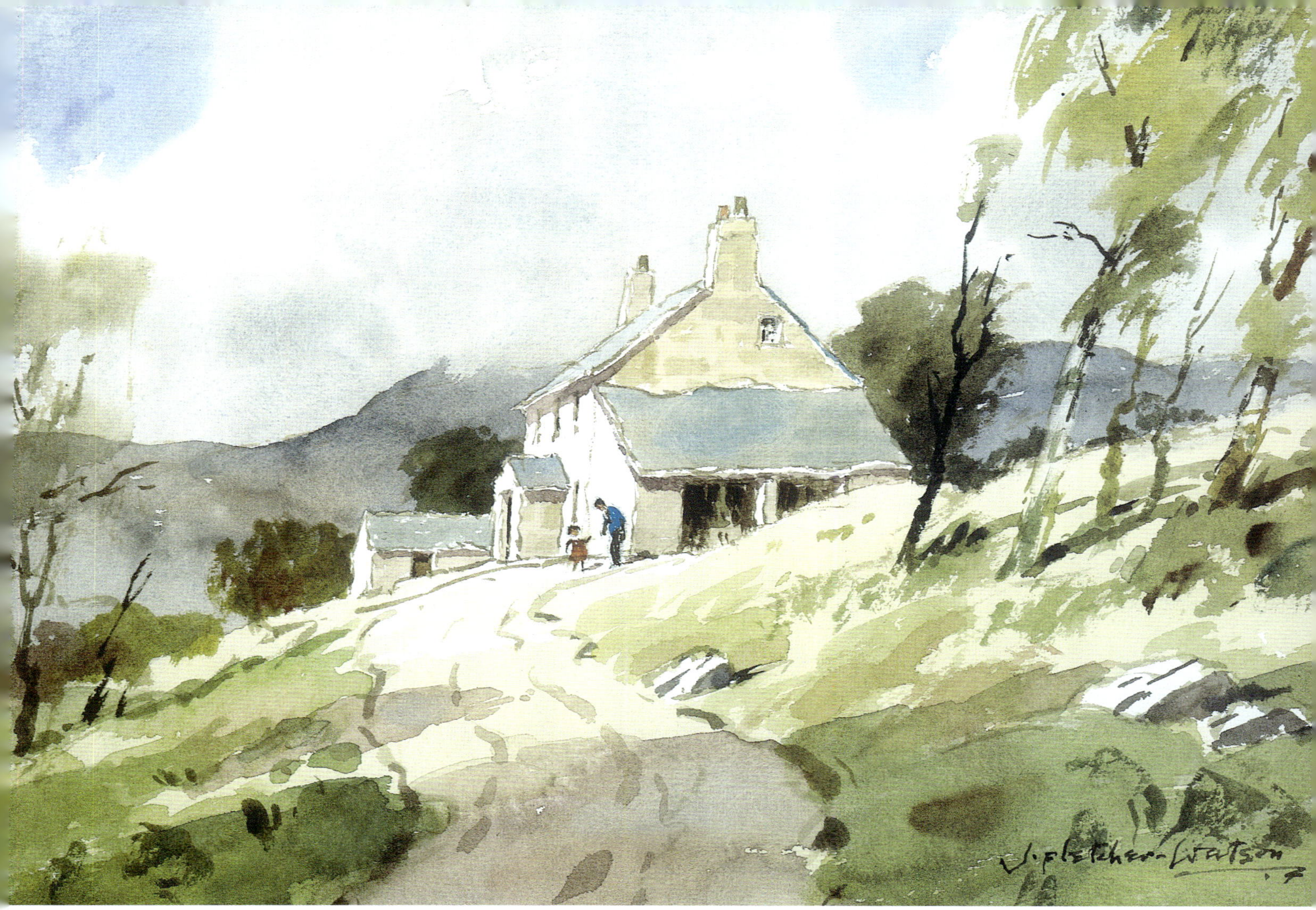

Figure 38
A Welsh farm cottage.
235 × 362mm (9½ × 14¼in)

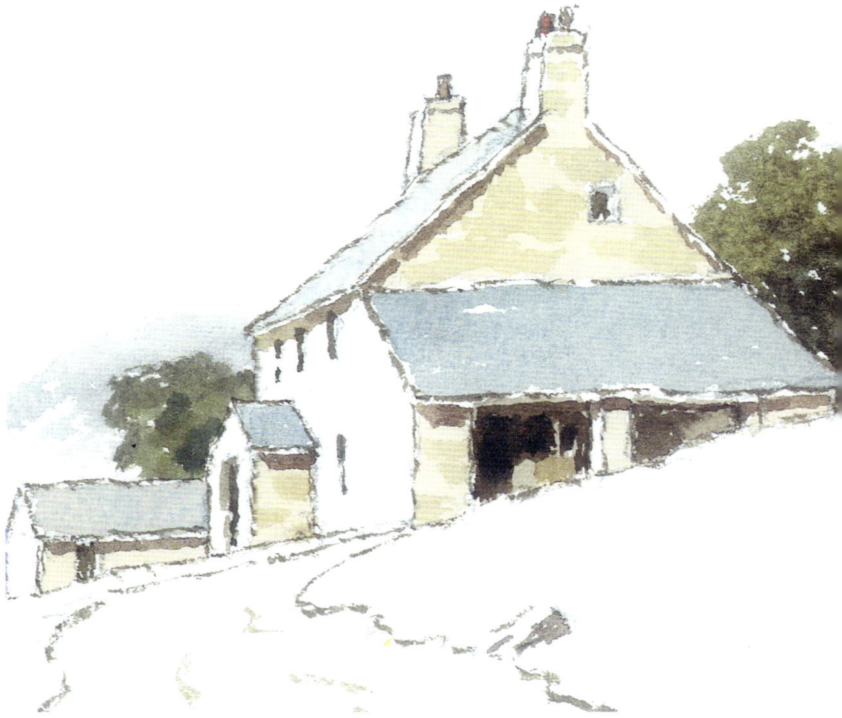

Figure 39
Detail of Welsh farm cottage.

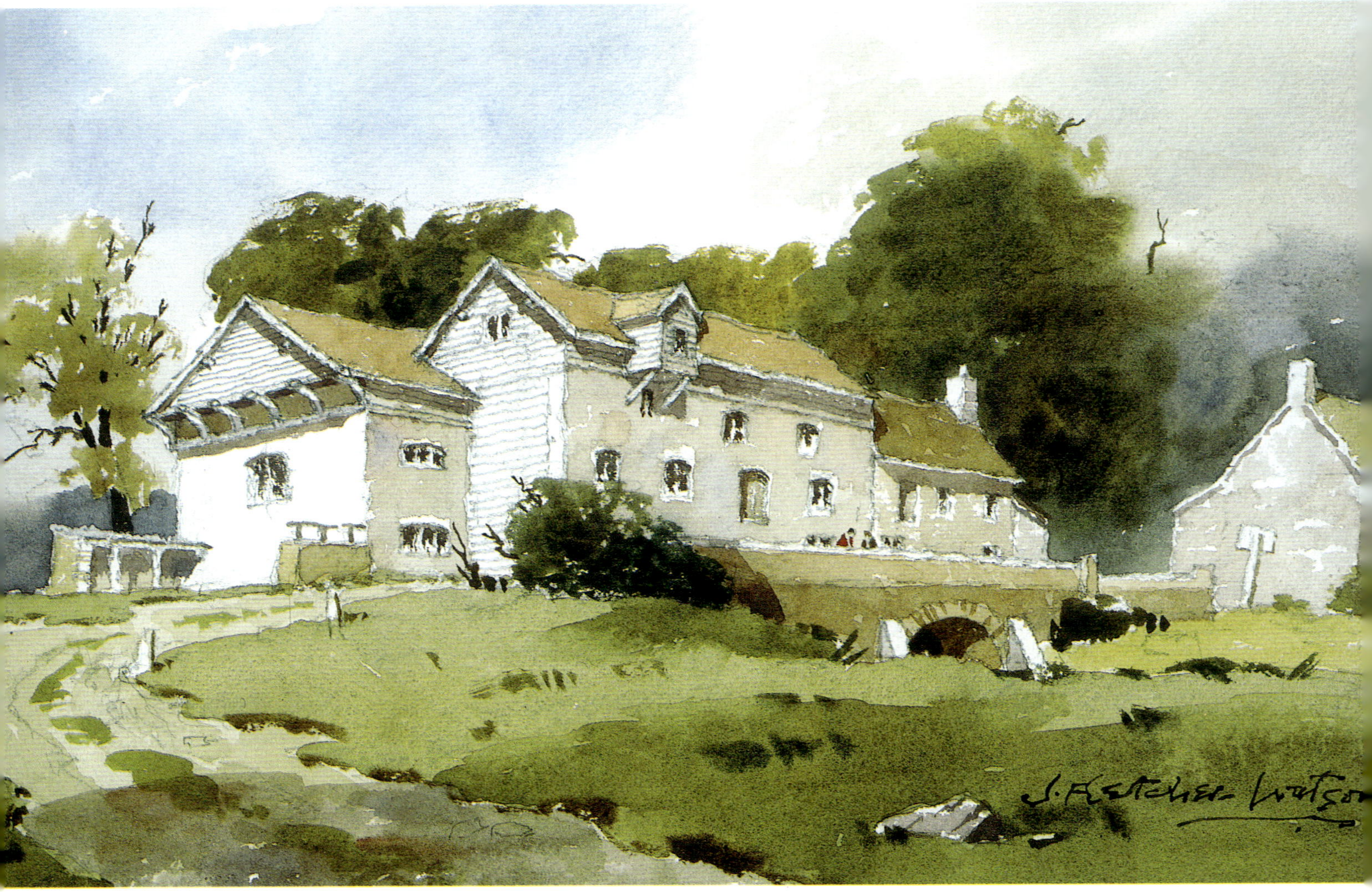

Figure 40
A Norfolk water mill, England.
235 × 362mm (9½ × 14¼in)

Another type of country building is shown in **figure 40**, *A Norfolk water mill*. This lovely old building is at Marlingford, near Norwich. As you will see, it is partly clad with weather-boarding and painted white, which is fairly typical of these mills.

The technique of painting this mill was first to make a careful pencil drawing. As you can see the pencilwork still shows on the weatherboarding, which was intentional. The perspective is important, as the viewpoint from where I was sitting was well below the farm road leading over the bridge. Some careful drawing was needed for the curved wooden brackets supporting the left-hand gable and also for the projecting gantry in the right-hand roof.

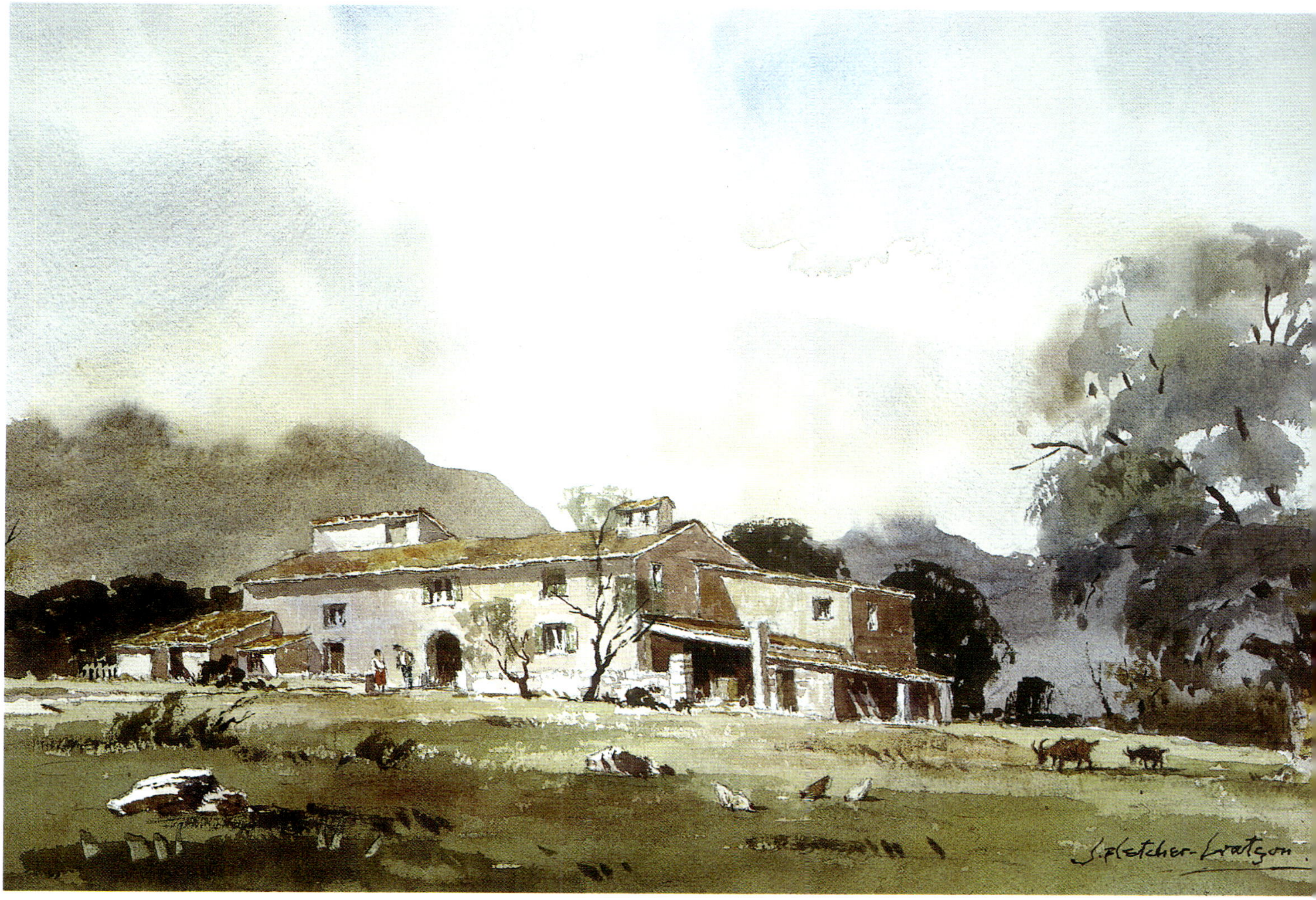

Figure 41
A Majorcan Farm.
266 × 476mm (10½ × 18¾in)

Incidentally, you will notice how valuable the mass of background trees is, giving a dark tone against the light walls of the mill and making the whole building stand out in bold relief.

The *Majorcan Farm* in **figure 41** is fairly typical of buildings to be seen in the northern part of the island. The various outbuildings have been added at different times over the years, making a charming group with the main building. The mountain in the background is also a very helpful feature and the large tree on the right balances the composition well. The rocks, goats and hens are movable features, which can be placed in exactly the right position, thus completing the overall harmony.

Figure 42, *Norham Castle, Northumbria*, shows a castle located on the outskirts of Norham village, which is easily accessible. I painted this on a recent trip where I was exploring Northumbria for the first time – and how rewarding this area was with its exciting old castles, rivers, bridges, unspoilt villages, rolling hills and stone outcrops.

I have selected this subject mainly for its simplicity. All we have here is an easy-to-draw castle tower, adjoining trees and a road. Note that the composition has the castle slightly to the right, well-placed trees, an uphill road and the big foreground shadow, cast by trees out of the picture on the right.

The colours used for the castle were varying tones of Burnt Umber and French Ultramarine, and for the rest of the picture Cadmium Yellow, Winsor Blue and Raw Sienna.

The ruined castle of Corfe (**figure 43**) stands on top of a hill and dominates the small village of stone-built houses and cottages. The castle itself dates back to the Norman period of the eleventh century. The village buildings are mostly fifteenth to eighteenth century, and taken all together the village is one of the most beautiful examples of unspoilt English domestic architecture.

Figure 42
Norham Castle, Northumbria, England.
266 × 476mm (10½ × 18¾in)

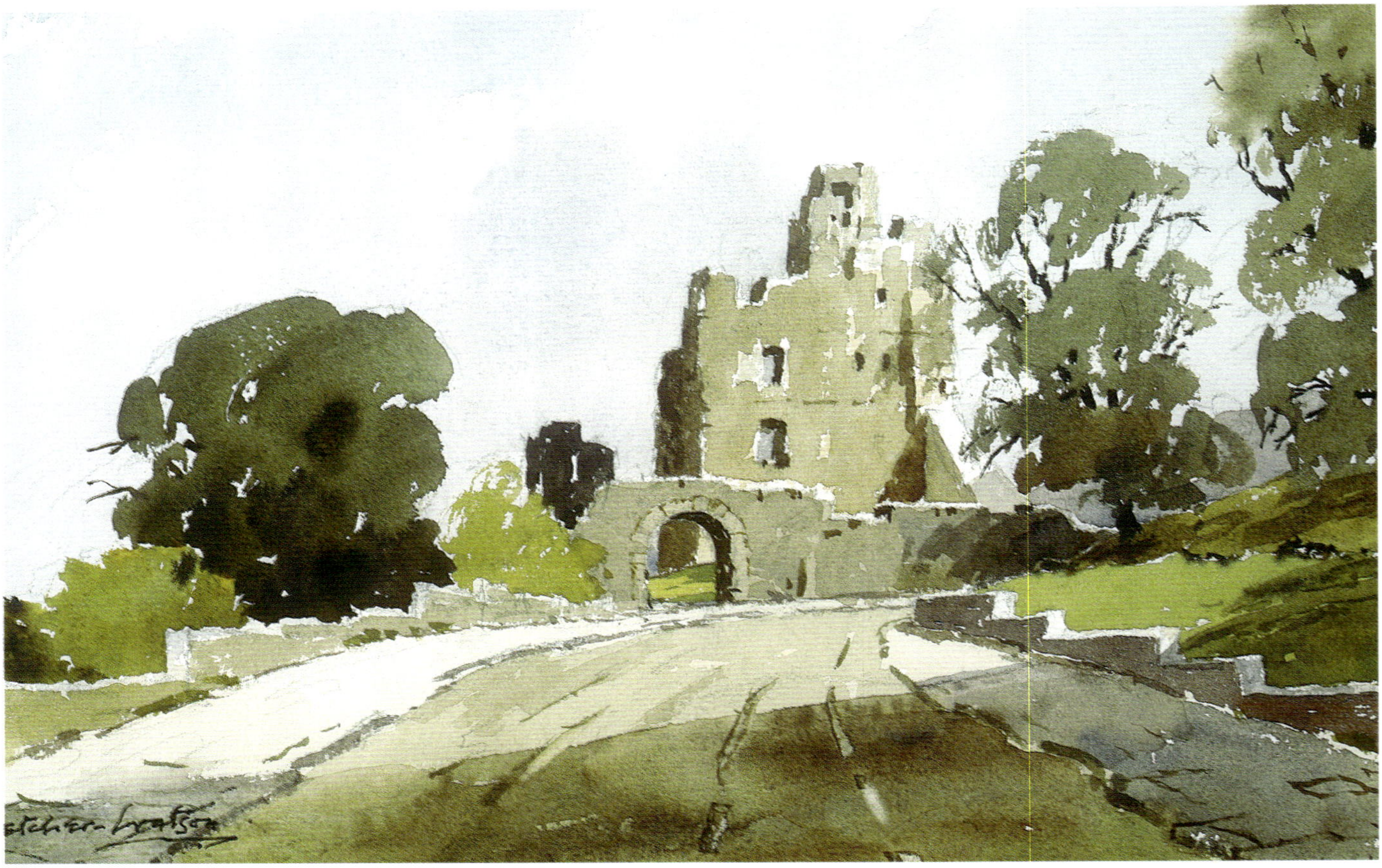

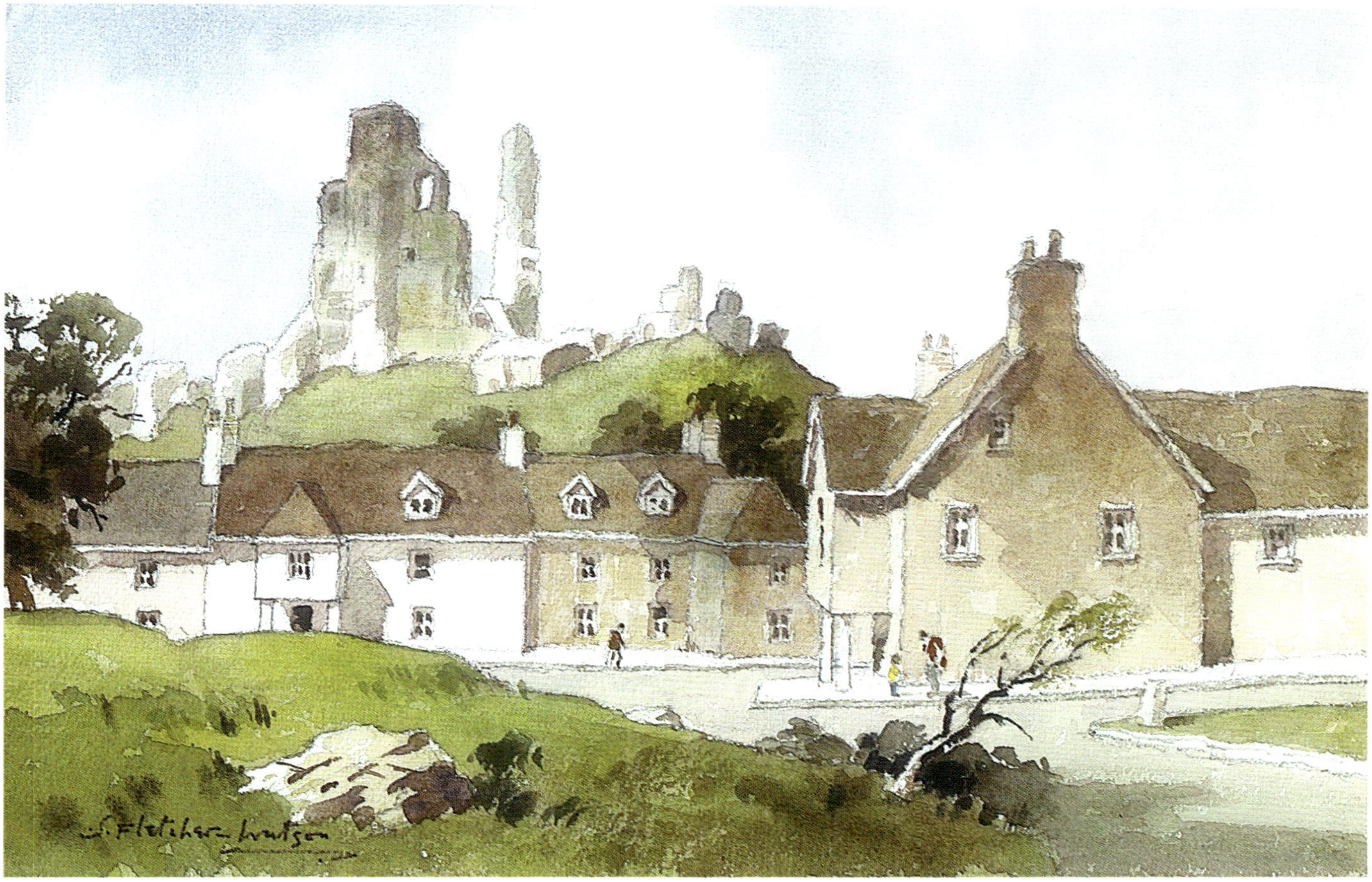

Figure 43
Corfe Castle, Dorset, England.
242 × 369mm (9½ × 14½in)

The paper I was using for the painting in **figure 43** was Whatman NOT and I started the drawing with a 3B pencil. First I sketched in the castle on its hill, followed by the various cottages. There were many possible views of the castle and I found it quite difficult to make a choice, but I finally settled on what is an extremely well-balanced view, as I think you will agree.

The painting work was as follows. First, of course, came the sky, which was fairly cloudy and I used Payne's Gray for these washes. There were plenty of gaps in the clouds, which produced an interesting combination of sunshine and shadows on the buildings. Especially notable are the cloud shadows on the ruin itself. The colour of the stone walls of the castle and cottages was a mixture of Cobalt Blue and Burnt Umber, and the stone-tiled roofs were all the same colour, but a darker mixture. The colour of the grass on the hill and in the foreground was Cadmium Yellow and Winsor Blue with a touch of Burnt Umber. The windows and door openings were painted with a mixture of French Ultramarine and Burnt Umber. This picture is a good example of a very limited palette that achieved the correct tone values on all the various parts.

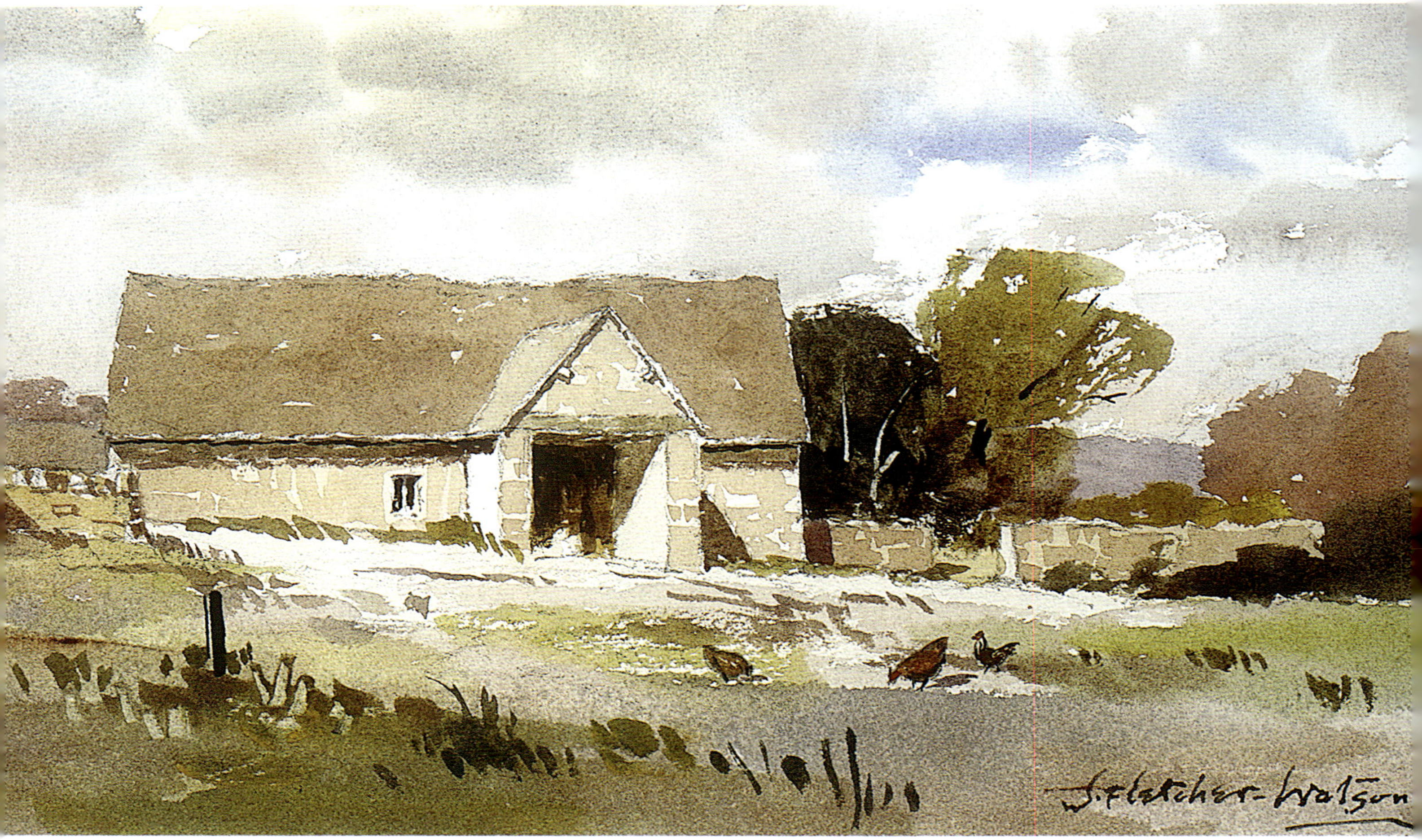

Figure 44 (above)
Barn in the Cotswolds, England.
235 × 362mm (9½ × 14¼in)

Figure 45 (right)
Farm buildings, Dedham, England.
318 × 477mm (12½ × 18¾in)

This chapter could not be complete without including buildings to be found on a farm. **Figure 44**, *Barn in the Cotswolds*, is very characteristic of the type of building to be found all over the Cotswolds. Architecturally it is a perfect specimen of stone walls and stone-tiled roof.

Another example, **figure 45**, *Farm buildings, Dedham*, shows an interesting group of barns and sheds. The buildings in themselves are not of great architectural merit, but it is their setting that adds such charm. The church tower can be seen over the treetops, and as soon as I saw this view, I knew it would be a winner. The composition was almost perfect and I took up my position just to the left of the farm track so that it ran into the picture from right to left. A minor adjustment was necessary to the big tree on the left, as it was too far away from the buildings, and I solved this by moving it a short distance to the right. The open-sided barn in the centre was the focal point and its interior was very dark indeed. I wanted an item of secondary interest in the buildings on the right, so I made a dark opening in the low blue-roofed shed. This gave just the desired strength of tone for the composition.

The painting process was fairly straightforward. The sky was, of course, washed in first. Then I tackled all the buildings, using various mixtures of Burnt Sienna, Cobalt Blue and Raw Sienna, and for the dark interior of the barn and shed, Burnt Umber and French Ultramarine. The straw bales in the barn were a weak wash of Raw Umber.

I next painted the various tree groups with mixtures of Raw Umber, Winsor Blue and Burnt Sienna. There was a distinct touch of autumn in the air and the trees reflected this. The foreground grass was painted using Raw Umber and a little Winsor Blue. I left the ground immediately adjacent to the barn white and unpainted, as the light earth was catching the sunlight.

The foreground cloud shadow was simply a darker mixture of the original grass colour, and over the track the shadow was Cobalt Blue and Light Red.

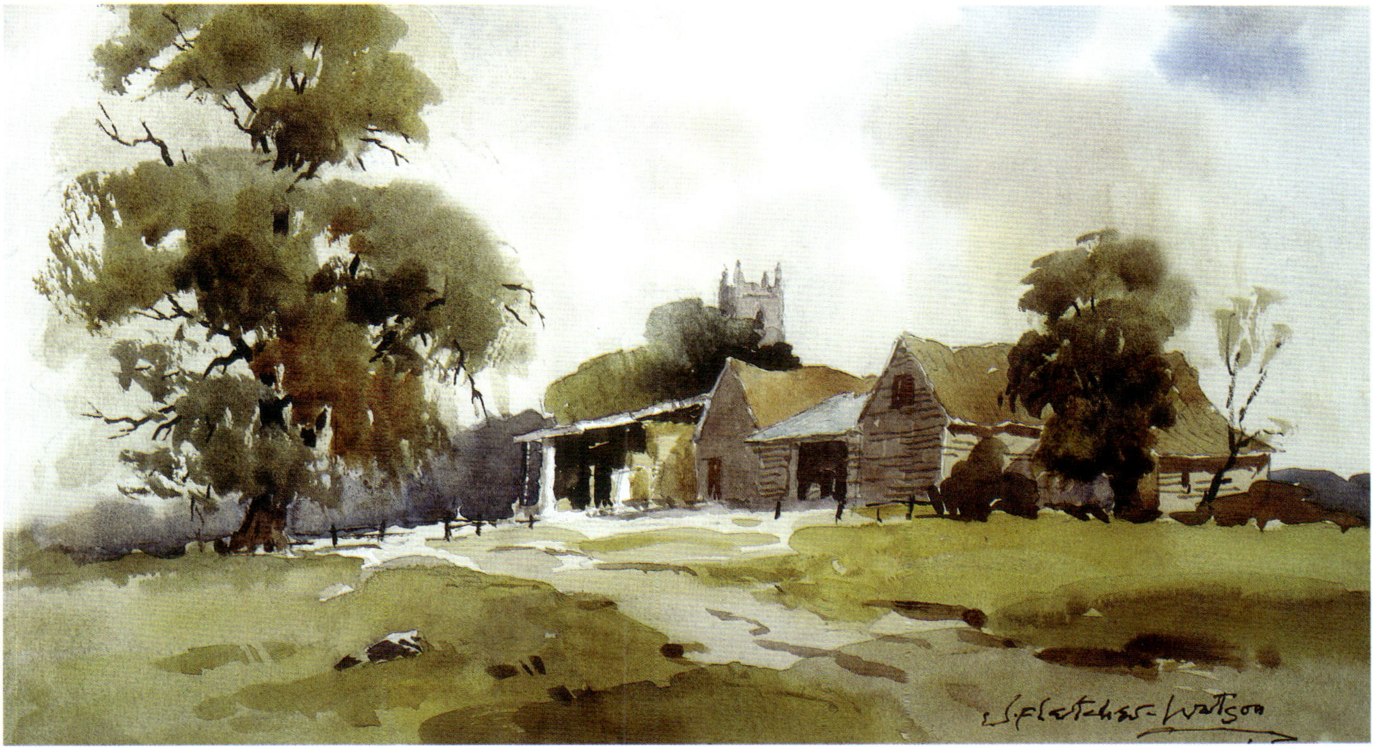

TIPS AND TECHNIQUES

- A background of dark trees can effectively define the building you are working on
- Even when working quickly, try to apply washes in an order that will build up the required colour and texture
- When painting buildings, there is no need to be too precise – too much detail may not actually enhance the overall effect
- When looking for a composition with buildings, the setting can give a picture as much charm as the buildings themselves

Chapter 6

TOWN BUILDINGS

Hill town, Crete; Roman ruin at Merida, Spain; St.Paul's Cathedral, London; Rouen, France; Roman bridge at Cordoba, Spain; ancient town in Normandy, France; city of Santiago de Compostela, Spain; quiet corners of England

In this chapter, I show how you can draw inspiration from a wide diversity of architectural styles. **Figure 47** (opposite) shows a remote and simple little habitation. These stone buildings are very typical of Cretan architecture and their simplicity lends charm. The small shop on the left with a sun-blind is in shadow, while the other buildings are thrown into sunny relief.

The drawing work was done with the small brush and brown paint used for the Welsh cottage in the previous chapter. **Figure 46** shows a detail of the central area, including the stone steps. It clearly demonstrates where a sketchy line is most effective. I used a limited palette of Raw Sienna, Burnt Umber and Cobalt Blue for most of the picture. For the figures, roof tiles and tree, I added Burnt Sienna and Winsor Blue. The key to success here is tone value. The darkest item is the door opening under the steps.

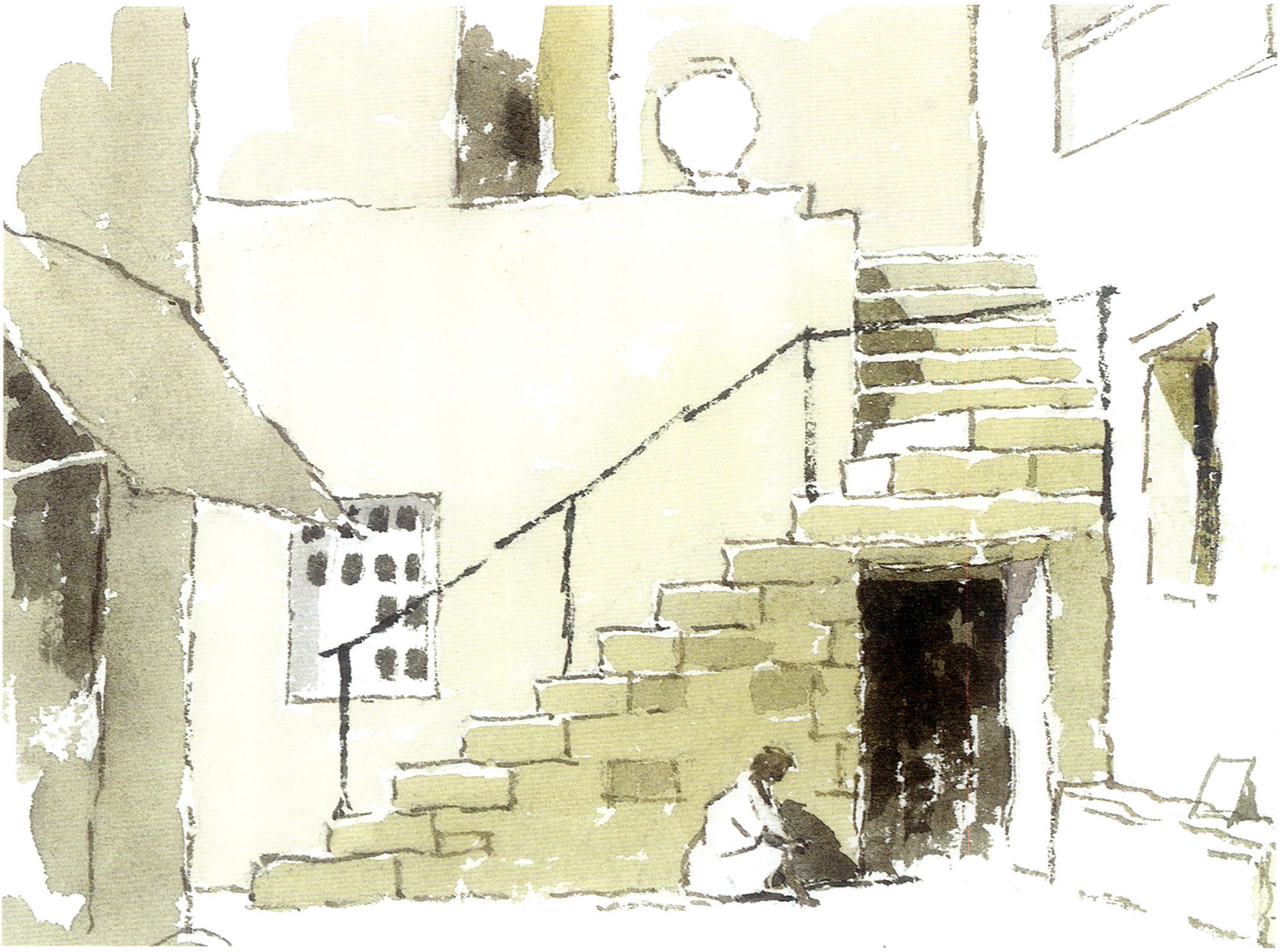

Figure 46
Detail of hill town, Crete.

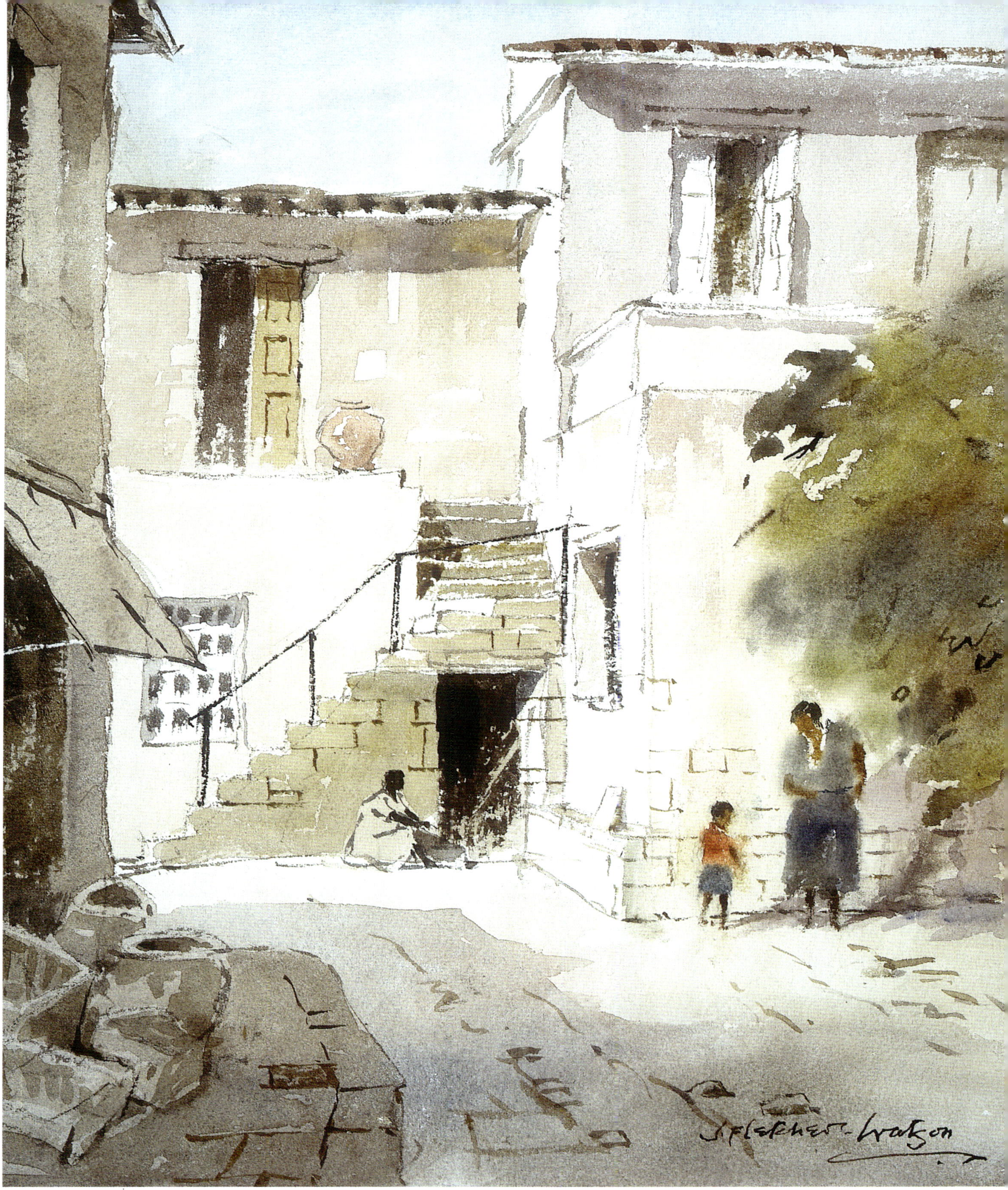

Figure 47
Hill town, Crete. 362 × 311mm (14¼ × 12¼in)

Moving now to Spain, **figure 48** was again a very simple scene crying out to be painted. It was essentially a strong sunlight subject; on a dull day it would be of less interest.

I was using a NOT surface paper and I drew the whole subject with a 2B pencil quite quickly and roughly (by which I mean that the lines were not dead straight). At the same time, it was drawn accurately enough to ensure that the archway was the right proportion. The very fact that this Roman structure was nearly 2,000 years old made one marvel! The main feature was its chunky stone quality. The general colouring was Burnt Umber mixed with French Ultramarine, giving various tones of grey-brown. Note how the stone paving joints help with the perspective and depth. The tree showing over the top was extremely useful, throwing the structure into splendid relief.

I mainly used a No. 8 brush, painting quite quickly with a strong mixture of colour, which gave the final result a freedom and simplicity that is so desirable in watercolour. This subject could easily have been overlooked, but with the sunlight and shadow it was transformed into something very special.

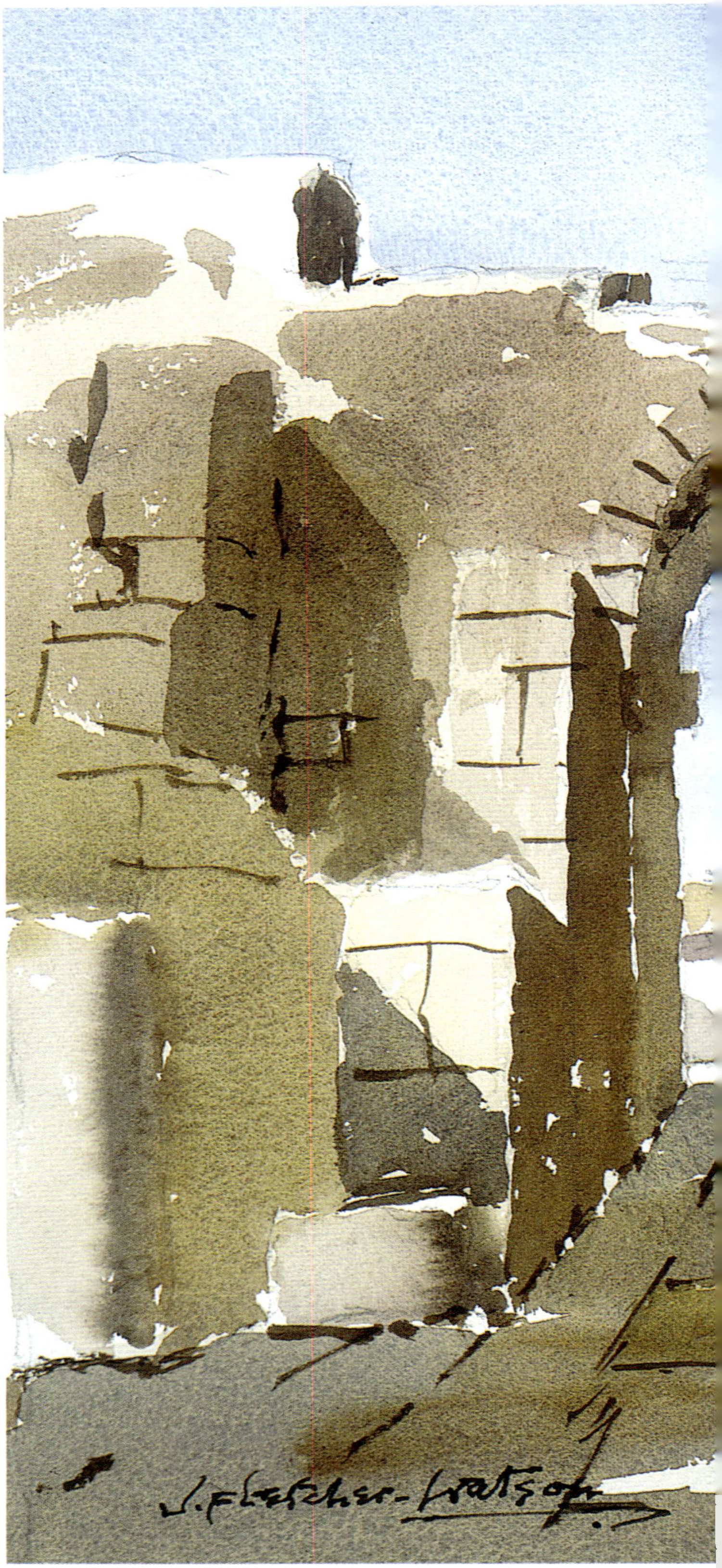

Figure 48
Roman arch amphitheatre, Merida.
318 × 477mm (12½ × 18¾in)

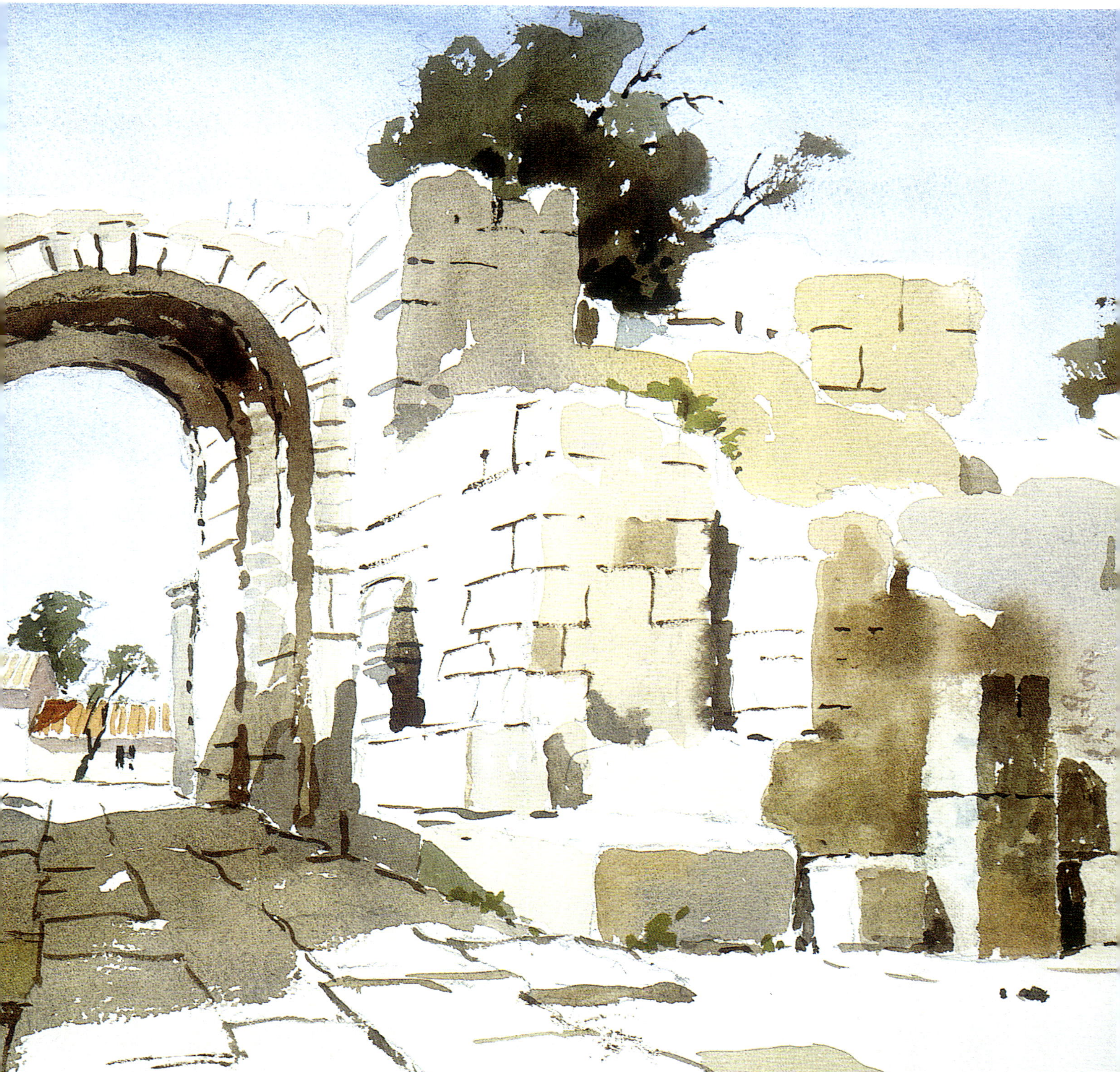

I was thrilled with this view of *St. Paul's Cathedral, London* (**figure 49**), seen from Ludgate Hill. I drew this on the spot some time ago and painted it back in the studio. There is a lot of architectural detail, which I have indicated without making the picture over elaborate. A knowledge of perspective is helpful when you are tackling a picture of this complexity.

Figure 50 is the famous *Gros Horloge* (Great Clock), positioned over the *Rue du Gros Horloge* in the centre of Rouen in Normandy. I enjoyed capturing the architectural detail of such an elaborate building, but I did not attempt to paint this picture on the spot. After a careful drawing to make a note of the important colours, I could manage the painting work in the studio.

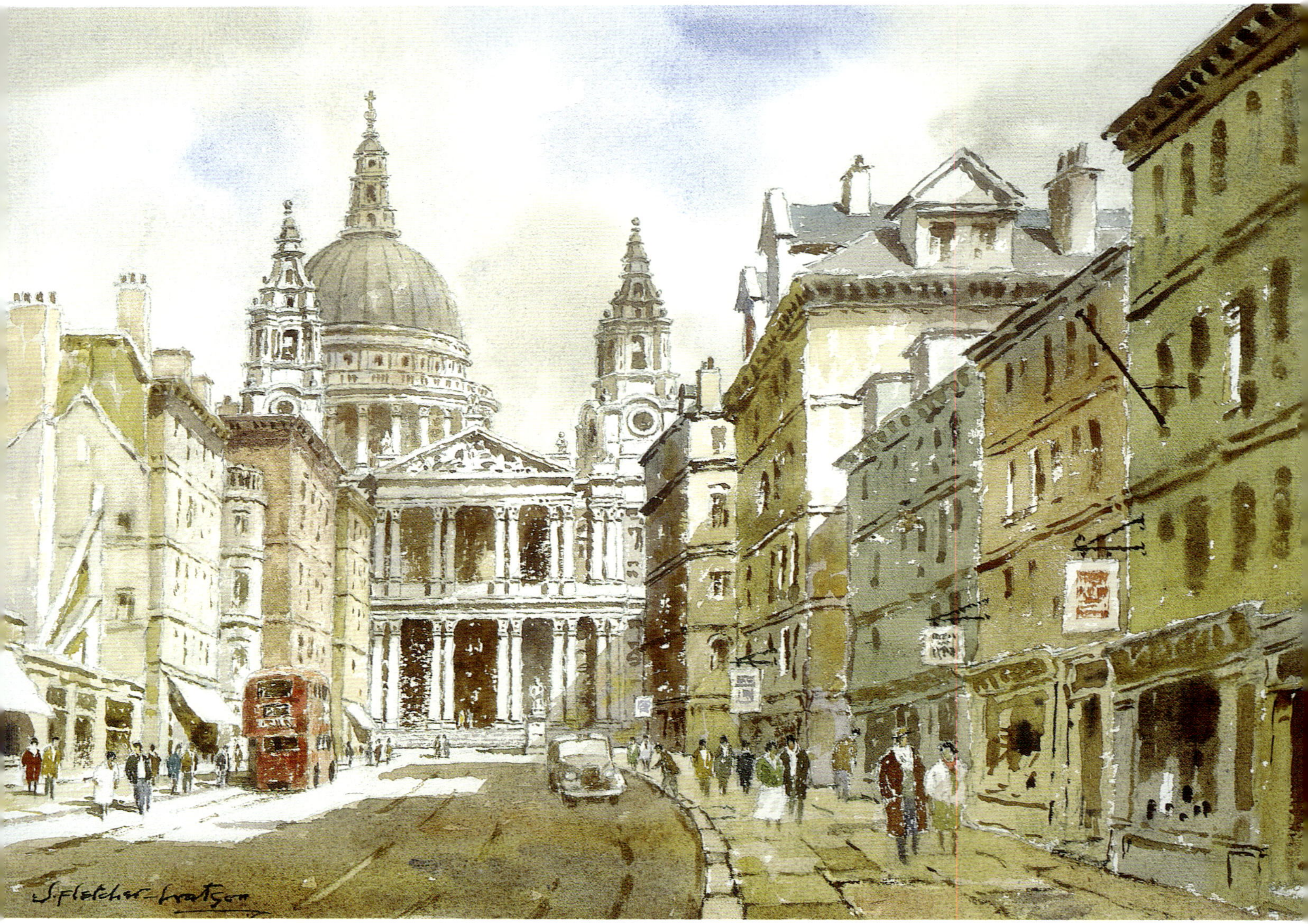

Figure 49
St Paul's Cathedral, London, England.
318 × 477mm (12½ × 18¾in)

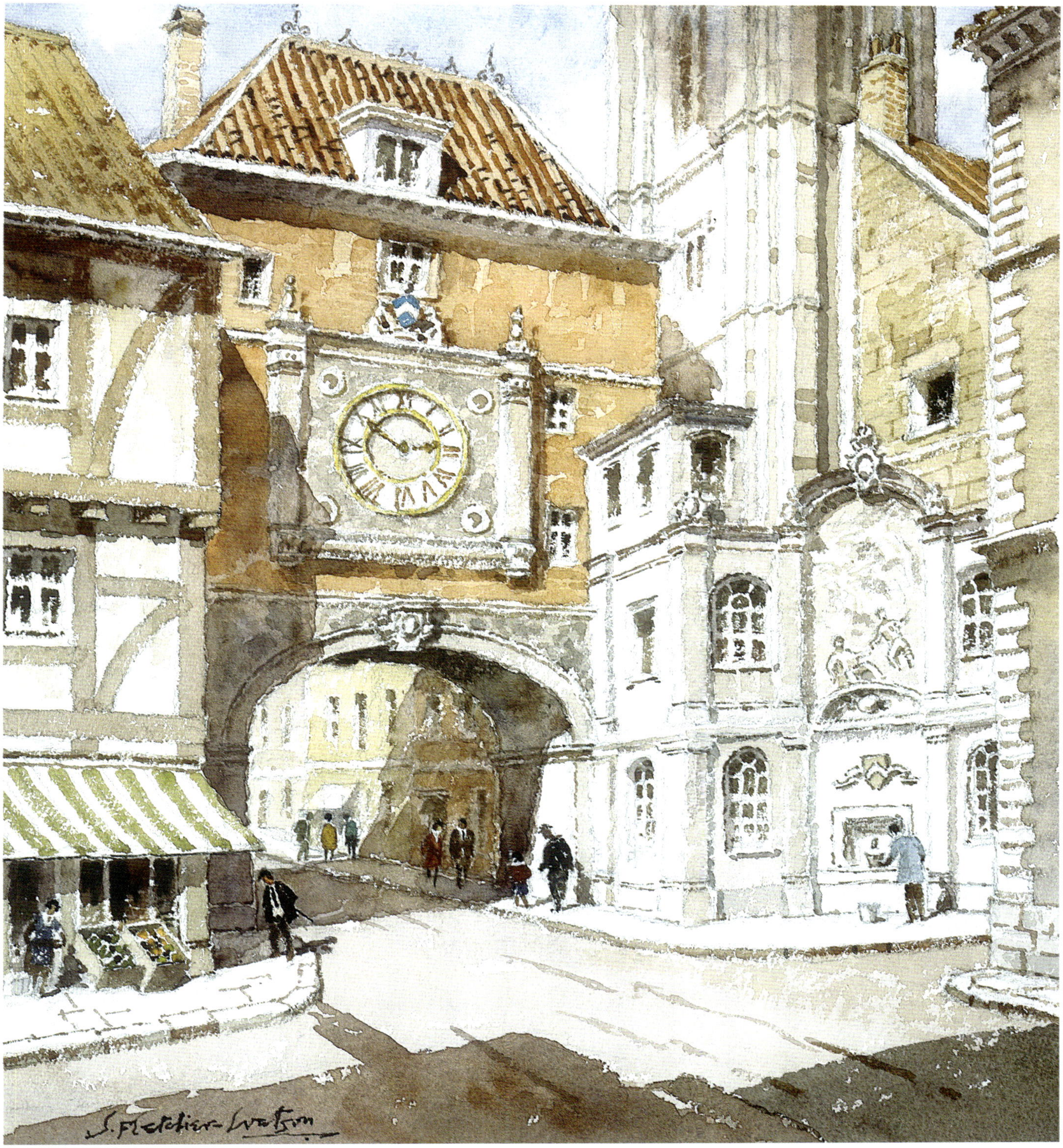

Figure 50
Rouen, Normandy, France.
362 × 311mm (14¼ × 12¼in)

Figure 51, *The Roman Bridge, Cordoba,* is another Spanish subject seen in the typically strong Spanish sunlight. Note the sharp shadows under the arches and the roof eaves of the central water mill.

I ventured off the main road down the sloping track, as some instinct told me I should find a good view down at water level, and I was rewarded with this superb composition. Everything was there, the arches, the solid stone buildings and the rugged foreground rocks, scrub and mud! What more could a painter want; the irregular skyline was calling out to be put down on paper and I revelled in this discovery!

I will not go through the whole painting in detail, but suggest that you first paint yourself the small area

Figure 51
The Roman Bridge, Cordoba, Spain.
318 × 477mm (12½ × 18¾in)

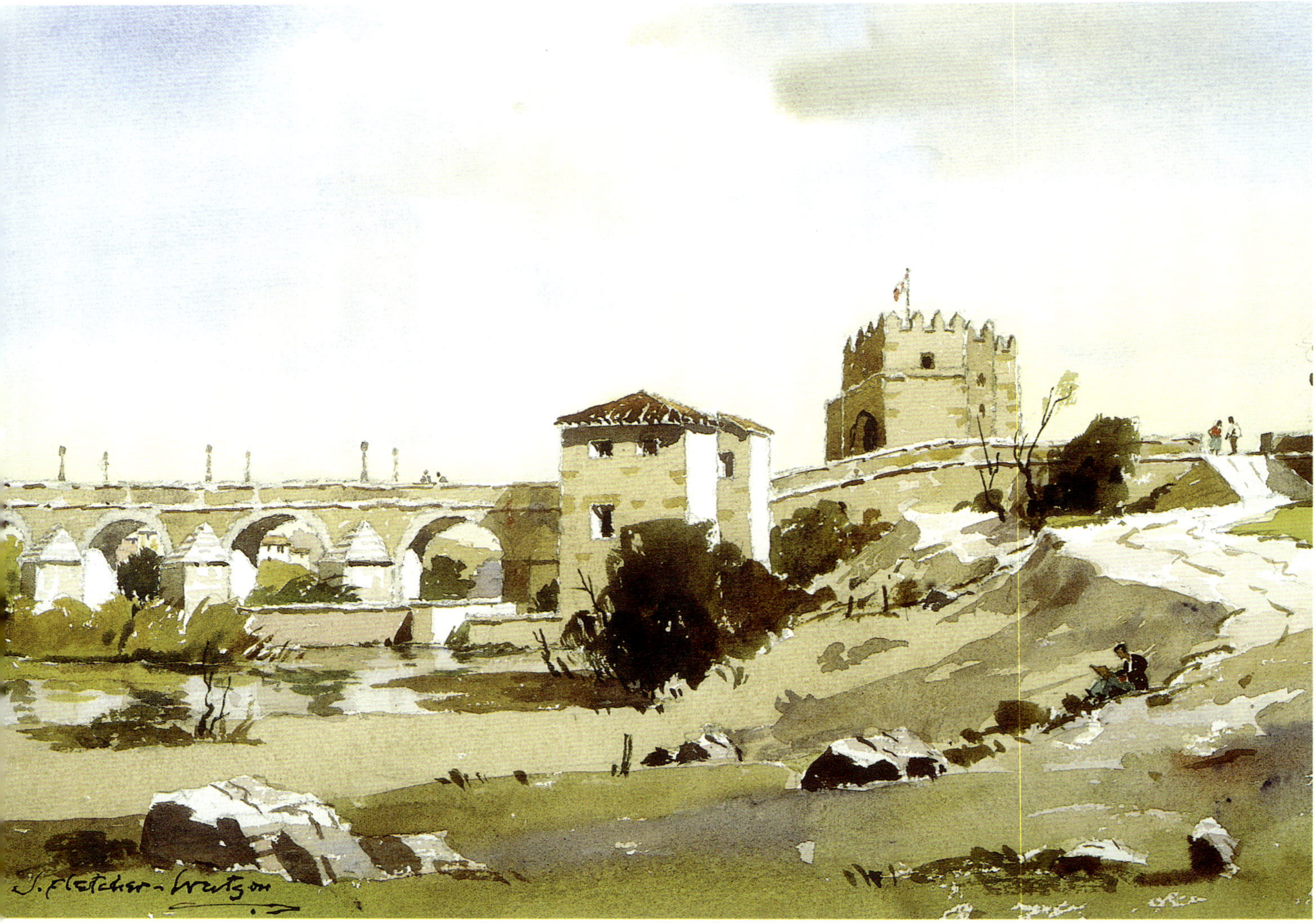

shown in **figure 52,** which shows the old Moorish mill building. Draw this on a small piece of watercolour paper about 178 × 254mm (7 × 10in) and then start painting. Begin with the red tile roof, using a No. 5 brush and a mixture of Burnt Sienna, and a touch of Cobalt Blue to form the sloping lines of Roman tiles. Then paint the walls of the mill and bridge with a No. 8 brush and a subtle mixture of Cobalt Blue, Light Red and Raw Sienna, which will give a warm, yellow stone colour. Now, with a No. 3 brush, draw in the thin shadow lines of the projecting stone string-course mouldings, using Burnt Umber. Follow this with the deep shadows in the windows and also the dark arch shadow, using Burnt Umber and French Ultramarine. For the strong sloping shadow cast by the millhouse onto the bridge, use the same colours but not quite such a dark mixture. This is the most important shadow of all, as it brings the whole picture to life. Finally the large bush in the foreground was painted using Burnt Umber and French Ultramarine again, but with a darker mixture and a No. 8 brush. Other minor details are touched in with suitable mixtures of the colours already mentioned.

You will find that this small exercise will teach you all you want to know for painting the whole picture on a larger piece of paper. Note the right-hand walls of the arch and the building are not painted at all, as the intense blazing sunlight makes them look quite white.

The colours used for the whole picture, including the greens and greys in the foreground and the blue-grey sky are as follows: Cadmium Yellow, Raw Sienna, Burnt Sienna, Burnt Umber, Light Red, Cobalt Blue, French Ultramarine and Winsor Blue.

Figure 52
Detail of the Roman Bridge, Cordoba.

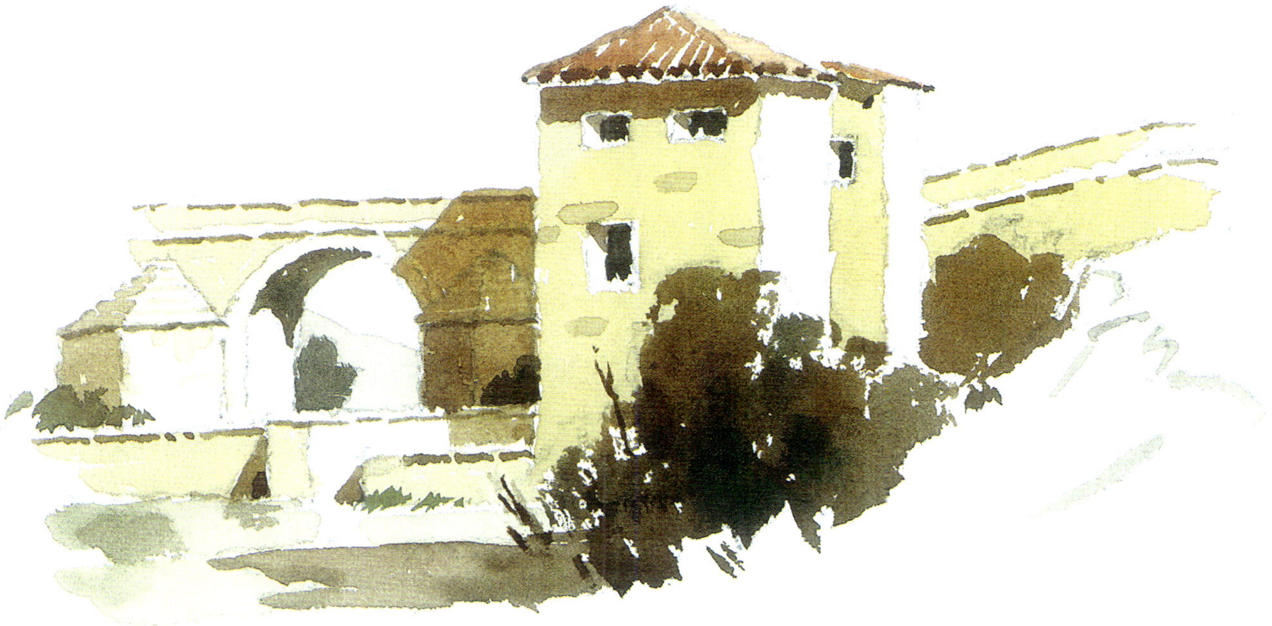

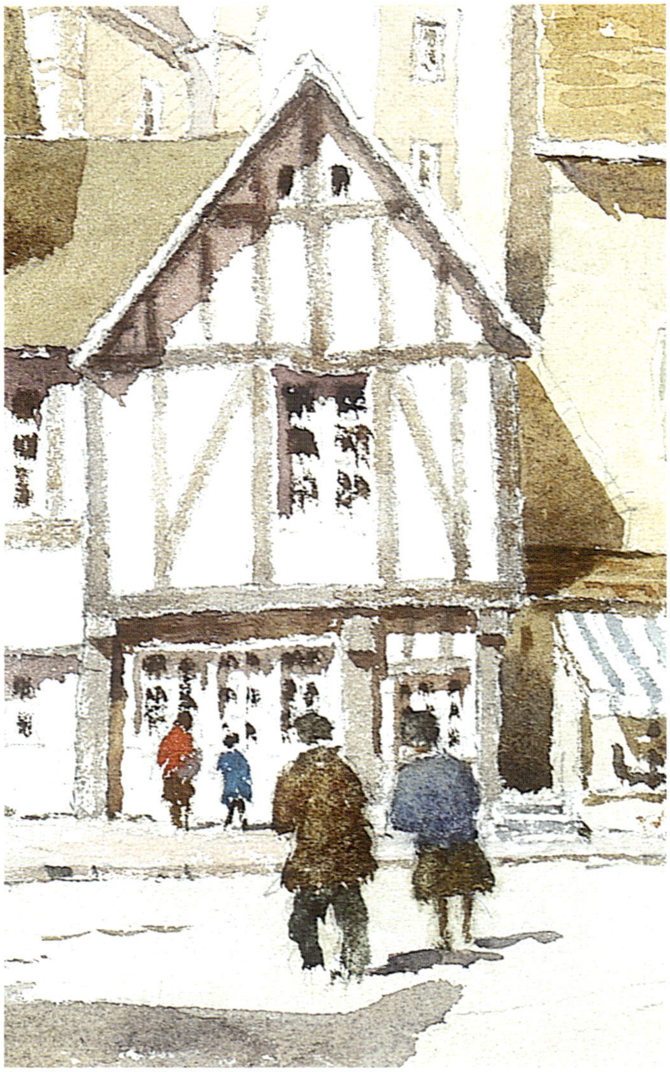

Figure 53a
Detail of house at Gaillon (**Figure 53**).

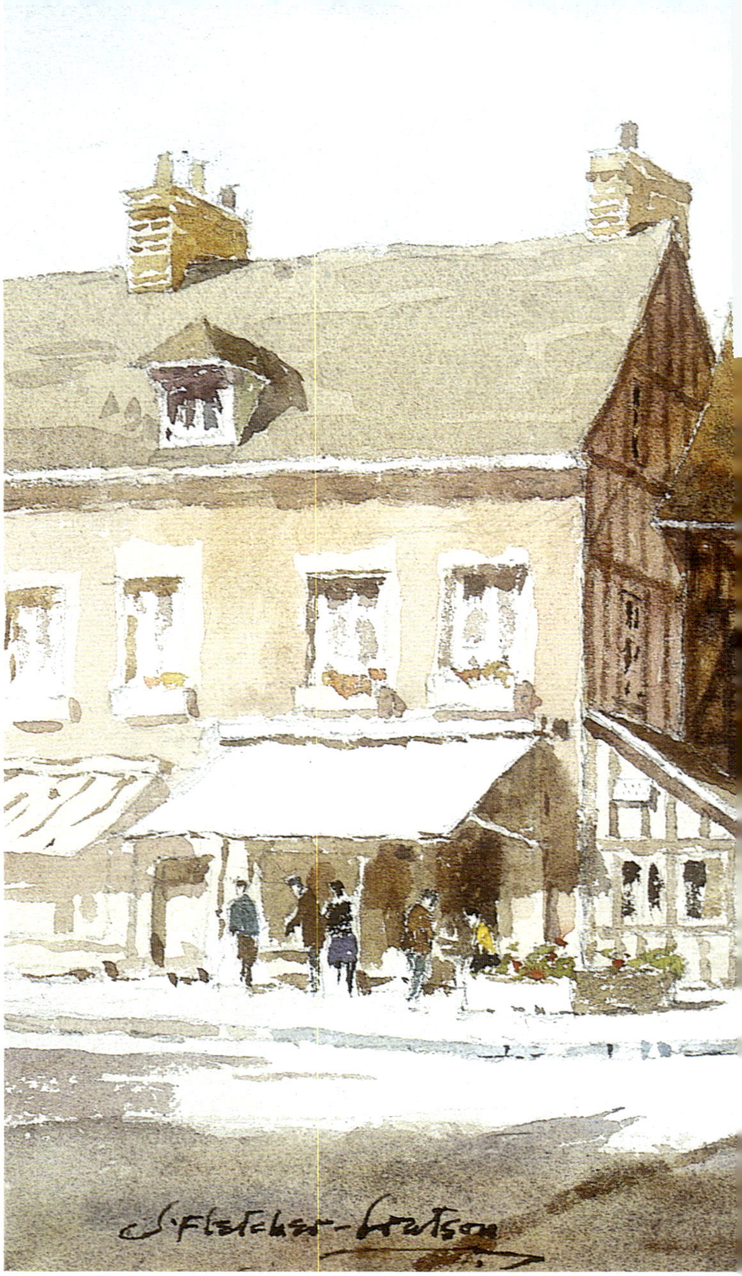

Figure 53
Gaillon, Normandy, France.
318 ×477mm (12½ × 18¼in)

Figure 53 shows seventeenth- and eighteenth-century architecture in northern France, with the steep roofs and spires of a medieval chateau in the background. The shadows were much more interesting when looked at from straight across the street rather than from a diagonal viewpoint. Incidentally, the perspective is also much easier with a frontal view.

I used Whatman 200lb paper with a NOT surface, suitable for detailed work. I first drew the whole scene with a 2B pencil, indicating the shadows, which can change surprisingly quickly. This is only necessary for a large subject like this when it takes a little while to reach the final stage of painting.

The positioning of figures is a very definite part of the composition. The two figures crossing the road were carefully kept to one side, as a central position would have made an unhappy focal point and divided the picture in two.

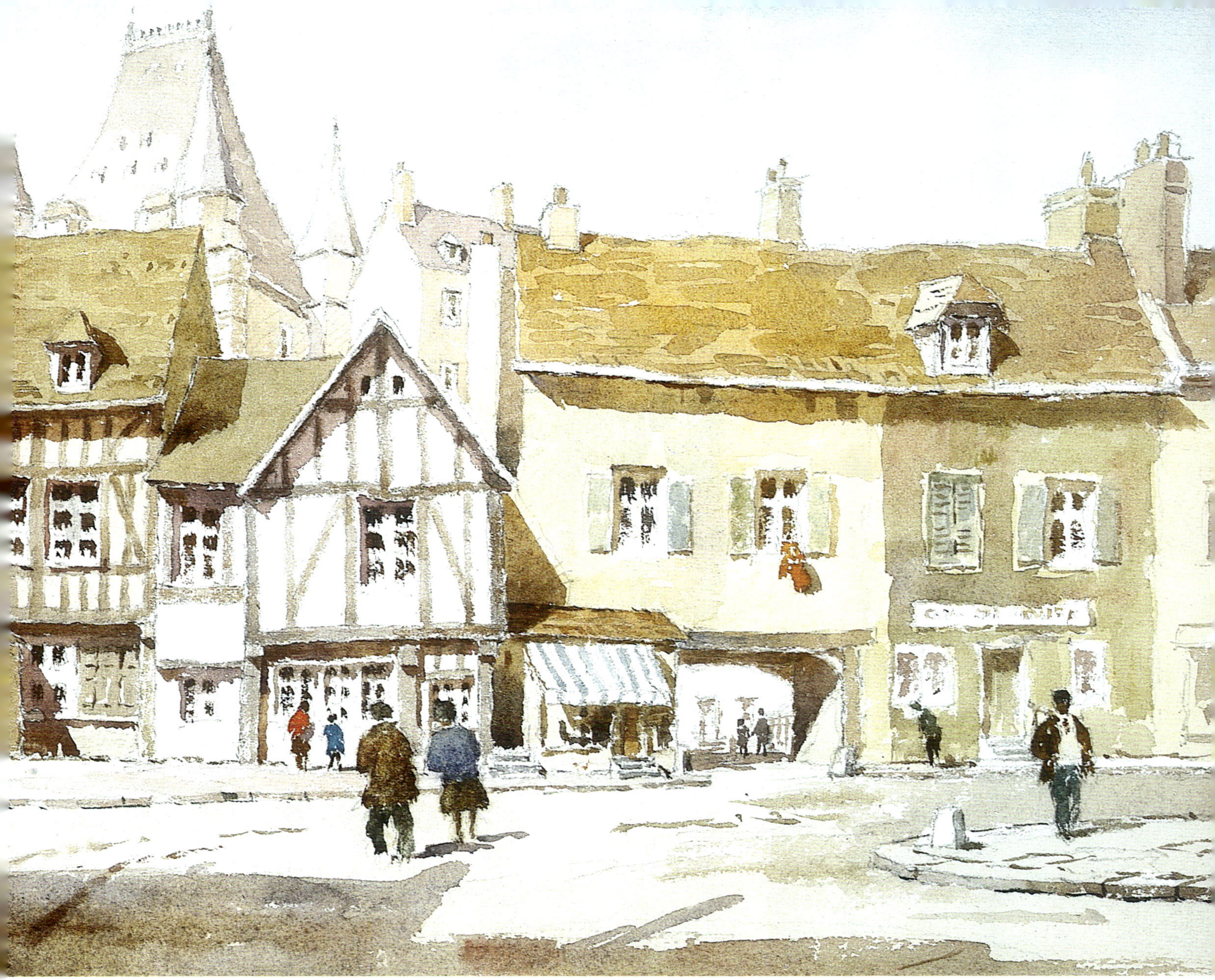

Having completed the drawing work, I started to paint the sky. Then I worked on the roofs and gave a light tone to the walls. The walls of the centre, gabled house were left unpainted to show the white of the paper. The next stage was to add the windows and doors. The figures were then painted in, and next the all-important shadows on the buildings and the foreground. Finally, wall textures were strengthened and shadows darkened selectively, which gave emphasis to certain parts of the picture.

Figure 53a gives you an idea of the painting technique. The heads of all the figures in the picture, both in the foreground and in the distance, are at the same level. By painting figures in this way you will ensure that you achieve the right perspective, thus giving a sense of distance to the picture. This is a golden rule of perspective and is well worth remembering.

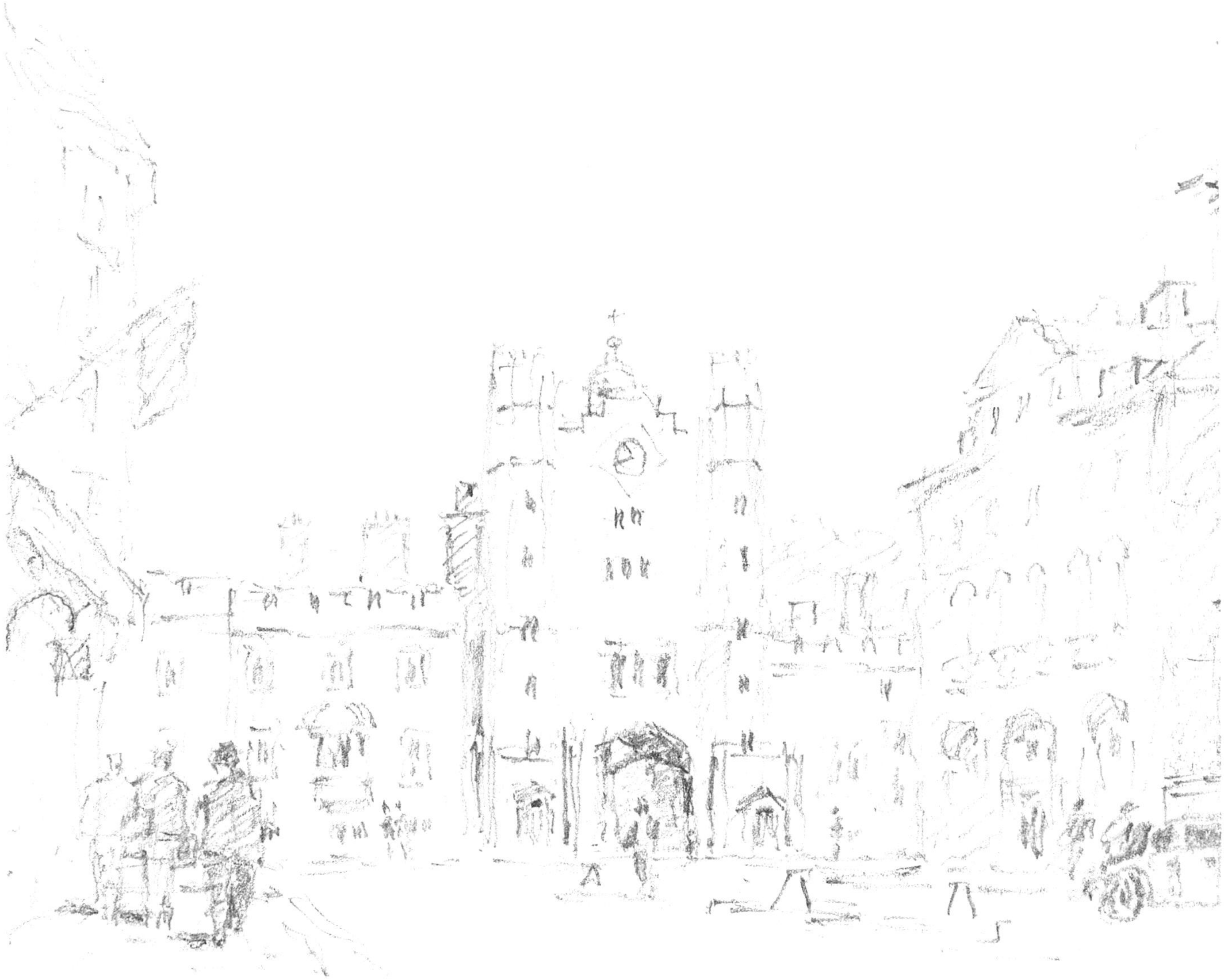

Figure 54, *Santiago de Compostela, Spain* (opposite), is a view of a wonderfully unspoilt city with narrow streets and spacious squares, which has to be seen to be believed. This particular view immediately caught my eye as a subject for an upright picture. Unlike **figure 53**, which shows a front elevation of a street, this was a view with strong perspective and depth, and it was reminiscent of one of Bonington's lovely street scenes.

Note the sky shape, which is broken up by the jutting-out roof eaves and the church pinnacle in the background. This picture is a good example of a vertical subject with lovely perspective and moving figures. Note the tone values, which are really strong in places, such as the arch on the right and the slanting shadow on the projecting building on the left. Observe the stone paving of the road, where the joints give perspective and depth in the same way as **figure 48**. Also note the strong shadows of the buildings, balconies and eaves, which give brilliance to the sunlit walls.

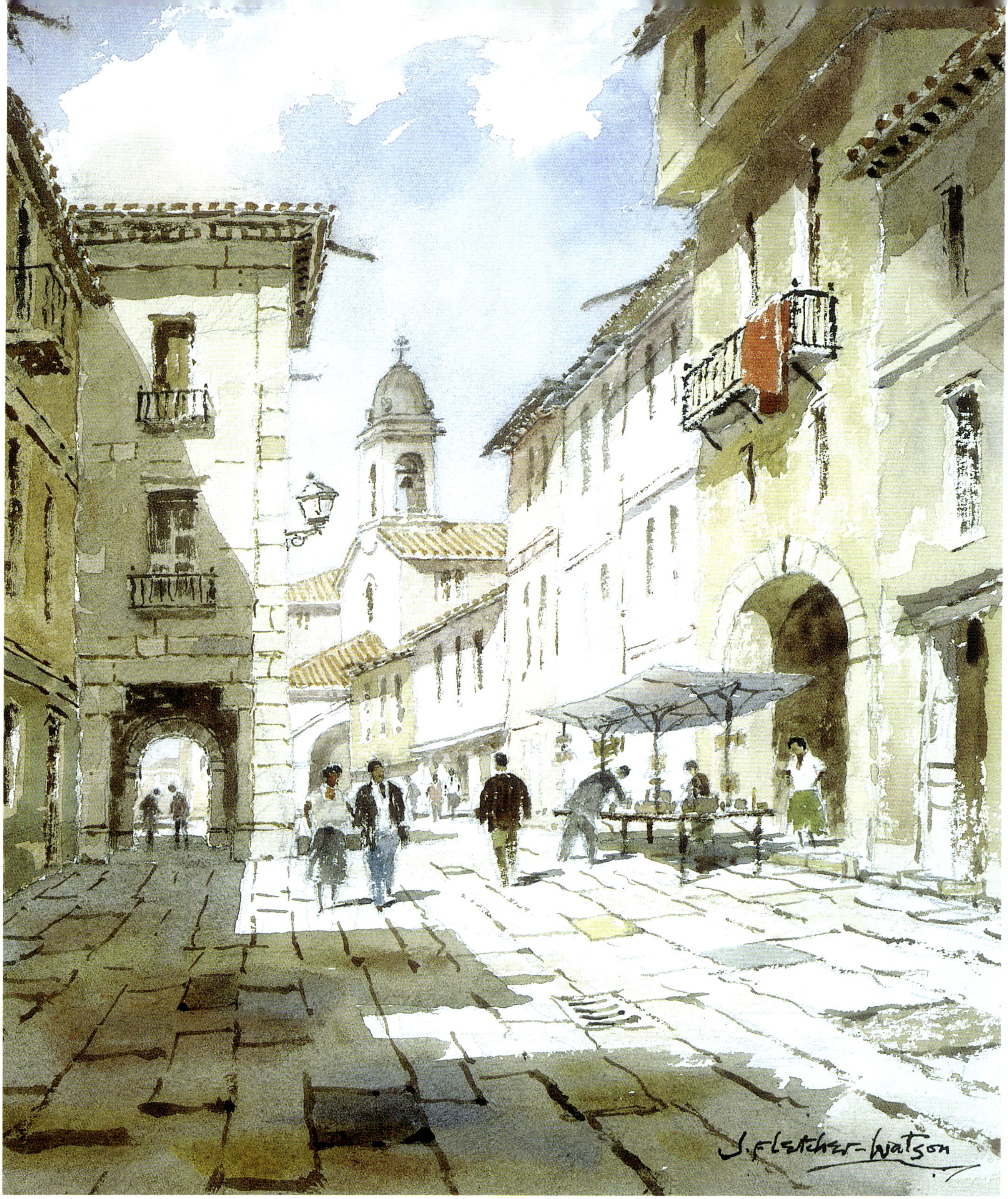

Figure 54
Santiago de Compostela, Spain.
368 × 317mm (14½ × 12½in)

This chapter concludes with two views illustrating simple country town architecture, which I don't think you would find difficult to paint.

Figure 55, *Castle Combe, Wiltshire,* is a delightfully unspoilt village, and this view of the central market place makes a pleasing composition. I have purposely left out cars and people to show the buildings to their best advantage (of course, it would be impossible to find such a deserted village today!). First I drew in all the buildings with a 2B pencil and then set to work on the painting, starting with the sky. It was a good cloudy day with sun, and the grey clouds were a mixture of Cobalt Blue and Burnt Umber for the grey, and a weak French Ultramarine for the blue areas. The walls of the buildings were various tones of yellow/grey, and the roof tiles or slates were various mixes of Cobalt Blue and Burnt Sienna. The dark green trees played an important part, especially the very dark tree behind the church. I used Winsor Blue and Burnt Umber and, in some places, a little Cadmium Yellow for these tree areas. The shadow colours on buildings and the foreground road were a very important element of the picture and consisted mainly of Cobalt Blue and Burnt Umber.

Figure 56, a backyard in Suffolk, was discovered by turning off the main street down a narrow alleyway to find it opened out into a lovely backyard. Here I found a stable and a pony looking out and beautiful unspoilt gables and dormer windows, and mellow old tiled roofs. The trees and church tower were an extra bonus and contributed to a really superb subject. Note how good the composition is with the strong tone of the trees on the right counterbalanced by the stable and dark shadows on the left.

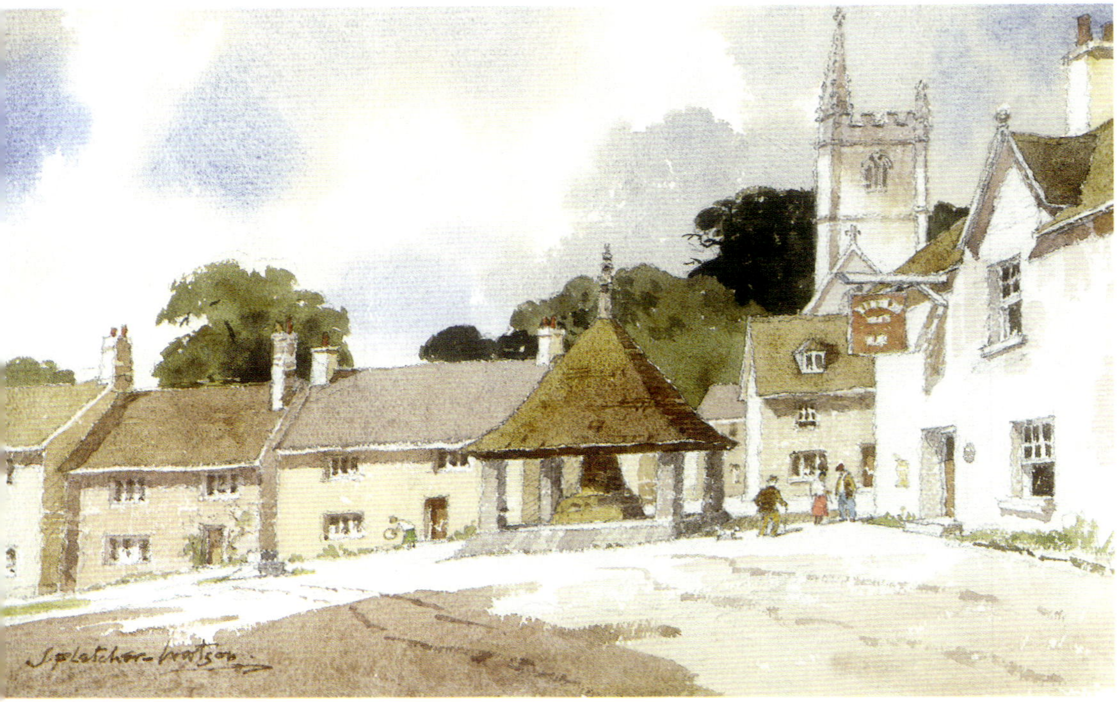

Figure 55
Castle Combe, Wiltshire, England.
235 × 362mm (9½ × 14¼in)

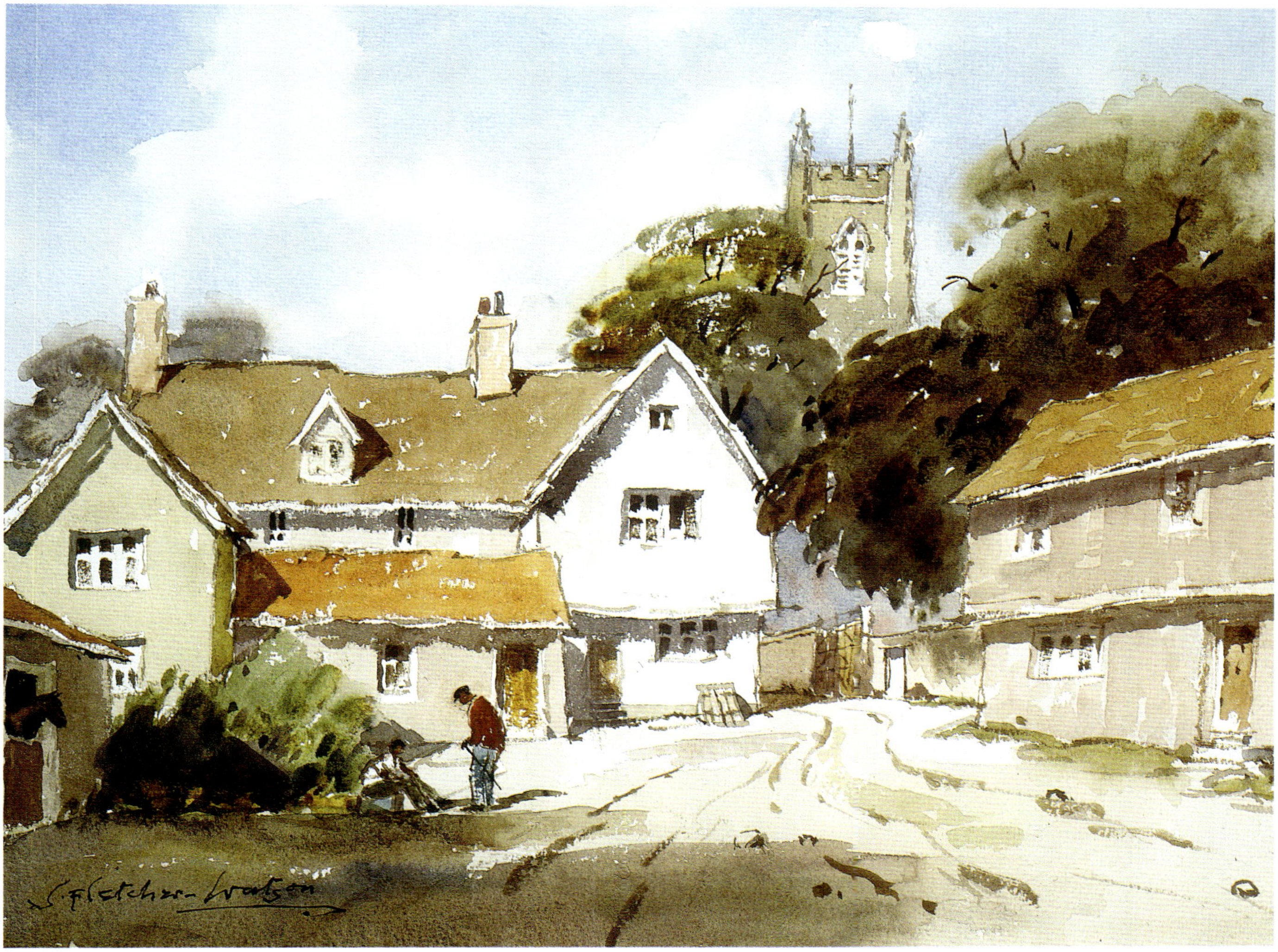

Figure 56
Backyard, Suffolk, England.
318 × 470mm (12½ × 18½in)

TIPS AND TECHNIQUES

- Tone values will invariably play a crucial part in the depiction of buildings in an urban setting, so it is important to plan the gradation of tones throughout the picture right from the beginning
- Lines from stone paving joints will help to focus the perspective and depth of a picture
- Having found a subject, remember to research every angle to paint it from – I often walk round my subject before selecting the best viewpoint
- When working with sun and shadows on a large subject, the light will change very quickly, so it is a good idea to indicate the shadows lightly in pencil before starting to paint

Chapter 7

MOUNTAINS

Mountain scenery with castles; bridges; lakes; low clouds

Mountain scenery has always had an enormous appeal for me, mainly, I suppose, because it is usually in completely unspoilt countryside. The picture of *Loch Awe, Scotland* (**figure 58**), shows a castle in dignified solitude in the heart of mountains and lochs.

In **figure 57** you see a close view of Kilchurn castle. Directly I came across this subject, I knew it was a must for a picture, but I was aware that I had to be careful not to produce a chocolate box painting. The composition was perfect once I had moved the castle slightly to the right. Then everything fell into place – loch, mountains, trees, castle and rocks.

After drawing the castle carefully and sketching in the rest of the picture lightly with a 2B pencil, I started the painting process.

1 The sky consisted of French Ultramarine and Burnt Umber for the grey clouds, with a touch of Raw Sienna added for the lower clouds. White cloud shapes were left on the white paper and Cobalt Blue painted in as necessary with the sky wash damp, but not too wet.

2 The mountains came next, with Cobalt Blue and Light Red used for the distant ones and Burnt Sienna and Burnt Umber added for the nearer ones.

3 The foreground and middle distance grass was then painted with Raw Sienna and French Ultramarine, using a light tone for the grass in sunlight before cloud shadows were added.

4 The castle was the next stage, painted in an all-over light grey wash using Cobalt Blue, Light Red and Raw Sienna. The shadows on the building were a stiffer, darker mixture of the same colours, using less water and more paint with a small No. 5 brush.

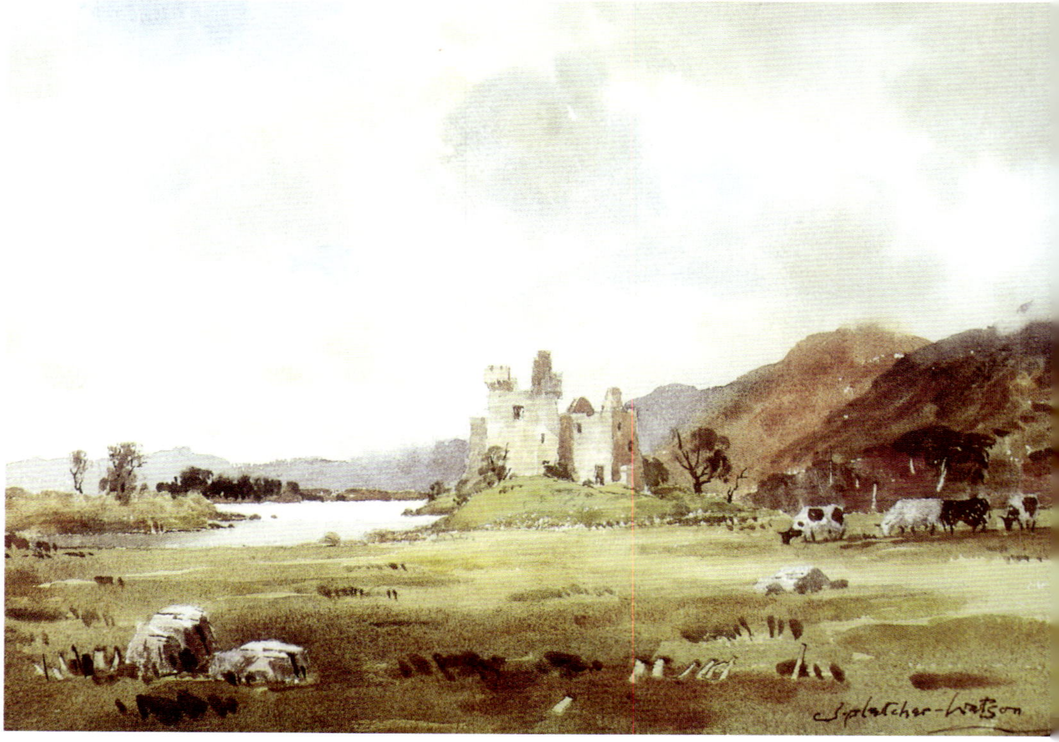

Figure 57
Kilchurn Castle, Loch Awe, Scotland.
318 × 476mm (12½ × 18¾in)

5 The rocks and castle were then painted with suitable dark grey shadows with Burnt Umber used for the cows on the right-hand side.

6 The various tree groups were composed of mixtures of Raw Sienna, Winsor Blue and Burnt Umber. The cloud shadows on the grassed areas were the same mixture as for the trees, using mainly Raw Sienna. A few foreground grass tufts were put in with stronger mixes of the same colour. Rather dry brushwork and a penknife blade gave a few light grass clumps.

Figure 58
Loch Awe, Scotland.
318 × 476mm (12½ × 18¾in)

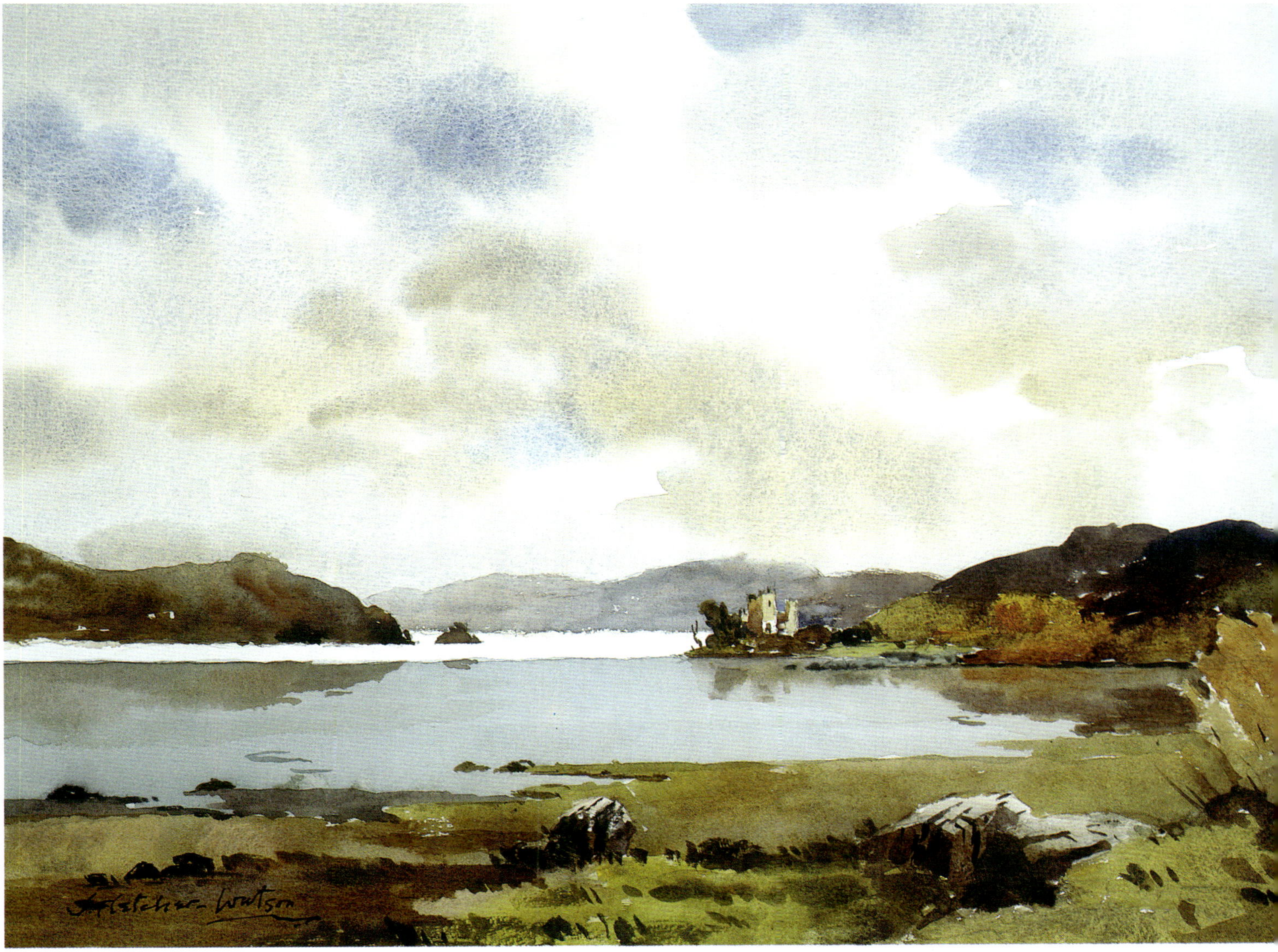

Figure 59 is a marvellous old stone bridge dating back to Roman times. I was actually sitting in the river bed to paint this picture on the spot, perched on a small rock.

The view I have chosen shows how greatly enhanced a subject can be with the addition of a mountain range. The bridge with the half-dry river bed and trees made a good picture, but the grey-blue background mountain range gives depth and grandeur. This is also an example of mountains on a sunny day with no low cloud to break the horizon. Note the cypress tree on the left, which is a lovely vertical foil to the horizontal bridge.

Figure 59
The Roman Bridge, Pollensa, Majorca.
318 × 476mm (12½ × 18¾in)

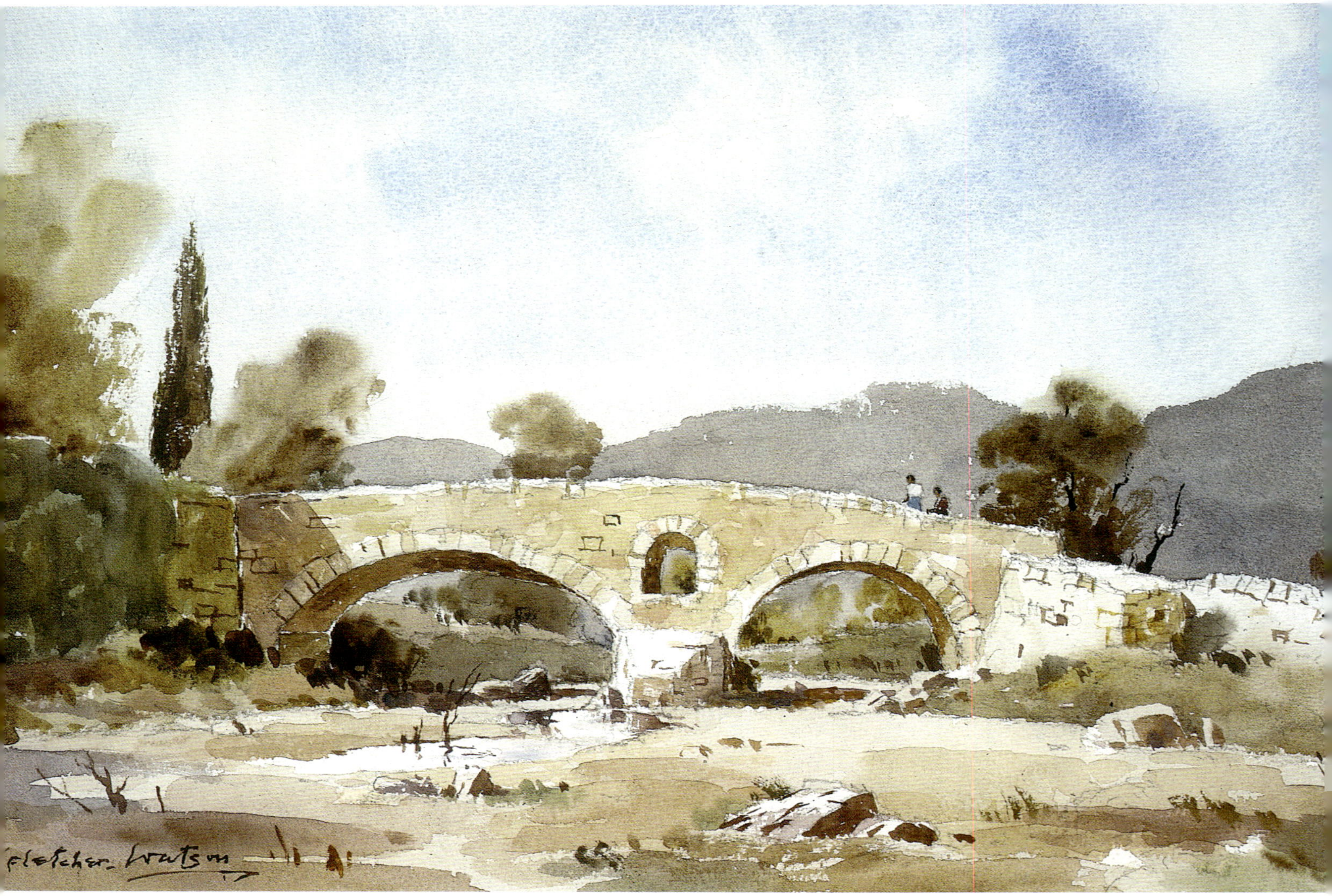

Another good example of a background mountain range is shown below in **figure 60**, *Regello hill village, Tuscany*. Again, the picture subject is delightful, with the central track leading towards the cypress trees and little cluster of houses with their terracotta roofs in the middle distance and the umbrella tree on the right. But it is the distant mountain which gives the extra quality that is so valuable.

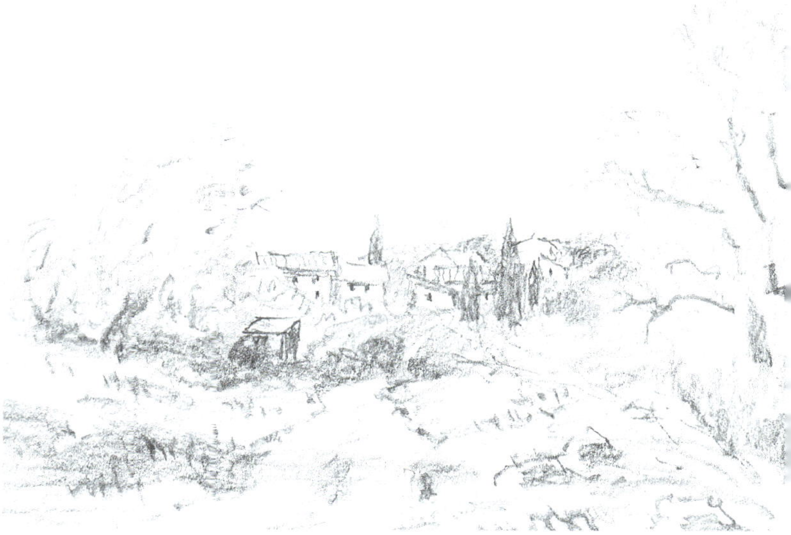

Figure 60
Regello Hill Village, Tuscany.
152 × 248mm (6 × 9¾in)

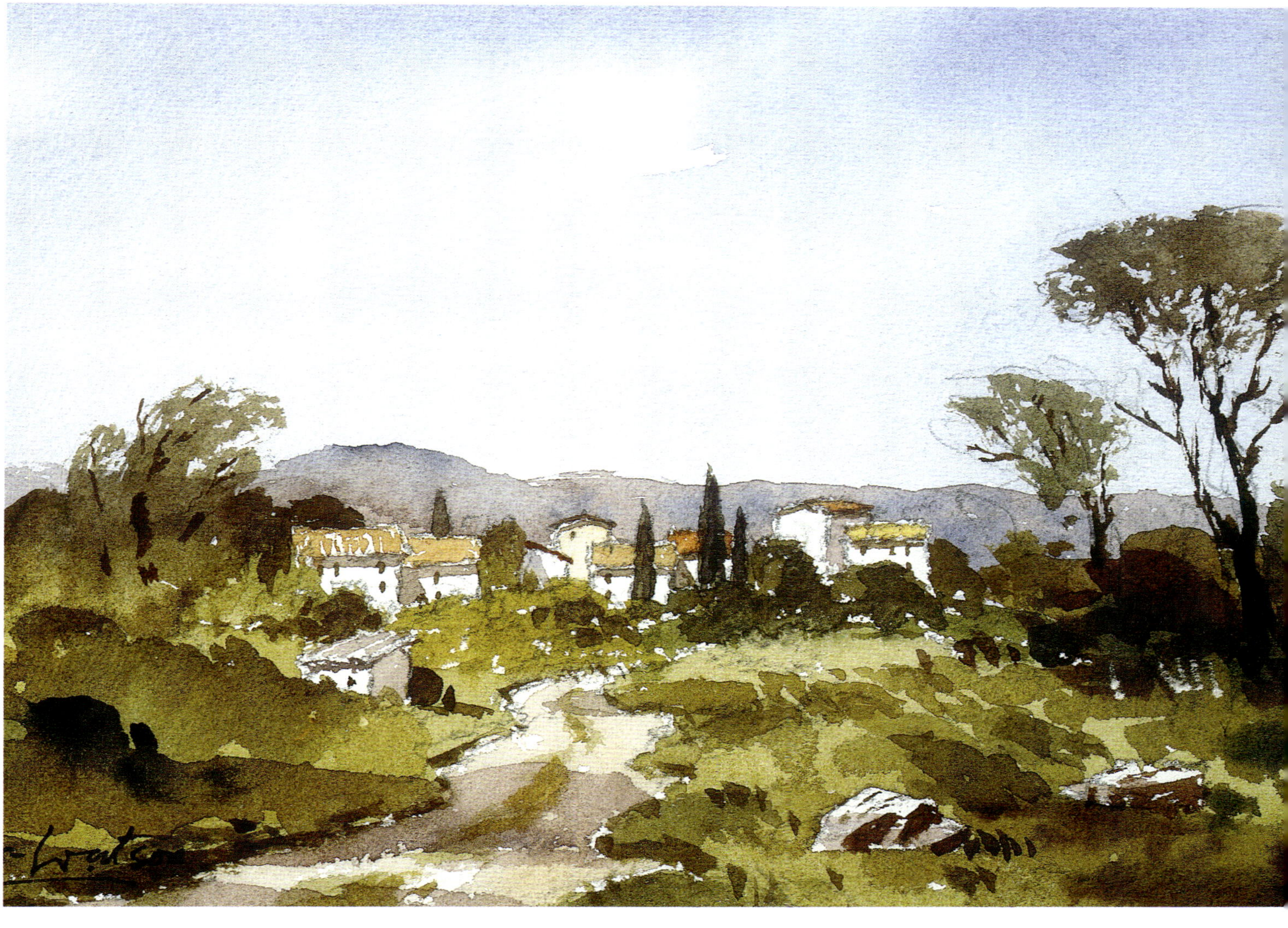

This picture of *Loch Ainort, Skye* (**figure 61**) emphasizes the isolation of a Scottish cottage in this remote area. The cottage is a splendid focal point in this beautiful mountain view, which I painted on the spot. The left-hand mountain, consisting of Burnt Umber and French Ultramarine, makes a strong background to the white cottage, and it is this that helps to create the impression of the great distance between the darker hills nearby and the lighter background mountains. Note the rocks and sheep adding foreground interest and helping the recession of water and distant mountains.

Up to this point, we have concentrated on distant mountains; now let us get a little closer to them. **Figure 62**, *Borrowdale, Cumbria*, shows a wonderful composition of individual mountains and foreground trees. It is a typical Cumbrian sky of low cloud covering the mountain tops, and there is a tremendous feeling of distance created by the progressively lighter tone values of the mountains. The trees themselves are invaluable to this picture and the darker tree in the centre gives an excellent focal point, leading the eye into the picture.

Figure 61
Loch Ainort, Skye, Scotland.
235 × 362mm (9½ × 14¼in)

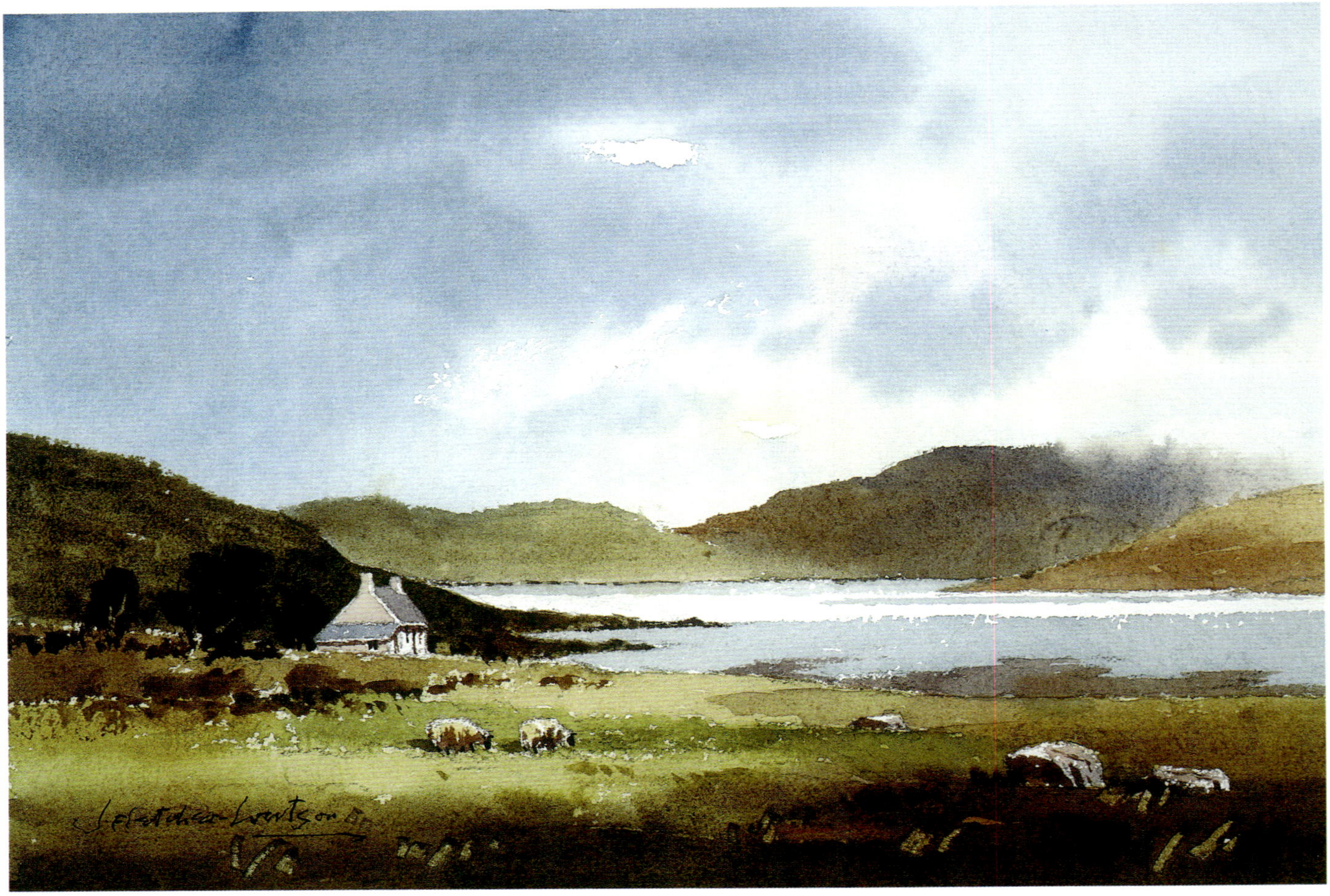

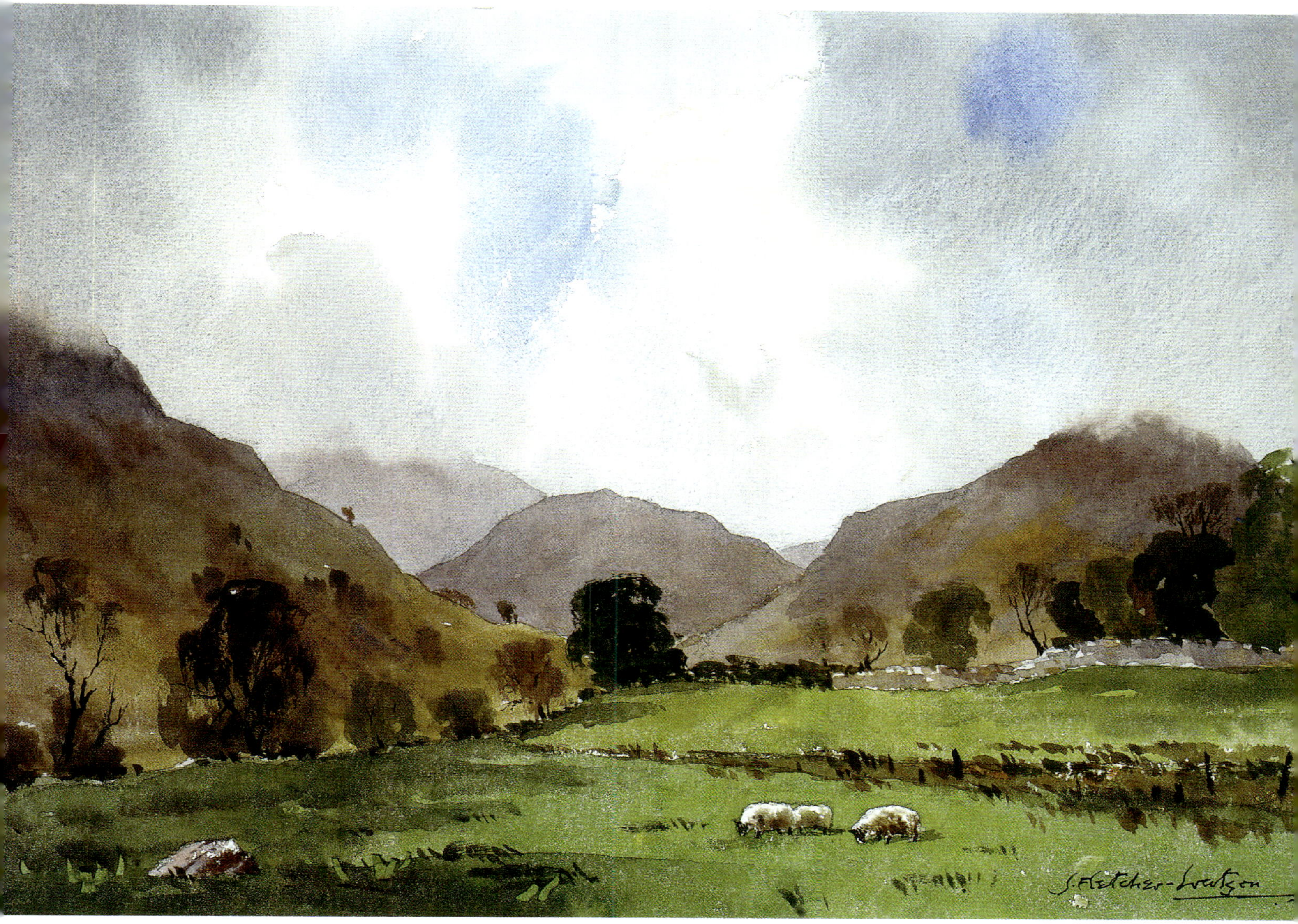

Figure 62
Borrowdale, Cumbria, England.
318 × 476mm (12½ × 18¾in)

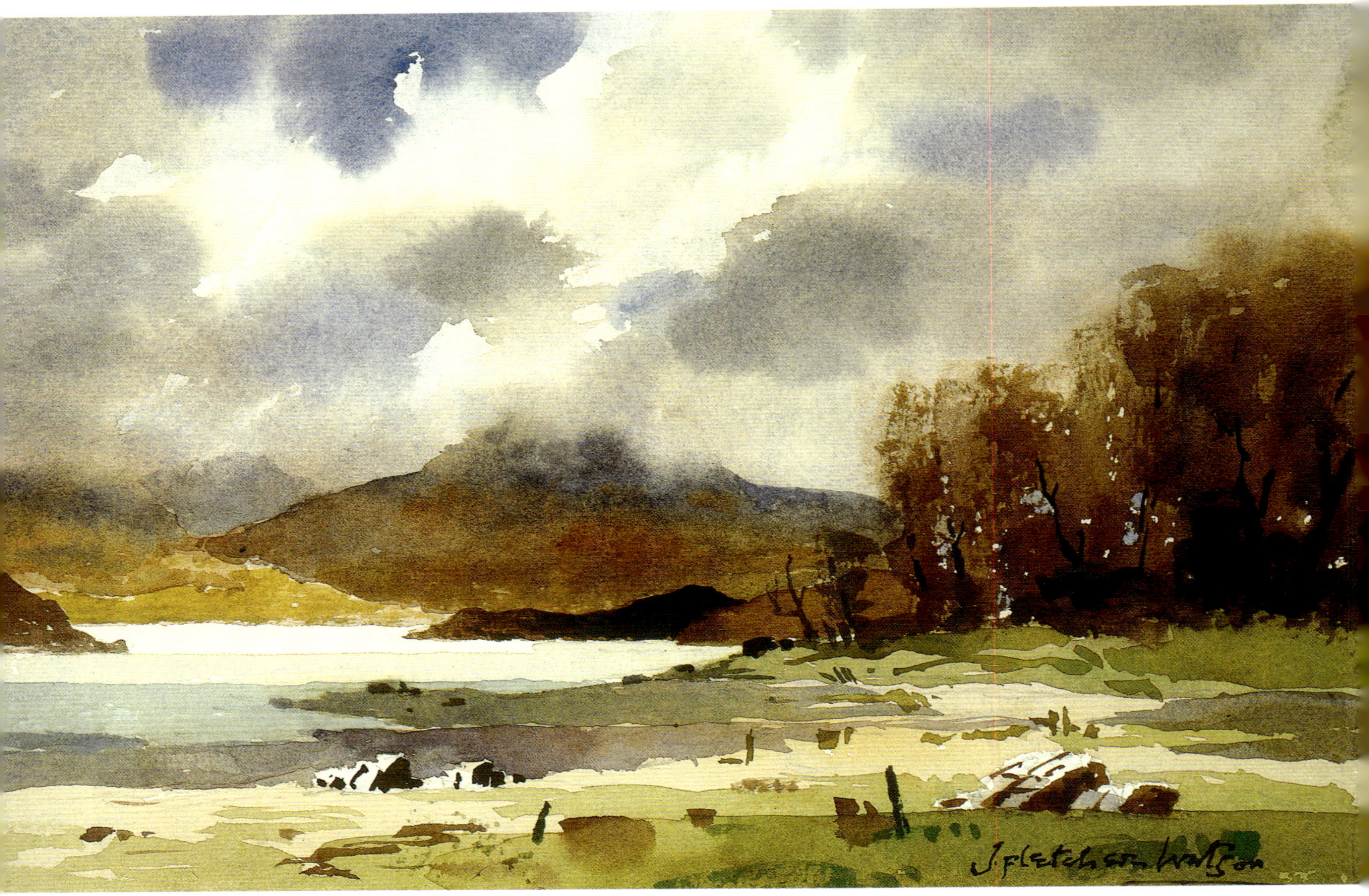

Figure 63
Loch Shieldaig, Scotland.
235 × 362mm (9¼ × 14¼in)

Moving now to **figure 63**, *Loch Shieldaig, Scotland*, we have here a composition of mountains, trees and a loch. This is a very exciting subject, and on this day of broken cloud and sun it was full of the most amazing colours. Autumn is the time of year that always shows Scottish mountain scenery at its best.

Some of the gravelly foreshore of the loch was positively purple in colour. To paint this I used a mixture of Rose Madder and French Ultramarine. Two of the island promontories in deep cloud shadow were painted a very dark brown, using Burnt Umber and French Ultramarine. On the far side of the water, there is a low piece of yellow land for which I used pure Raw Umber. This was most striking against the dark background mountains, as it was lit up by a gleam of sunlight.

Mixtures of Raw Sienna and Winsor Blue were used for the foreground, and Burnt Umber and Winsor Blue

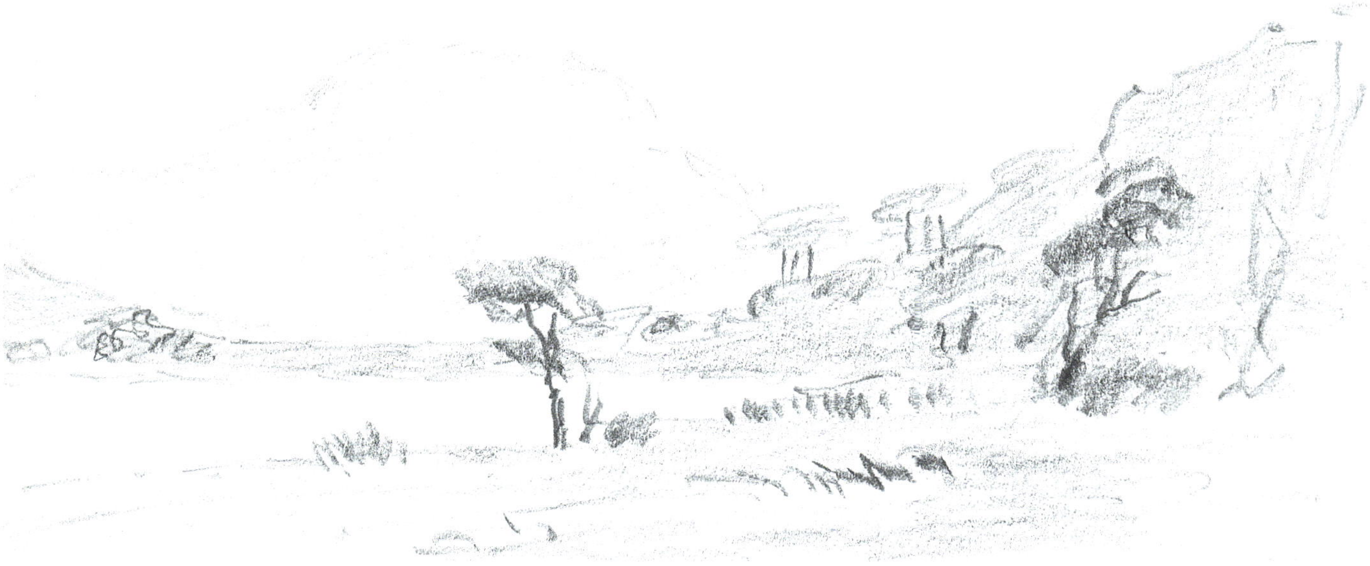

for the woods. The mountain was mostly painted with Burnt Umber and French Ultramarine.

Good composition is particularly important in relation to mountain scenes, and you will often find dramatic recession in the varying shapes of near and distant mountains. There are several more examples of mountain scenes featured in the following chapters.

TIPS AND TECHNIQUES

- Mountains scenes offer great inspiration to the painter
- A mountain range can either be a subject in itself, or give a dramatic background to another subject
- Remember to avoid creating hard edges when painting distant mountains. They will look more effective with softer, slightly diffused outlines

Chapter 8

WATER AND REFLECTIONS

Cotswold rivers; Scottish loch; Cumbrian lake; Italian waterway; Cumbrian waterfall

First of all, I would like to show you the rule governing reflections that can be seen in calm water, such as in a lake or a slow-moving river. **Figure 64**, *Snow on the Windrush River*, shows a block of trees in the centre, some way back from the water's edge and on the right is a group of trees quite near the water. Water in snow scenes can look quite dark.

Figure 64
Snow on the Windrush River, England.
235 × 362mm (9¼ × 14¼in)

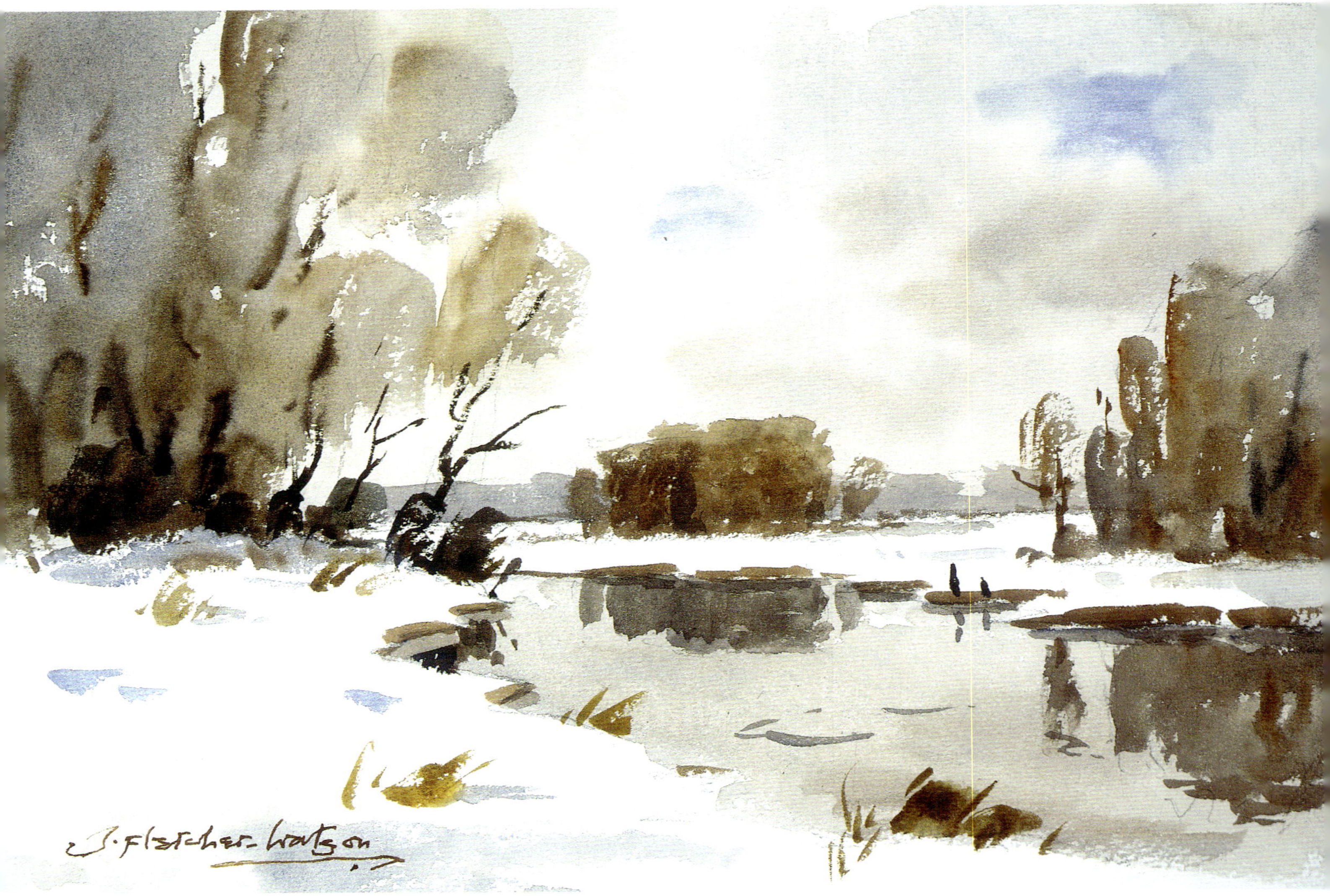

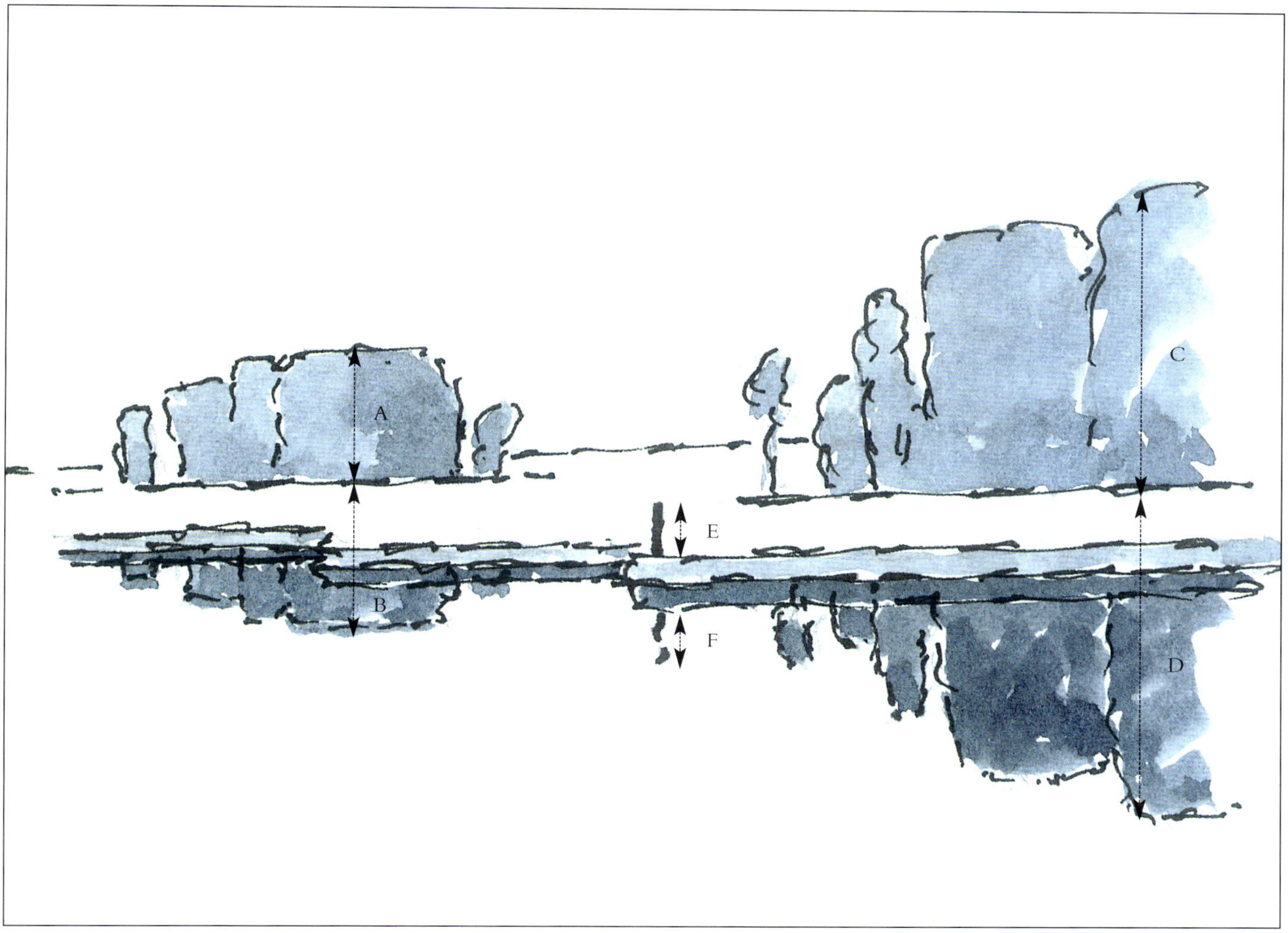

Figure 65
Reflections diagram.

The diagram in **figure 65** shows you how to measure the depth of the tree reflection in the water. The height of the trees at A is measured vertically downwards as shown at B. You will see that measurement B is taken from a point slightly below the base of the trees, so as to allow for the depth of the ground which is the equivalent of the depth of the river bank. The result is that far less of the trees will show reflected in the water than can be seen above ground.

If we look at the trees at C, we find that the depth of reflection at D is much greater owing to the trees being nearer the river bank. And again the post at E reflects its full height at F, because it is right on the edge of the water.

Figure 66, *Loch Etive, Scotland*, shows another example of reflections. The reflection of the mountain in the water is only about one-third of its full height, because of its great distance from the water's edge. The brown trees on the right, though, are reflecting about two-thirds their height in the water, as they are only a short distance from the bank.

When choosing a subject with water, I always look out particularly for features on the far side of the water that give a reflection. Even a tree stump or bush is better than nothing, as it will help to give the water a more liquid appearance. Reflections of the sky can also contribute to this effect, especially if there are several patches of blue.

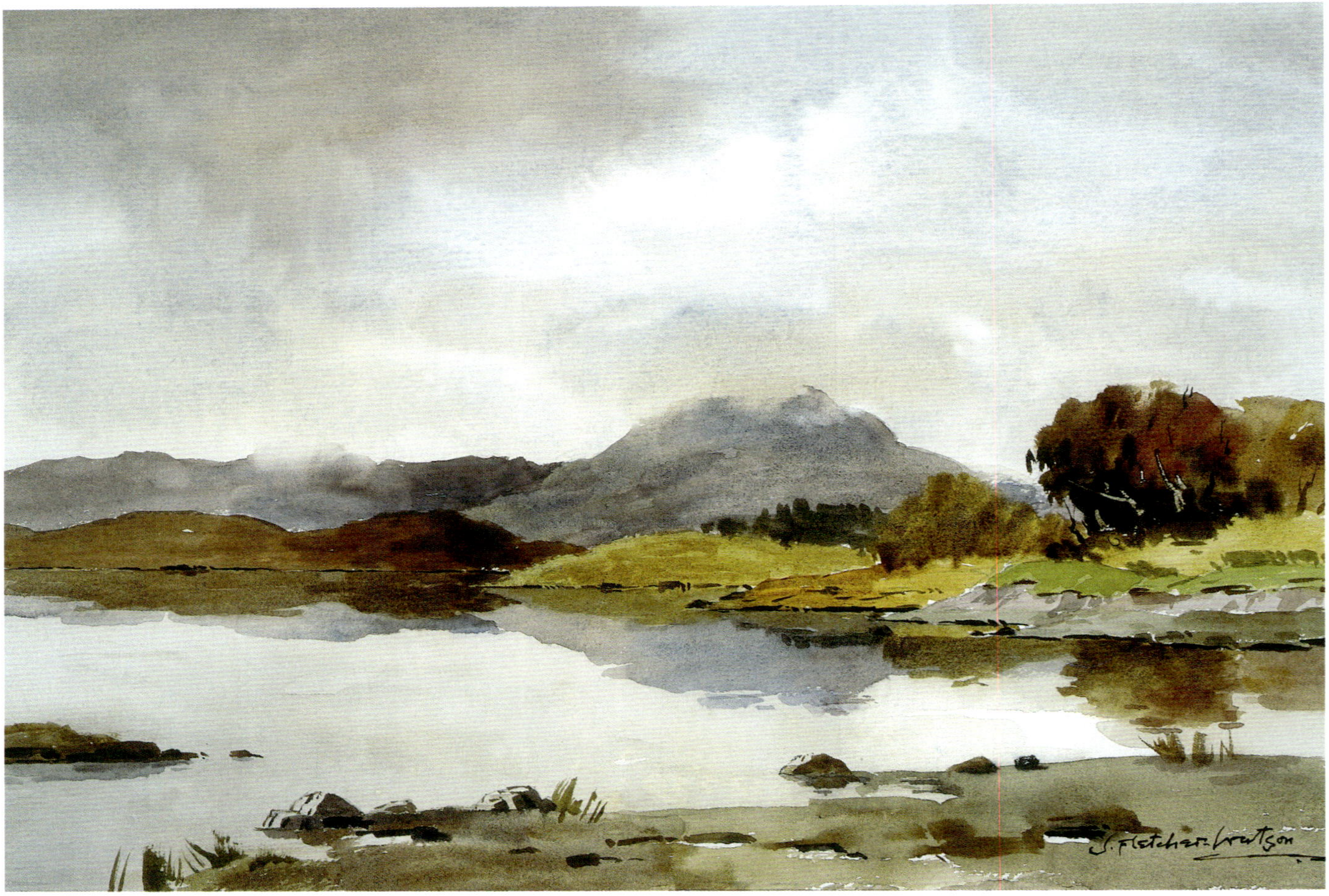

Figure 66
Loch Etive, Scotland.
330 × 482mm (13 × 19in)

An excellent example of trees reflected in water is shown in **figure 67**, which was painted when the Windrush river was flooding over its banks. The leaning tree on the left, with its bent and twisting branches, makes an interesting mirror-image reflection in the water. Remember that you will get a kink or two in a branch reflection owing to the moving water.

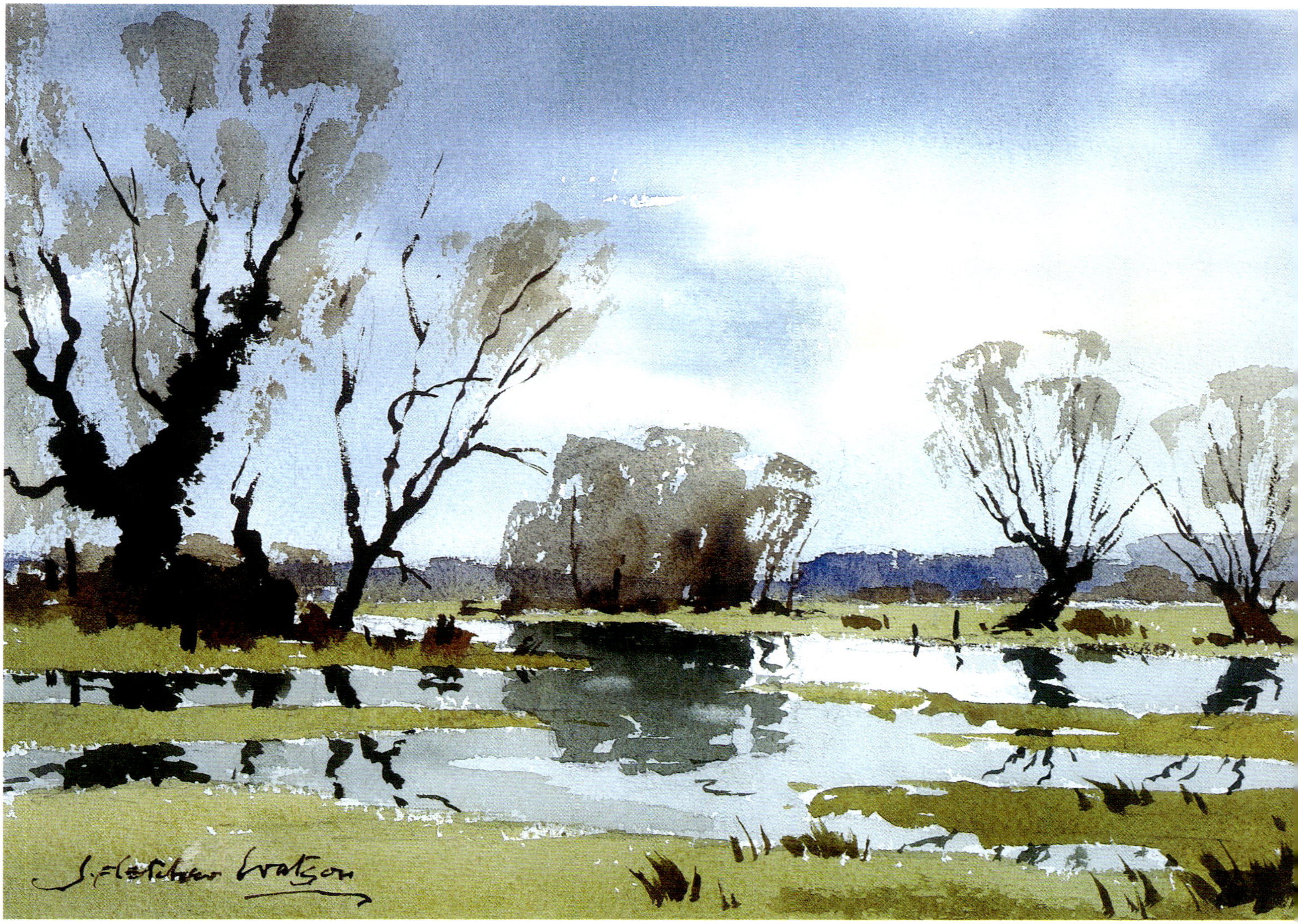

Figure 67
Flood water on the Windrush, England.
235 × 362mm (9½ × 14¼in)

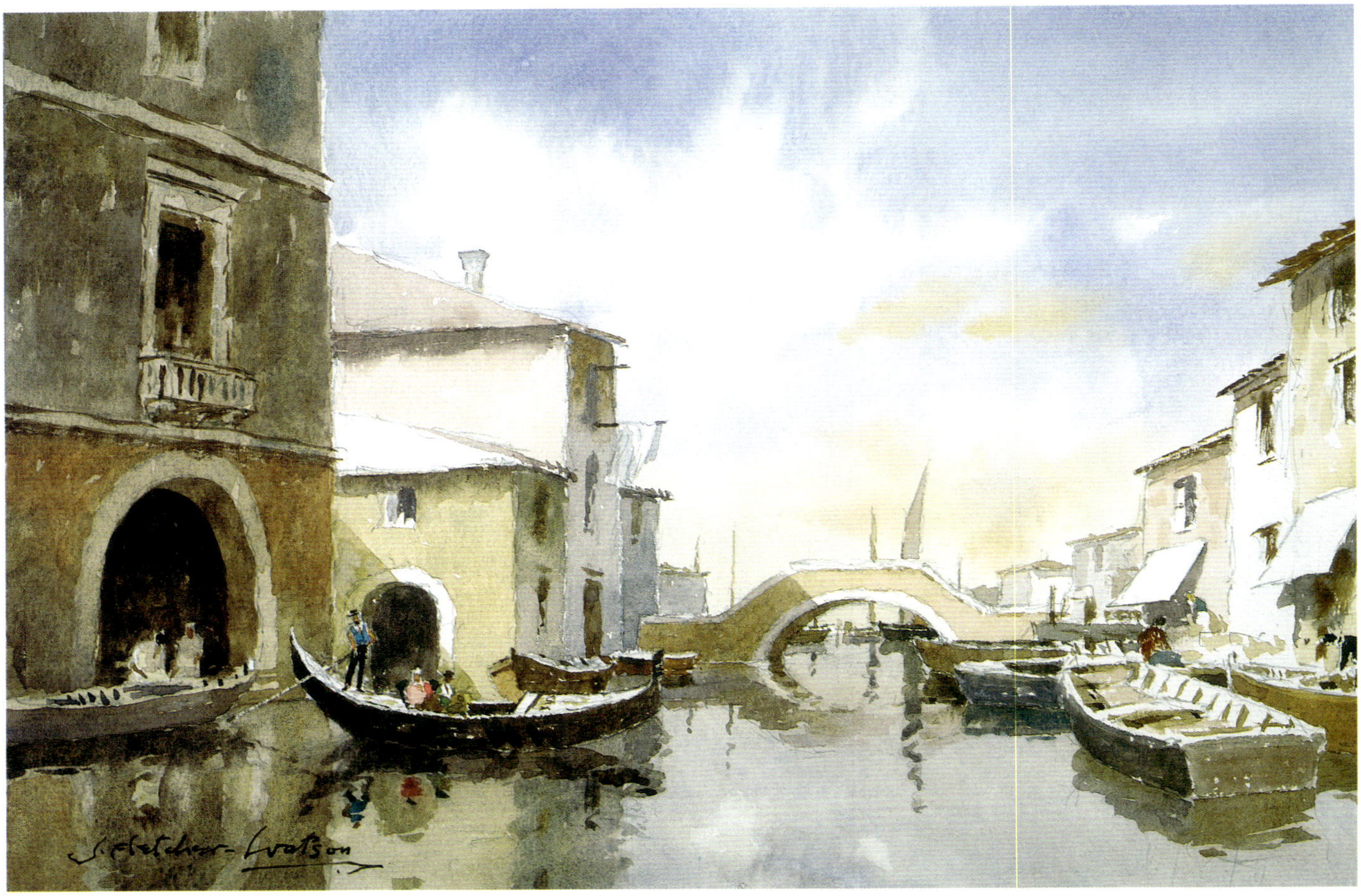

Figure 68
Chioggia, Italy.
235 × 362mm (9¼ × 14¼in)

Water reflecting boats and buildings is always an interesting subject and **figure 68** shows the lovely Italian town of Chioggia near Venice. The sky buildings and boats were all painted first and then I could think about the water. It had a slight movement and the reflections were therefore painted with wavy edges. The gondola on the left side was painted last, as this was strong in tone value and fairly close to me. I was careful not to overdo the detail both for the actual buildings and boats and their reflections, otherwise the whole picture would have become fussy and restless.

Side canal, Venice (**figure 69**) is a further example of water reflections with buildings. The sun is coming from the right side, so the buildings on the left are in full sunshine and the right-hand buildings are in shadow, which is reflected in the water.

The water is nearly always moving in Venice, which accounts for the fact that the building reflections are slightly broken up. In this picture, the canal was painted with a weak wash of Payne's Gray. Then, after it had dried, a darker mix of the same colour was used for the reflections.

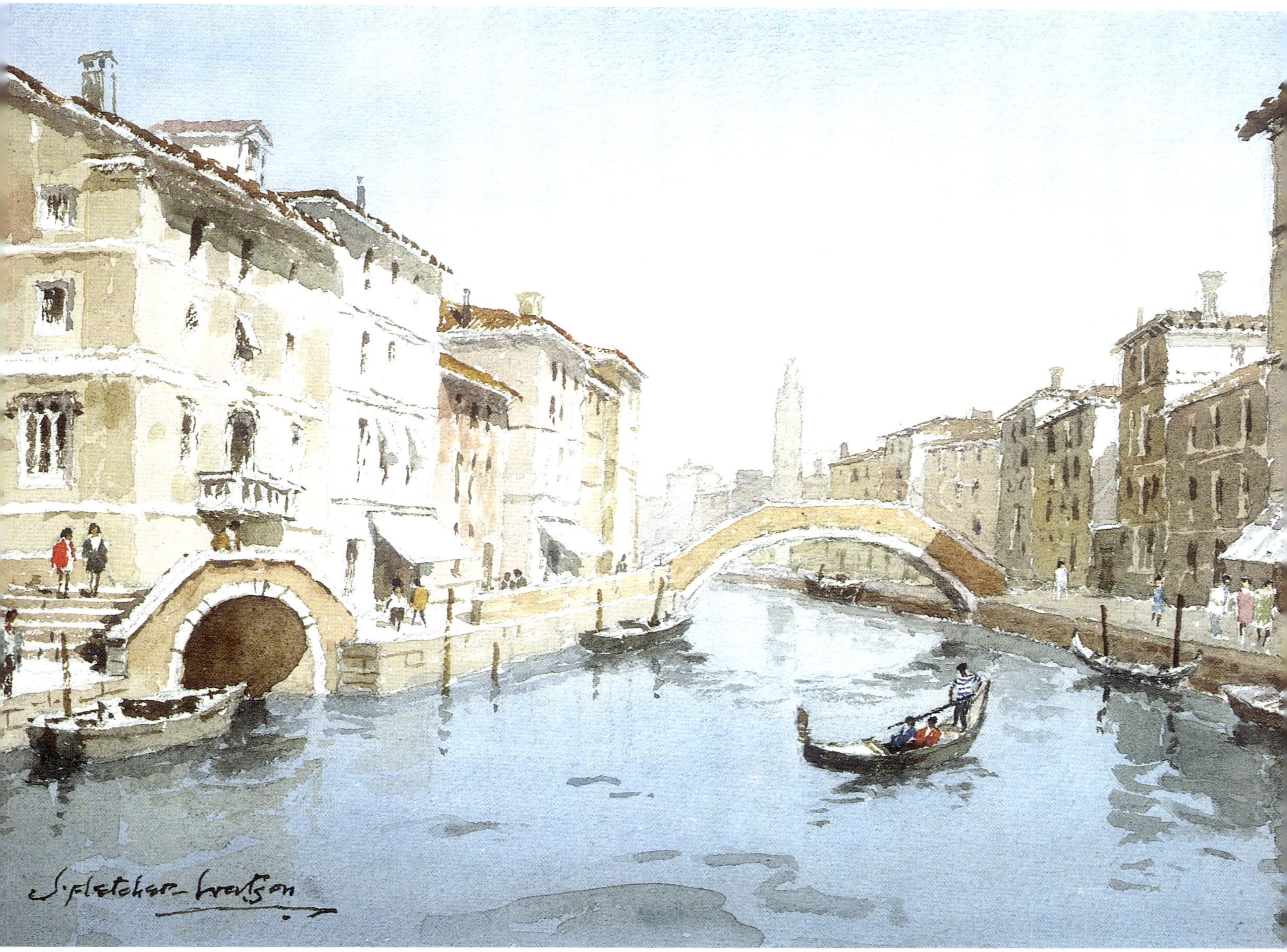

Figure 69
Side canal, Venice.
318 × 476mm (12½ × 18¾in)

Figure 70, *Windrush River, near Burford,* was painted from a position where the river was fairly wide, and the reflections included not only the church spire and trees, but also a considerable amount of sky. A good cloudy, sunny sky with pronounced blue areas is always an attractive feature when seen in a water reflection. I moved up and down the bank looking for a good wide area of water in order to arrive at a suitable vantage point for achieving this expanse of sky.

Figure 70
Windrush River, near Burford, England.
235 × 362mm (9¼ × 14¼in)

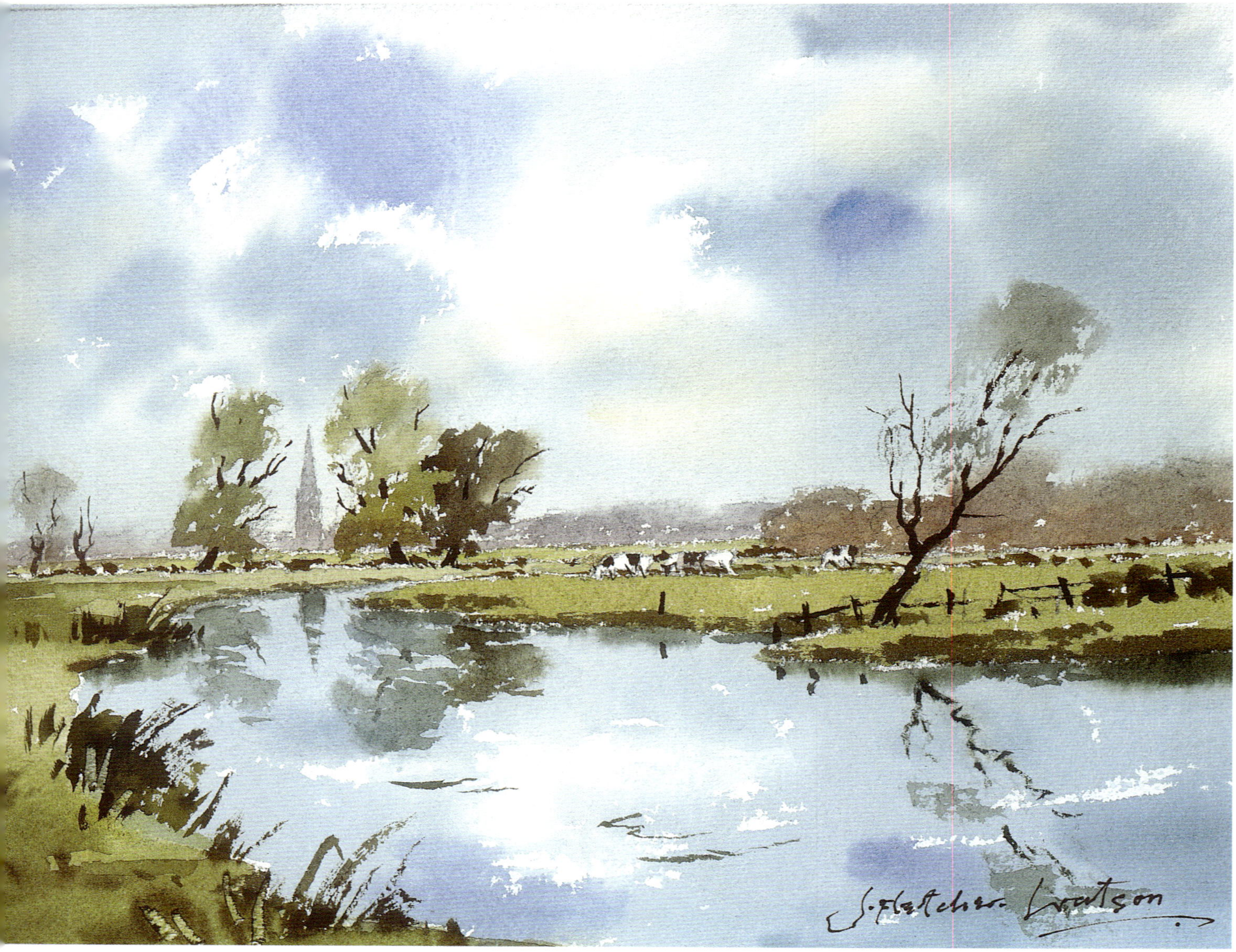

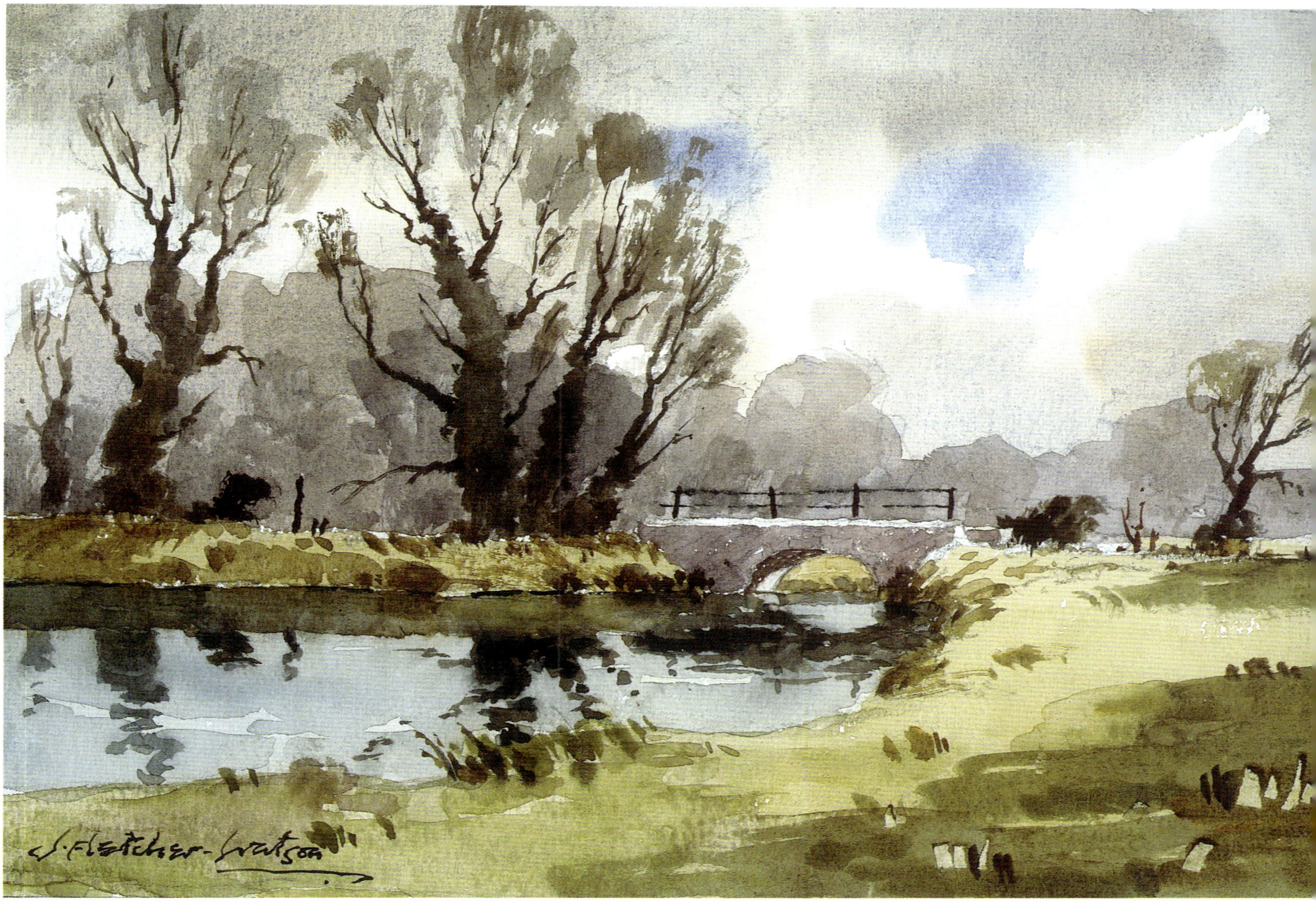

Figure 71
Sherborne Brook, Gloucestershire, England.
235 × 362mm (9¼ × 14¼in)

This picture of *Sherborne Brook* (**figure 71**) shows a smaller river and, because it has slow-moving water, the reflections of bridge and trees are fairly strong. The group of three tightly growing willow trees in the centre of the picture have their trunks covered in ivy, which is a very dark tone and makes a good reflection in the water.

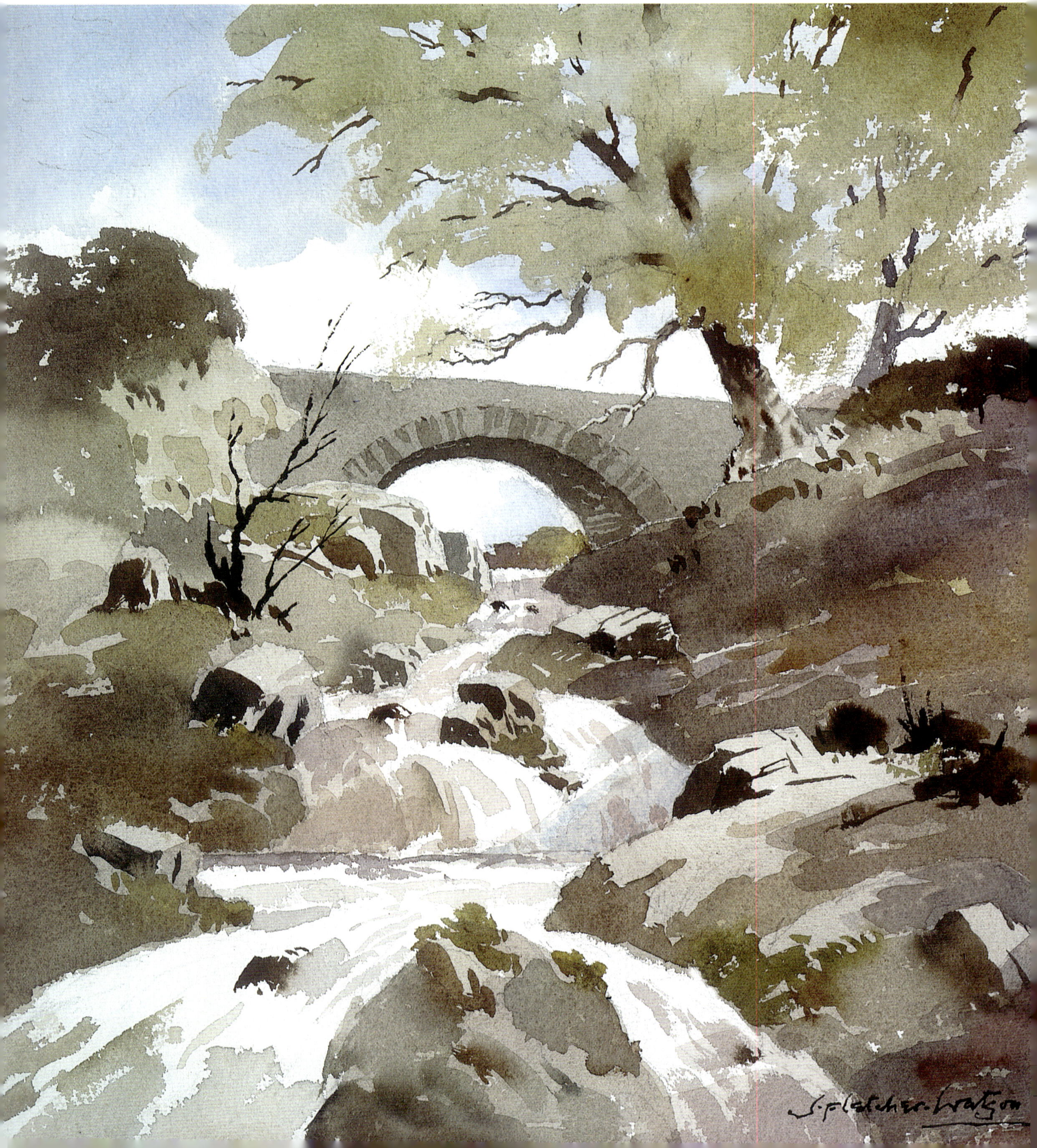

Figure 72, *Cumbrian waterfall*, is a really good example of dealing with fast-moving water. I found this exciting little view with a stone footbridge quite by chance in the Borrowdale district of the Lakes. At first, it seemed a daunting subject to paint, but once I had got it all carefully drawn in pencil, the painting work was less difficult.

After laying in the blue sky, I used cool grey-green mixtures with Raw Sienna, Burnt Umber, Cobalt Blue and a touch of Winsor Blue for the bridge, trees and banks and then the rocks. Next came the water, which was mainly light grey from mixtures of Cobalt Blue, Light Red and touches of Raw Sienna. The smooth horizontal surfaces were left white while the racing sloping parts were streaky grey. It all came together finally with some really dark touches for the rock shadows and the small tufts of grass.

I would like you to note the composition of this painting, which is unusual. The focal point is the bridge, which is positioned high up in the picture. The arrangement of rocks and small waterfalls is carefully planned to give an excellent balance.

TIPS AND TECHNIQUES

- Remember the rule governing reflections in calm water – the reflection of any object will always be measured from its base, even if this is hidden from view
- When looking for a subject with water, look for elements that will give an effective reflection, which will enhance the quality of water
- A water reflection will benefit from a cloudy sunny sky with definite blue areas
- Do not overdo painted detail for subjects and their reflections

Figure 72
Cumbrian waterfall, England.
362 × 311mm (14¼ × 12¼in)

Chapter 9

LANDSCAPES

Cumbria; Norfolk; Scotland; Snow in the Cotswolds

This chapter tries to show how it is possible to go far beyond mere topographical representation for a landscape painting. I would like to remind readers that we have all inherited a wonderful watercolour tradition handed on to us by Turner, Cotman, De Wint and Constable, as well as later painters such as Winslow Homer and Sargent. Take inspiration from them and remember, this tradition is still developing.

Everything we have been talking about in preceding chapters – including light coming from the sky, colour, shapes and composition – come together in a magical landscape picture before our eyes. Having dealt with the techniques for the individual items in a landscape, such as skies, trees, buildings and mountains, I will now consider the landscape as a whole. In order to make the whole picture satisfactory, it is important to suppress unnecessary detail and to achieve a balance between colour, tone and composition so that all these things contribute rather than compete with one another.

I have chosen **figure 73**, *Crummock Water, Cumbria*, as an example which I feel meets this requirement. The picture was painted on a most beautiful day with strong cloud formations and bright sunlight. Burnt Umber and French Ultramarine were the only colours used for the sky. This demonstrates what a variety of tones can be obtained with only two colours.

The composition of this picture gives a happy balance, with the dark brown mountain on the left and the slightly larger mass of dark trees on the right. These two masses were purposely made different sizes. The focal point is the lake and distant grey-blue mountain, and I used a Cobalt Blue and Light Red mixture for the latter. The foreground is brought to life with cloud shadows and rocks judiciously placed.

This all sounds so simple when expressed in a few words, but there is a lifetime of experience behind it. I am hoping to give you some short cuts so that you can produce an exciting picture after a comparatively brief period of practice.

Of course, finding a subject is the secret of good landscape painting and you must develop the knack of transferring a subject immediately on sight onto a piece of watercolour paper. This must be done in your mind's eye as you look at a view. Try practising this every yard of the way on your next country walk. And don't forget artist's licence, which means being able to move observed objects slightly or even to leave them out altogether. This is quite permissible within reason, but don't take it to extremes.

Try not to choose too complicated a subject to start with – you could find it an uphill struggle. Instead, choose a very simple subject, which will lead to success.

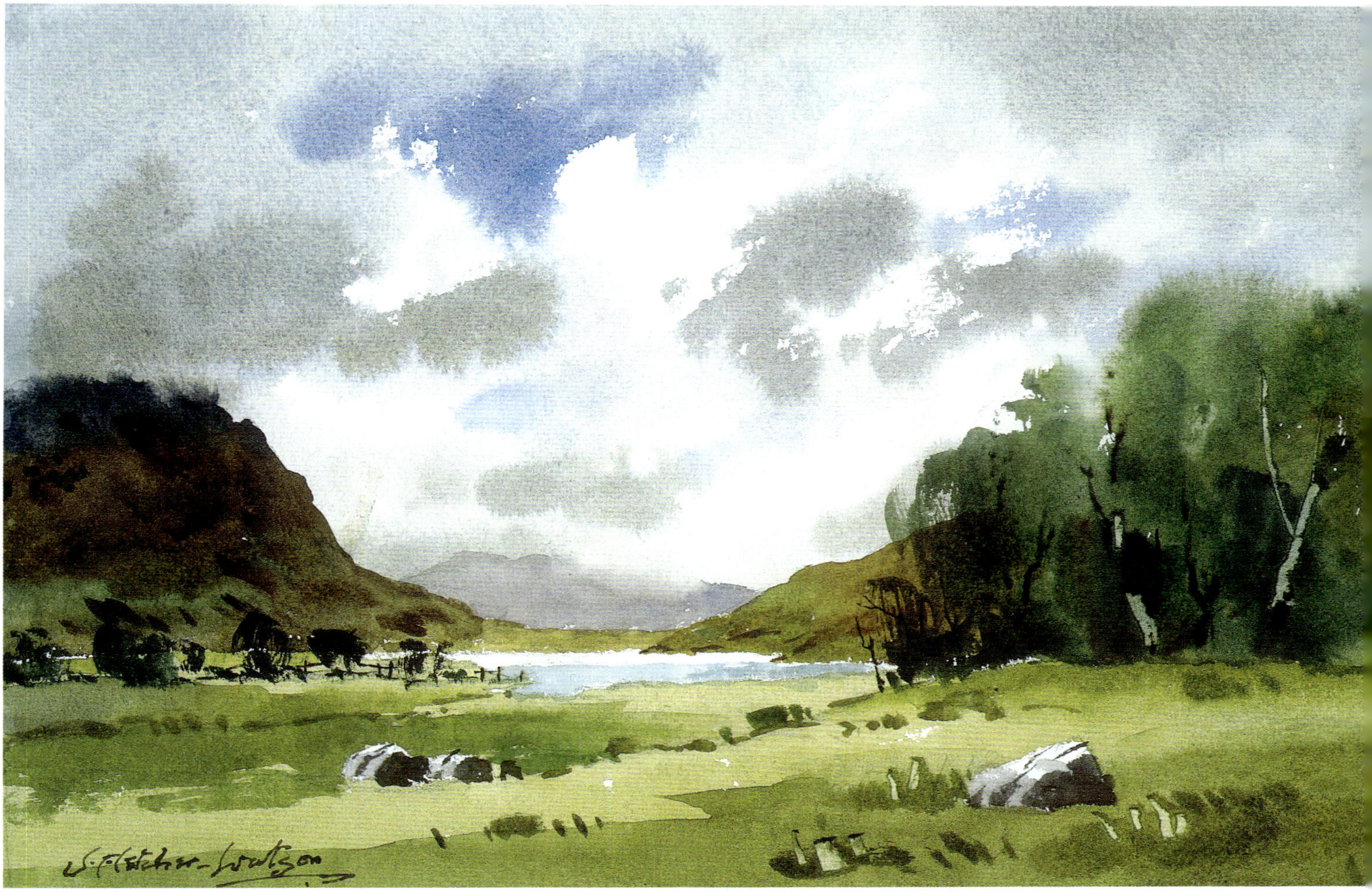

Figure 73
Crummock Water,
Cumbria, England.
235 × 362mm (9¼ × 14¼in)

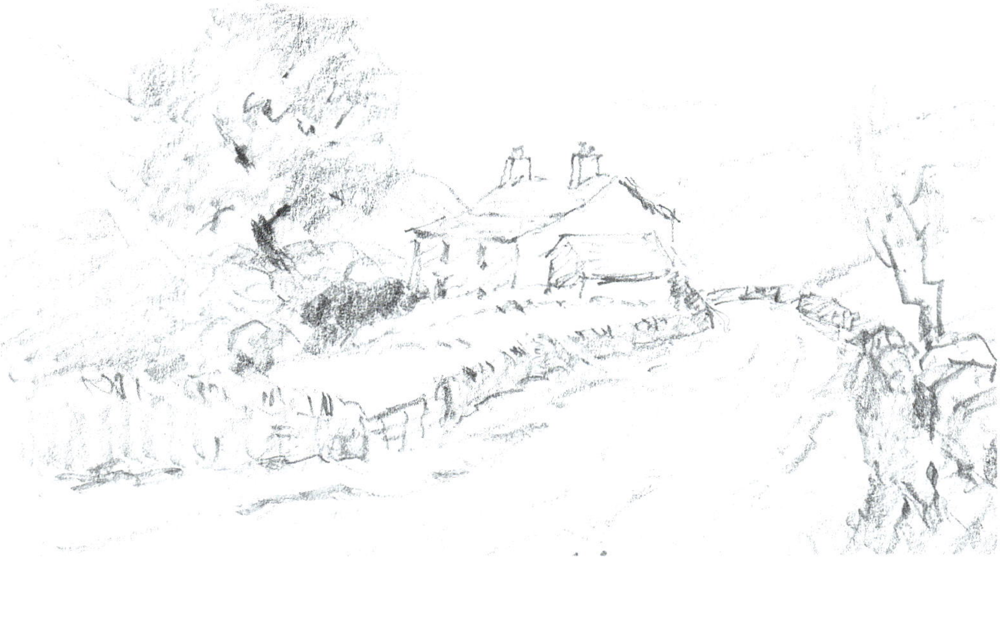

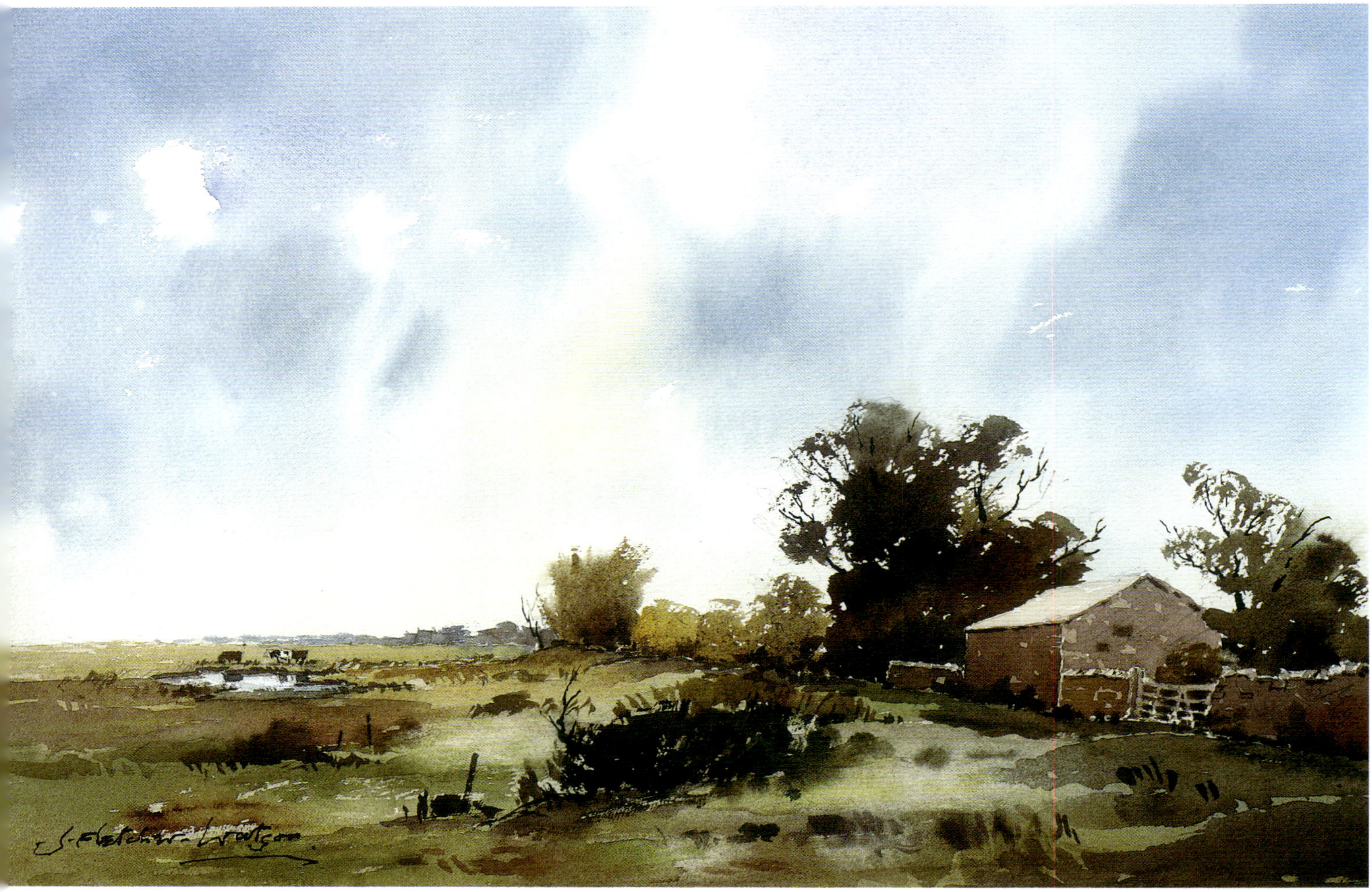

Figure 74
Brancaster Marshes, Norfolk, England.
235 × 362mm (9¼ × 14¼in)

This picture of *Brancaster Marshes* (**figure 74**) is a great mixture of tone values. The sky has soft grey clouds, painted in Payne's Gray and one or two touches of blue (French Ultramarine), and the landscape has some very strong trees and shrubs, which are boldly painted in. You can see how effectively the dark and light tones work together, with the dark tree positioned directly behind the light roof. Remember to be brave with colour tone values so as to give punch to a picture.

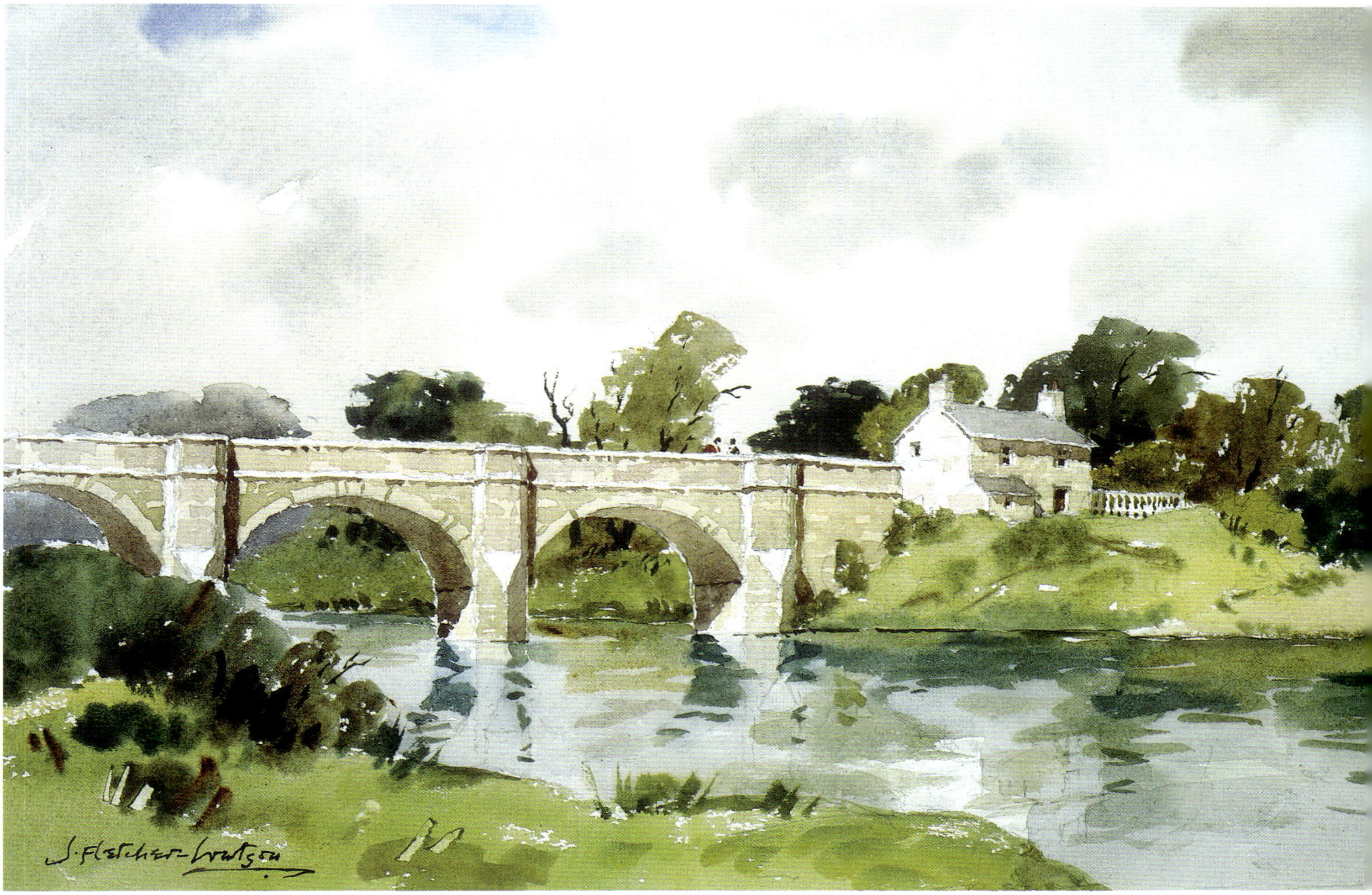

Figure 75
The River Tweed, Scotland.
318 × 476mm (12½ × 18¾in)

The River Tweed was an attractive picture to paint as the stone bridge and stone cottage are both pleasing features, and they are very much highlighted by the darkness of the background trees. This famous fishing river is quite fast flowing, hence the reflections in the water are fairly blurred but indicate the water movement. This picture was painted in early summer when the trees are a rich variety of greens, and the reflections from the sun are strong, making a bright, colourful landscape.

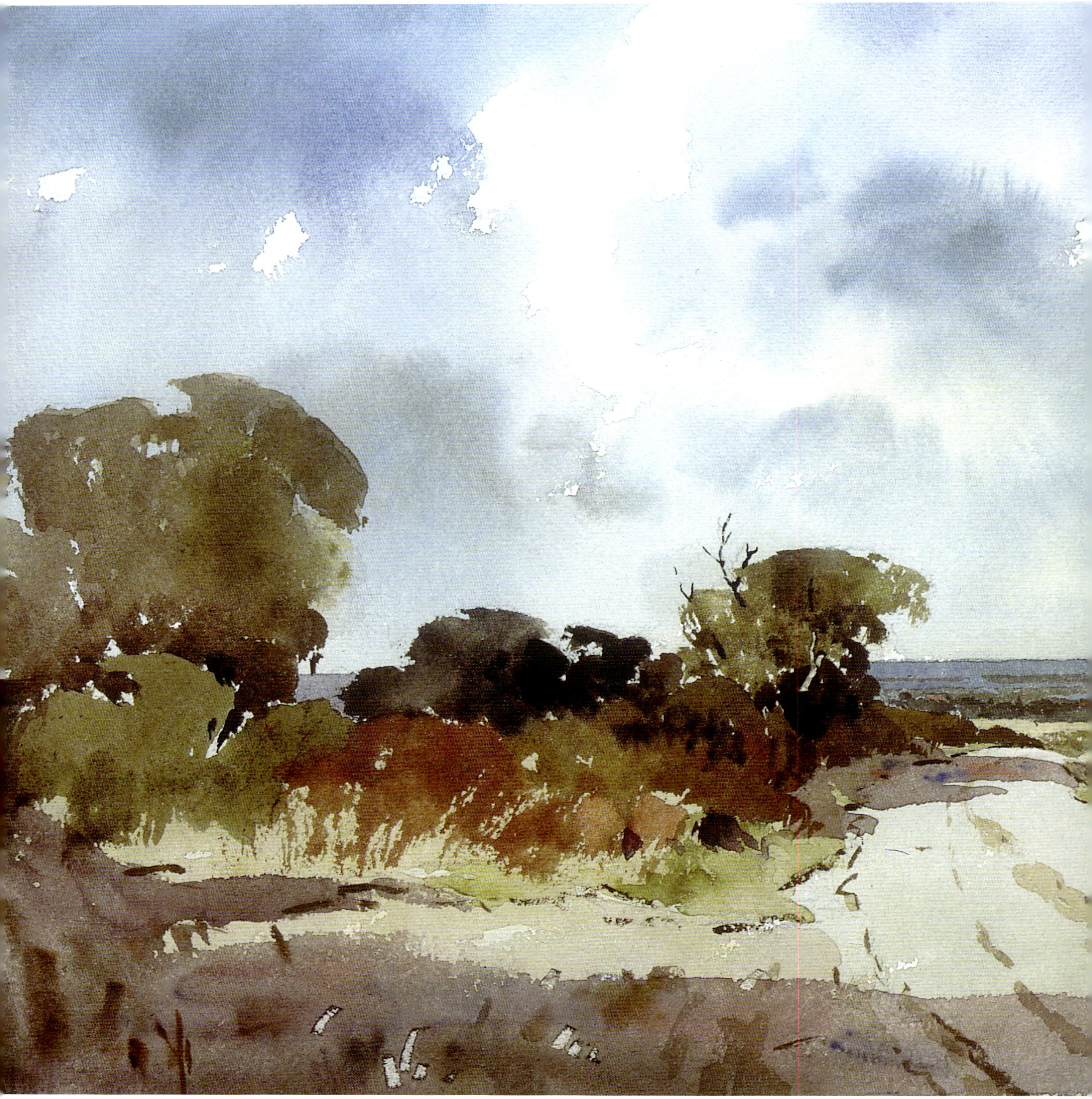

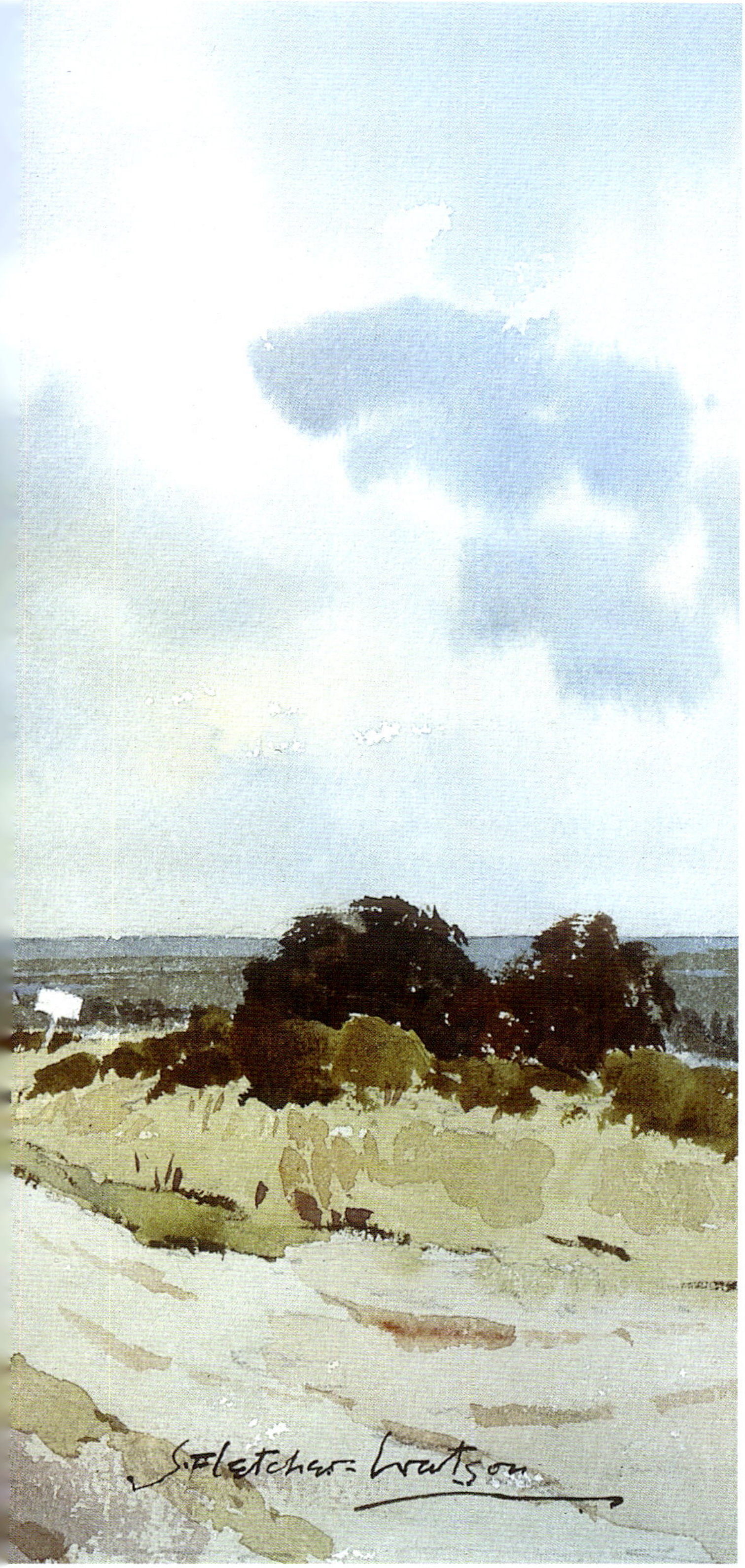

Figure 76, *Above Brancaster, Norfolk*, is an autumn picture that could be said to typify the English landscape. Many people would pass this by, seeing nothing worth painting, but that is where the experienced eye of the artist is useful. If it had not been for the sun and cloud and tree shadows falling across the road, it would have had little interest. But the autumn colouring and the particularly attractive light, which often occurs in Norfolk, made this an irresistible subject that I longed to put on paper.

The various trees and grassed areas were painted with mixtures of Raw Sienna, Burnt Sienna and Winsor Blue. The rather dark, shadowy trees were created with Burnt Umber and Winsor Blue, and Payne's Gray was added for some of the extra-dark foliage.

Figure 76
Above Brancaster, Norfolk, England.
318 × 476mm (12½ × 18¾in)

Figure 77, *Runham Mill, Norfolk*, shows a windmill in a landscape. This is a rare subject to find, but fortunately there are windmill societies that protect and maintain a few examples, most of which are the larger type of corn mill.

This is an ideal subject for those of us who wish to paint a picture in the tradition of pure landscape. Here we have a big sky with a low horizon, giving a great sense of distance, and a fascinating vertical feature in the form of a marsh-draining mill built of

Figure 77
Runham Mill, Norfolk, England.
318 × 476mm (12½ × 18¾in)

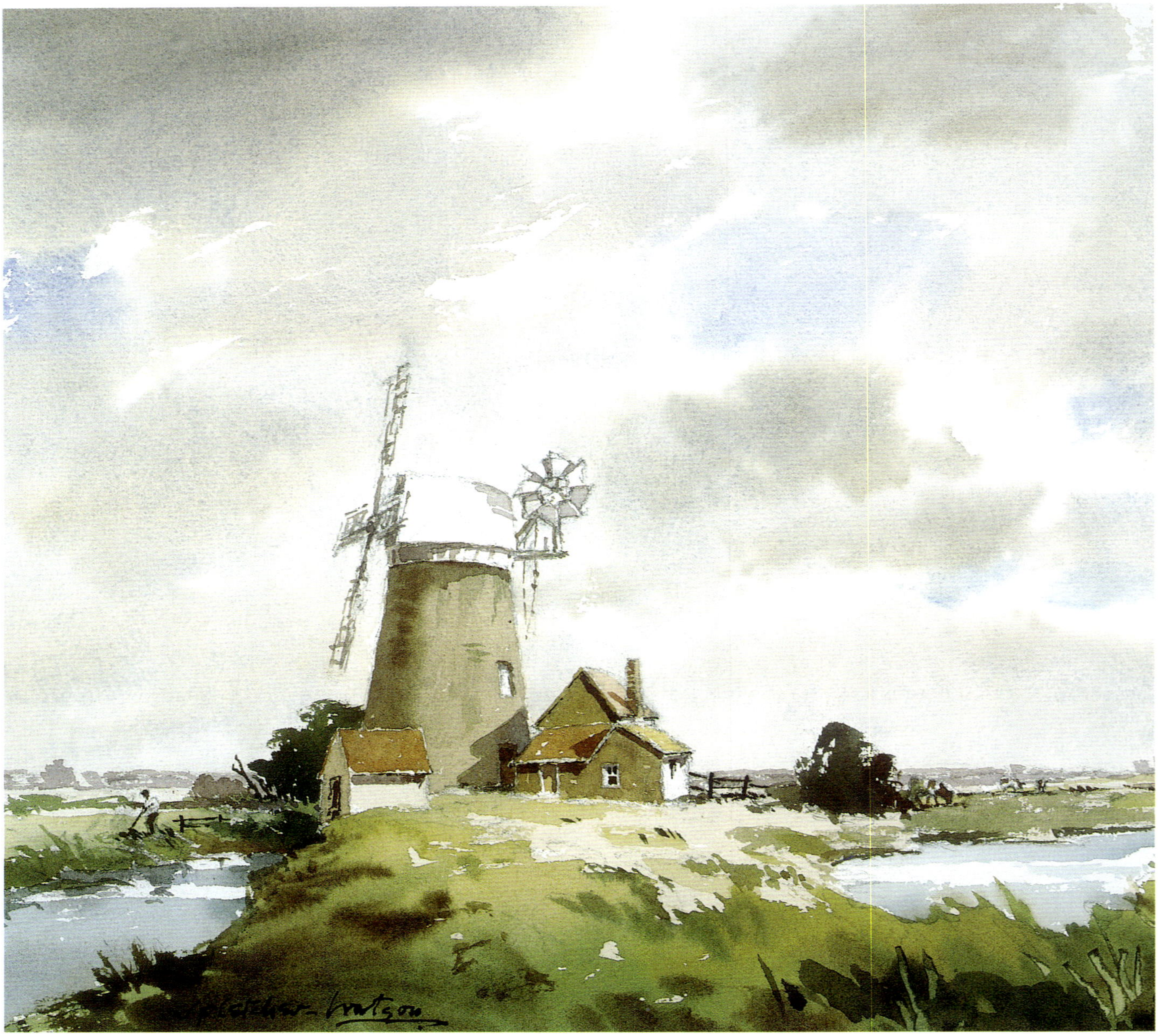

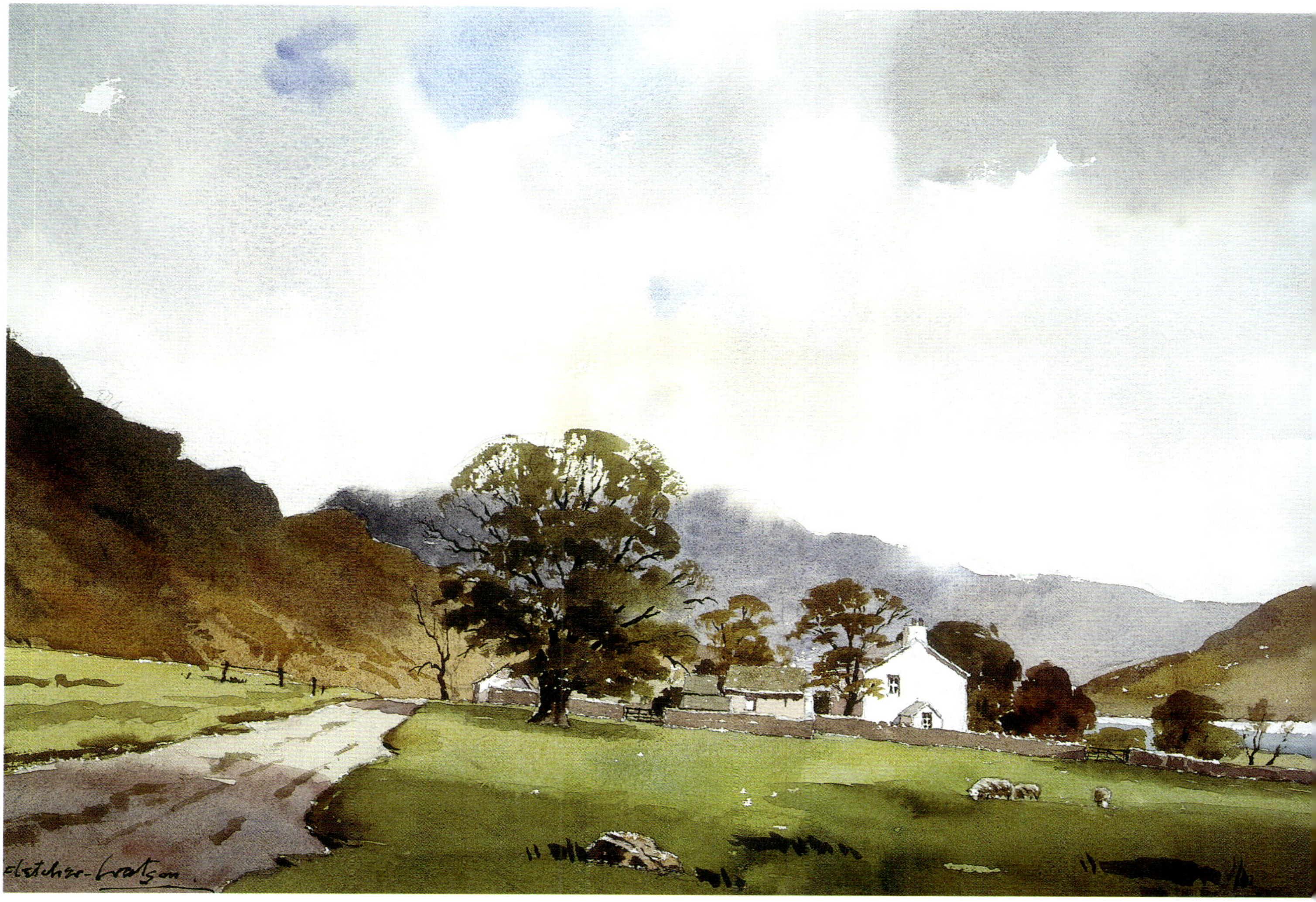

Figure 78
Near Crummock Water, Cumbria, England.
318 × 476mm (12½ × 18¾in)

brick and timber. There is a wind blowing, which is indicated here by the bent foreground grasses, and this adds to the atmosphere of the scene.

This view *Near Crummock Water* (**figure 78**) makes a perfect subject for landscape painting, with the background of mountains going into the distance and the attractive farm building as a splendid focal point. The road carries the eye into the picture and the cloud shadows on the foreground grass and road give perspective and depth to the subject. There is an interesting range of colour in this picture with the brown mountain on the left, painted with Burnt Umber and French Ultramarine, changing to a blue-grey mountain in the distance. The very dark green tree in the centre of the picture is a useful balance to the farmhouse on the right.

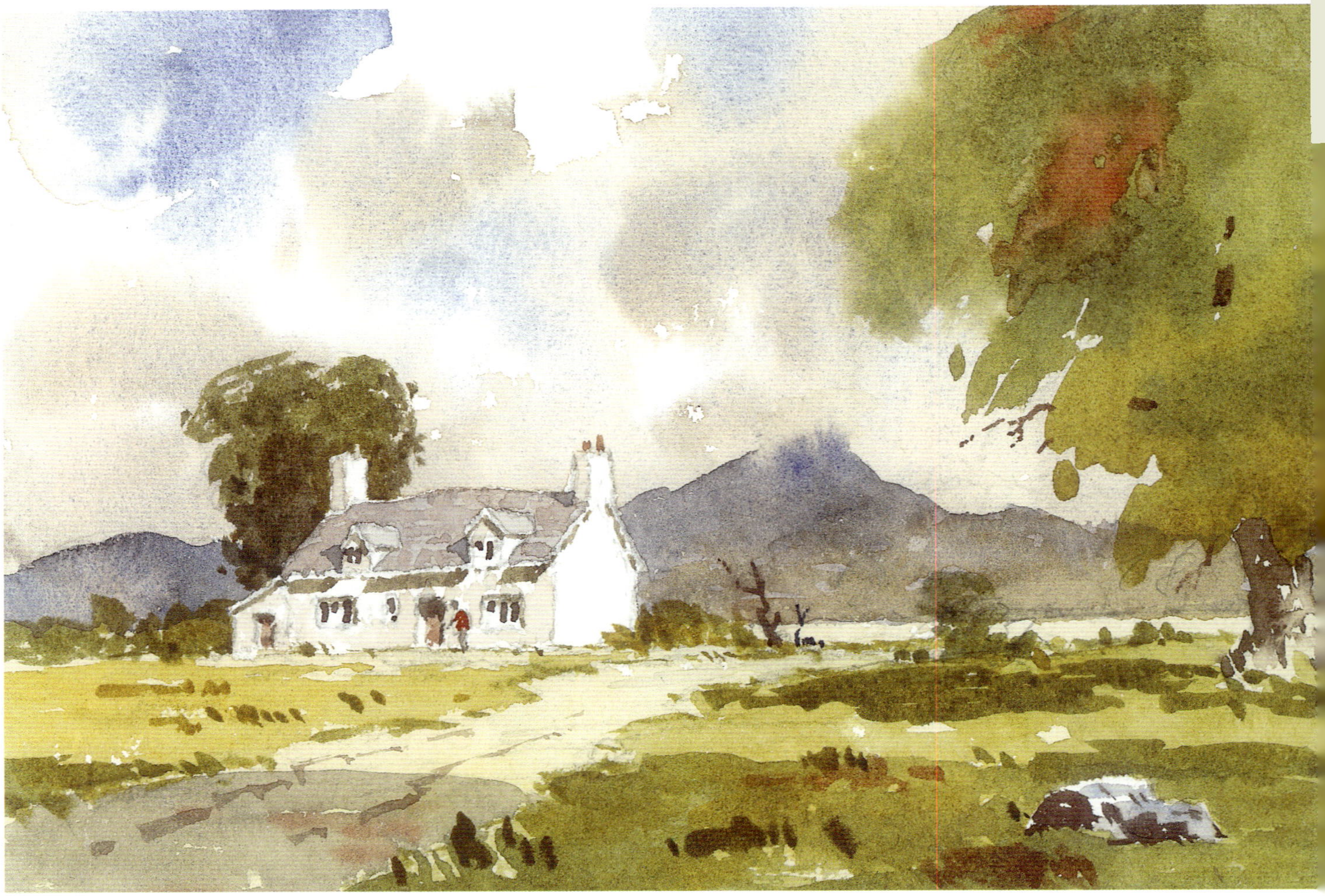

Figure 79, *Cottage by a Scottish loch*, is a picture painted with only three colours, Raw Sienna, Light Red and French Ultramarine (although almost any yellow, red and blue would be suitable). This is an extremely good exercise to give yourself, as it will make you concentrate on the *tone values* as much as the colour. In this case, I used Saunders-Waterford 300lb paper, which has a slightly cream colour and absorbs washes extremely well. The painting process was as outlined below.

1 As it was a fairly small picture and I did not require a thick line, I used a B pencil. The cottage was drawn first, positioned slightly to the left, followed by the line of the loch and background mountain. Next the small tree behind the cottage, the large tree to the right and the rough unsurfaced track in the foreground were added.

2 The painting began with the sky, mixing first French Ultramarine with Light Red, to give a rather hard grey, and then adding a little Raw Sienna to make a softer, warmer colour of grey for the clouds. I first damped the sky area with clear water and then applied the grey wash, leaving suitable white spaces. I brought the wash right down to the foot of the mountain and carefully painted round the white cottage.

Figure 79
Cottage by a Scottish loch. 146 × 203mm (5¾ × 8in)

Raw Sienna

Light Red

French Ultramarine

Next I dropped in the blue sky patches, with the paper still half-damp, using pure French Ultramarine in varying strengths. Finally I mixed a slightly darker grey with the three colours and over-painted some of the grey clouds, which brought the whole sky to life.

3 The mountain was then painted with a mixture of French Ultramarine and just a touch of Light Red. This gave it a slightly purple colour, but I added some neat blue near the top of the high mountain. I used the trick of the low cloud over the mountain top as previously described.

4 Once everything was dry, I tackled the cottage. The roof was done first, using French Ultramarine with a little Light Red and Raw Sienna added. I made it a warm grey so it was distinct from the mountain. I kept playing with the three colours until it was right. Then came the windows and doors, using stiffer mixes to give a darker tone. The shadows under the roof eaves and door openings were also added.

5 Then I worked on the trees and shrubs. The tree behind the cottage was the darkest green, a stiff mixture of French Ultramarine and Raw Sienna. The big tree on the right was painted with the same two colours, but the yellow was made more dominant. I dropped in a little neat Light Red near the top to give the autumn colouring, which was starting to show. The very dark shadow on the trunk of the big tree was a strong mixture of all three colours.

6 The foreground grass was painted with a mixture of Raw Sienna and a little French Ultramarine. The shadows were a stronger mixture of the same two colours, but for the track shadow I used French Ultramarine with a touch of Light Red. The dark rock shadows were painted with all three colours, using a very stiff mixture which produced the almost black colour required.

I strongly advise any of my painting friends who have never tried this 'three colour only' system to experiment with this idea. It does teach you a great deal about composition, tone values and generally building up a harmonious picture.

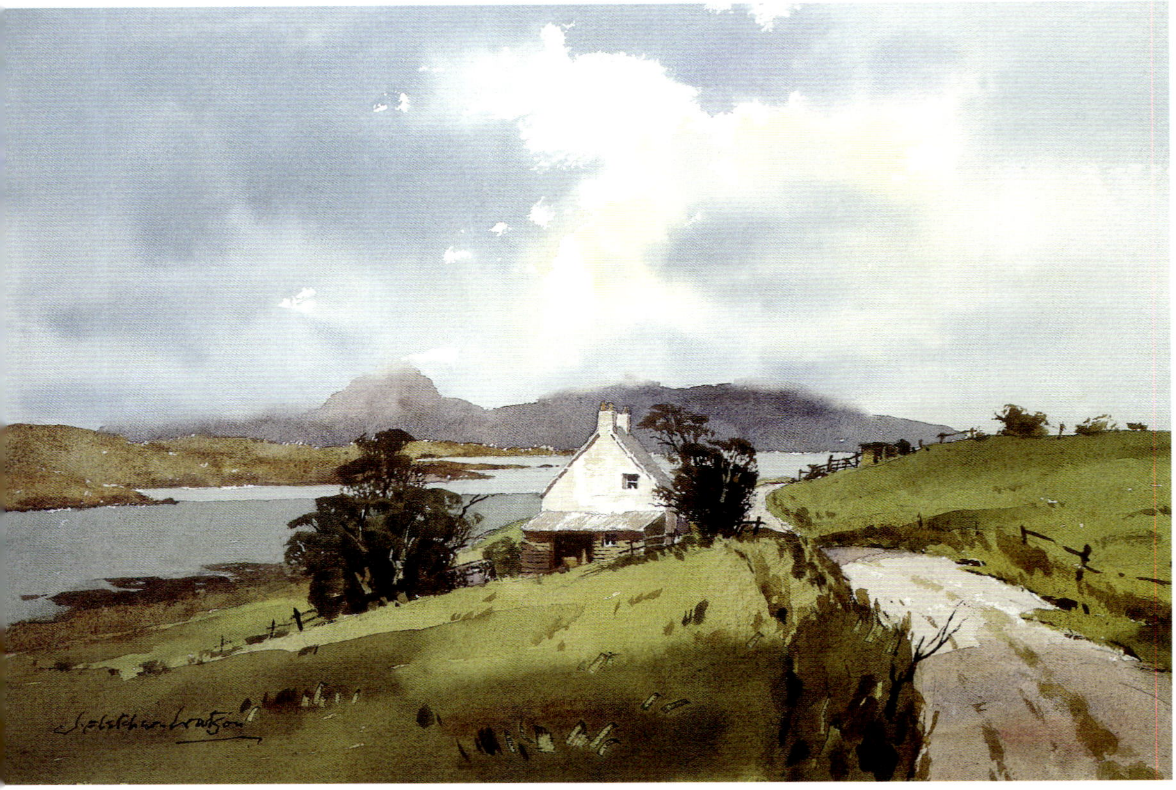

Figure 80
Loch Caroy, Skye, Scotland.
235 × 362mm
(9½ × 14¼in)

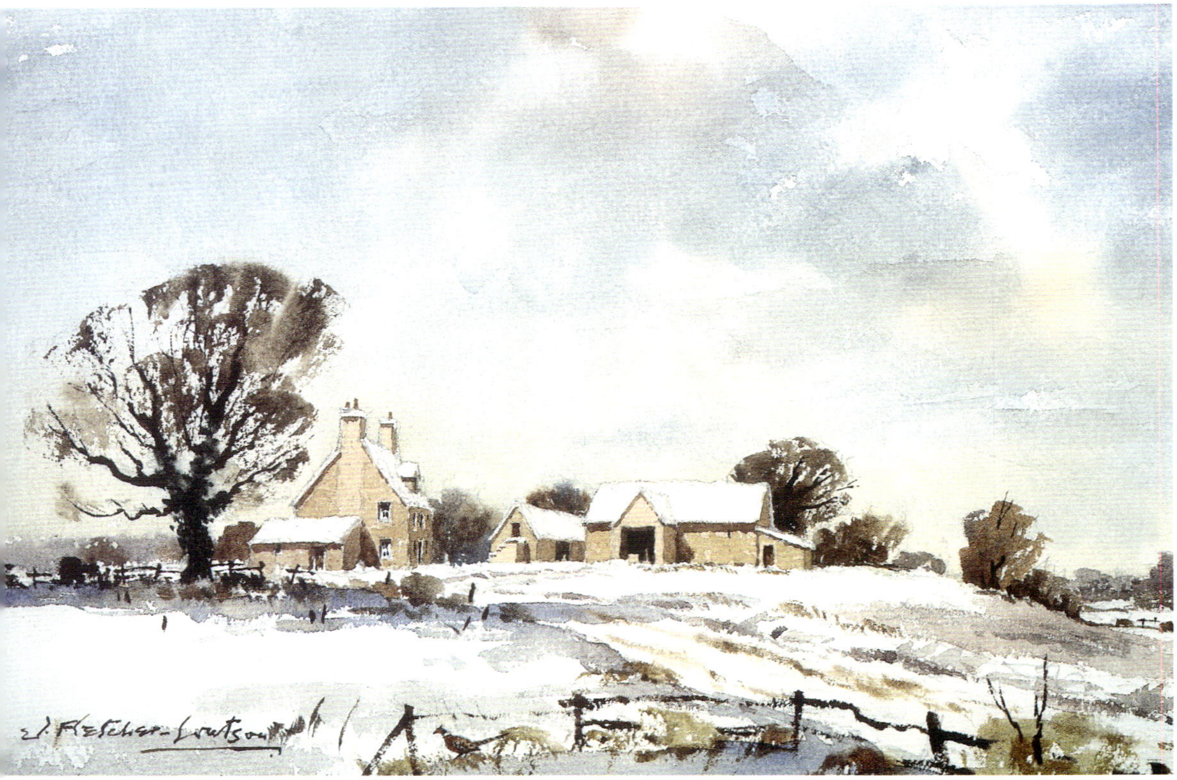

Figure 81
Snow in the Cotswolds, England.
235 × 362mm
(9½ × 14¼in)

Both **figure 80** and **figure 81** are good examples of buildings in a landscape. I painted *Loch Caroy, Skye* on a bright, blustery day. Hence the interesting cloudy sky with bright patches as well as the lovely variety of tones of green shadow on the grass. In contrast, *Snow in the Cotswolds* required more browns and greys with blue shadows on the snow. It was painted in the studio from a pencil sketch I made in my car.

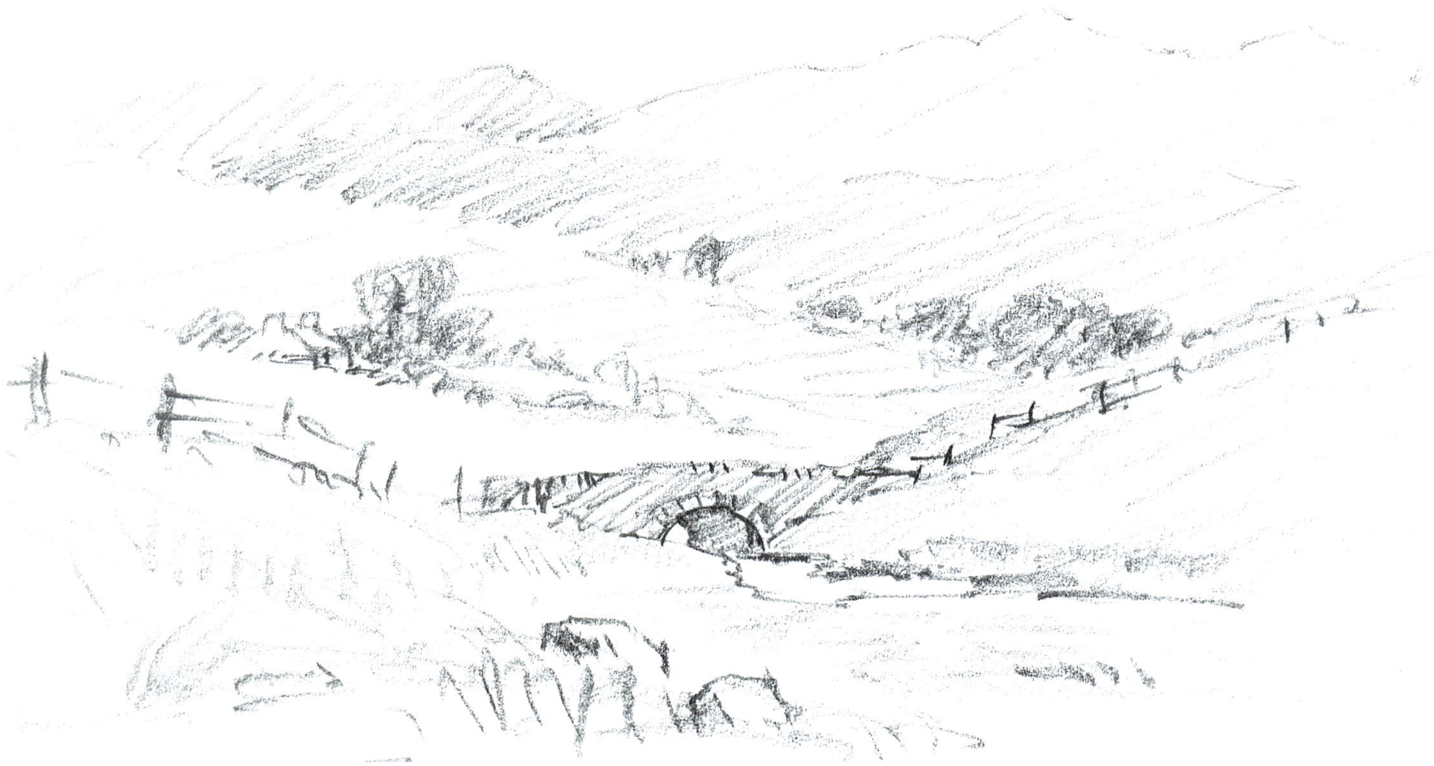

TIPS AND TECHNIQUES

- Avoid unnecessary detail in a landscape composition in order to achieve a pleasing balance between all the different elements
- Remember to define a focal point in a landscape: this will give the painting the correct balance
- When selecting a subject, it can be effective to first translate it onto watercolour paper in your mind
- Avoid over-complicated subjects when starting to paint landscapes. Even when you are more experienced, a simple subject can often give the best results
- Landscapes can be painted using a three-colour system of French Ultramarine, Light Red and Raw Sienna. This simple system helps you to develop skills in composition, tone values and the balancing of a painting

Chapter 10

SPECIFIC SUBJECTS

The Forum, Rome; Regello, Tuscany; Lugo, Spain; Deia, Majorca: church interiors; a Spanish street on toned paper; perspective

This chapter gives illustrations of slightly more advanced subjects, which are fun to tackle when you have reached a greater level of confidence.

Figure 82, *The Forum, Rome*, is the most splendid architectural subject imaginable. The Forum is like a gigantic outdoor museum of Roman remains, and the ground is strewn with old pieces of cornice or columns. There were many paintable views, but I eventually settled on the one shown here, as the distribution of trees was excellent in showing up portions of buildings. (Most importantly, I could sit in a bit of shade as it was a very hot day.) Thankfully my wife, Gill, produced a cool drink at suitable moments!

A subject of this level of complexity must be considered very carefully before you start drawing and painting it, or the result could be a restless, unsatisfactory picture. I think I managed to avoid this successfully by carefully balancing the composition and by featuring the dark trees and bushes, which are an immense help in making architectural features stand out. This is especially the case with the central group of columns through which the dark tree can clearly be seen.

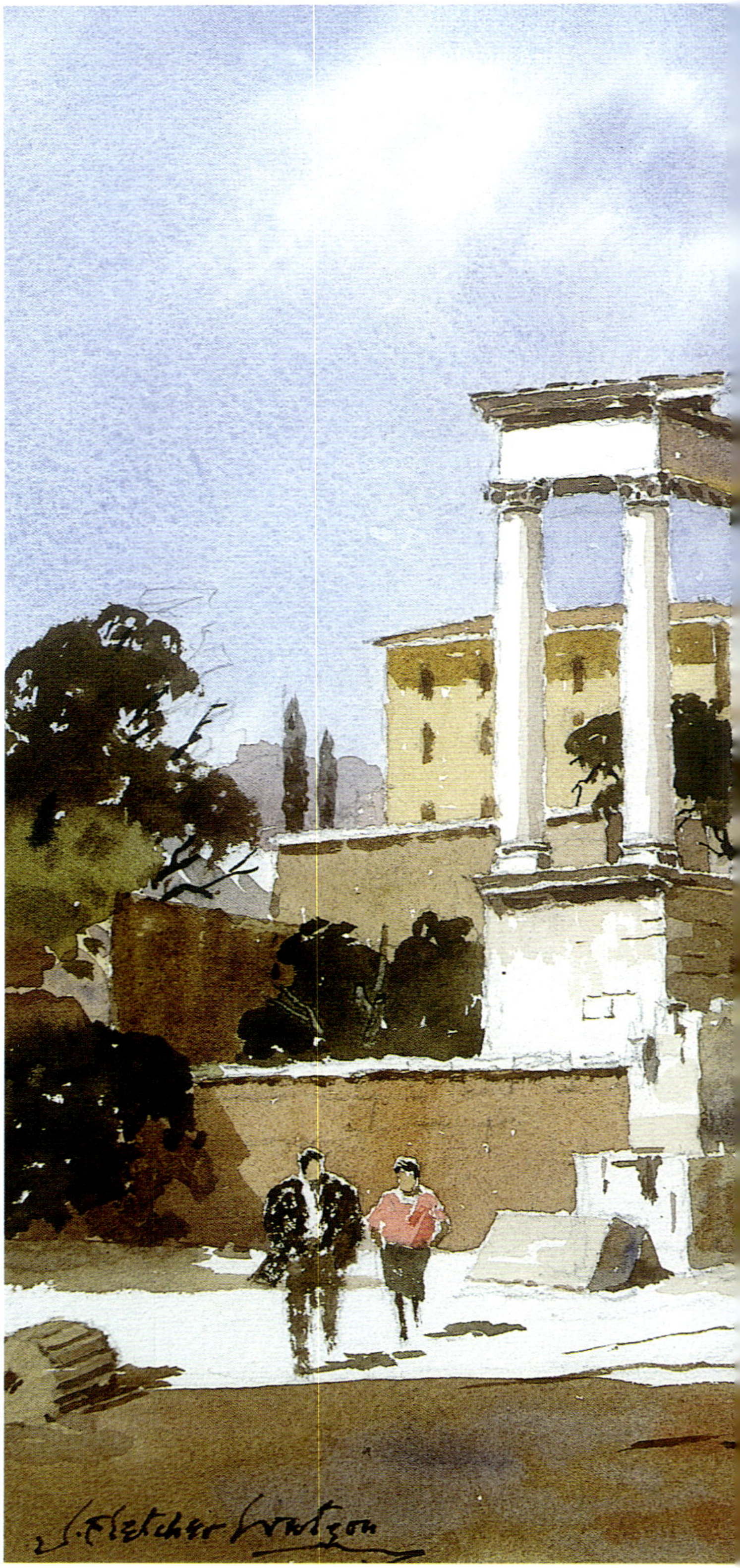

Figure 82
The Forum, Rome.
318 × 476mm (12½ × 18¾in)

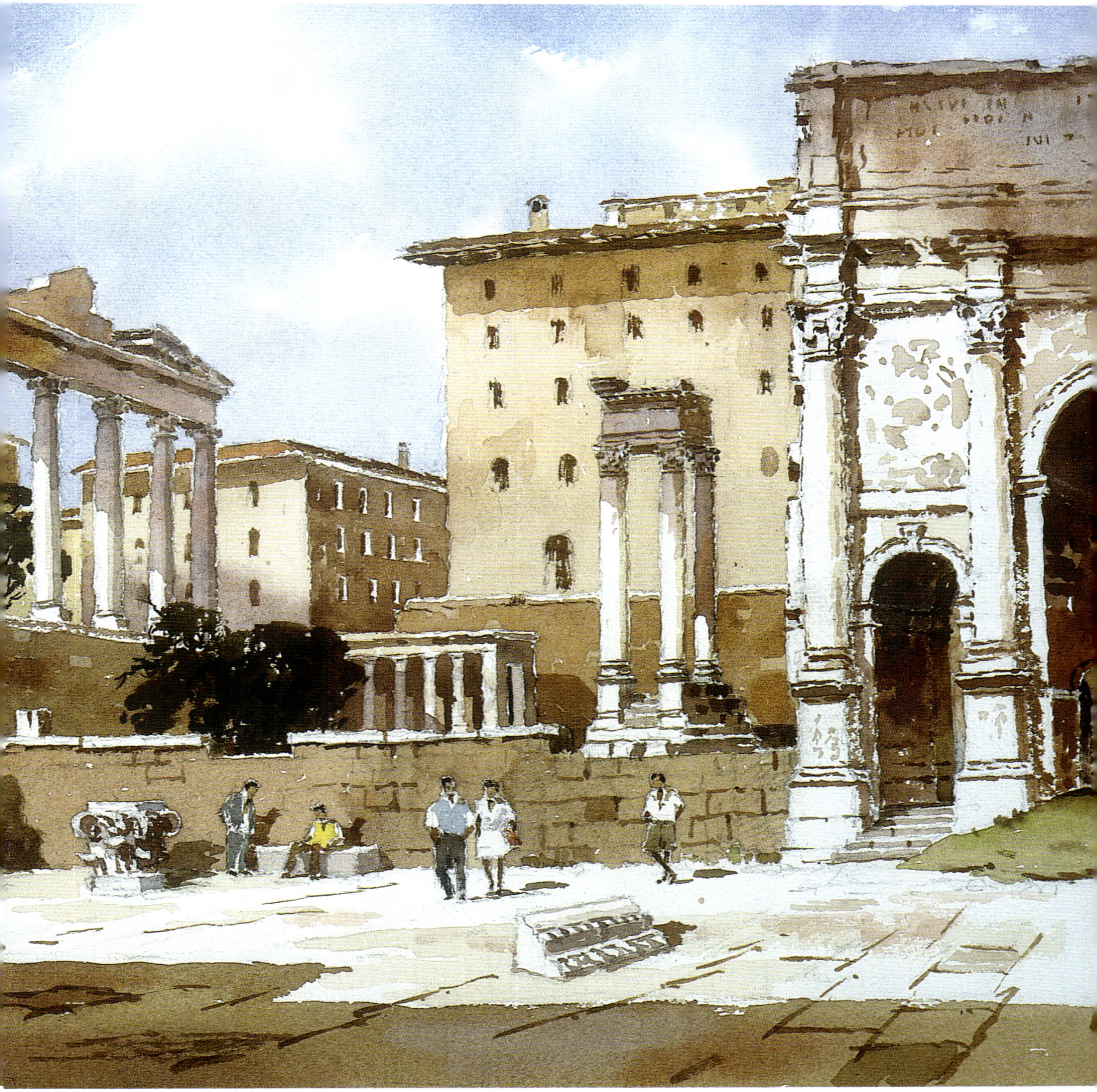

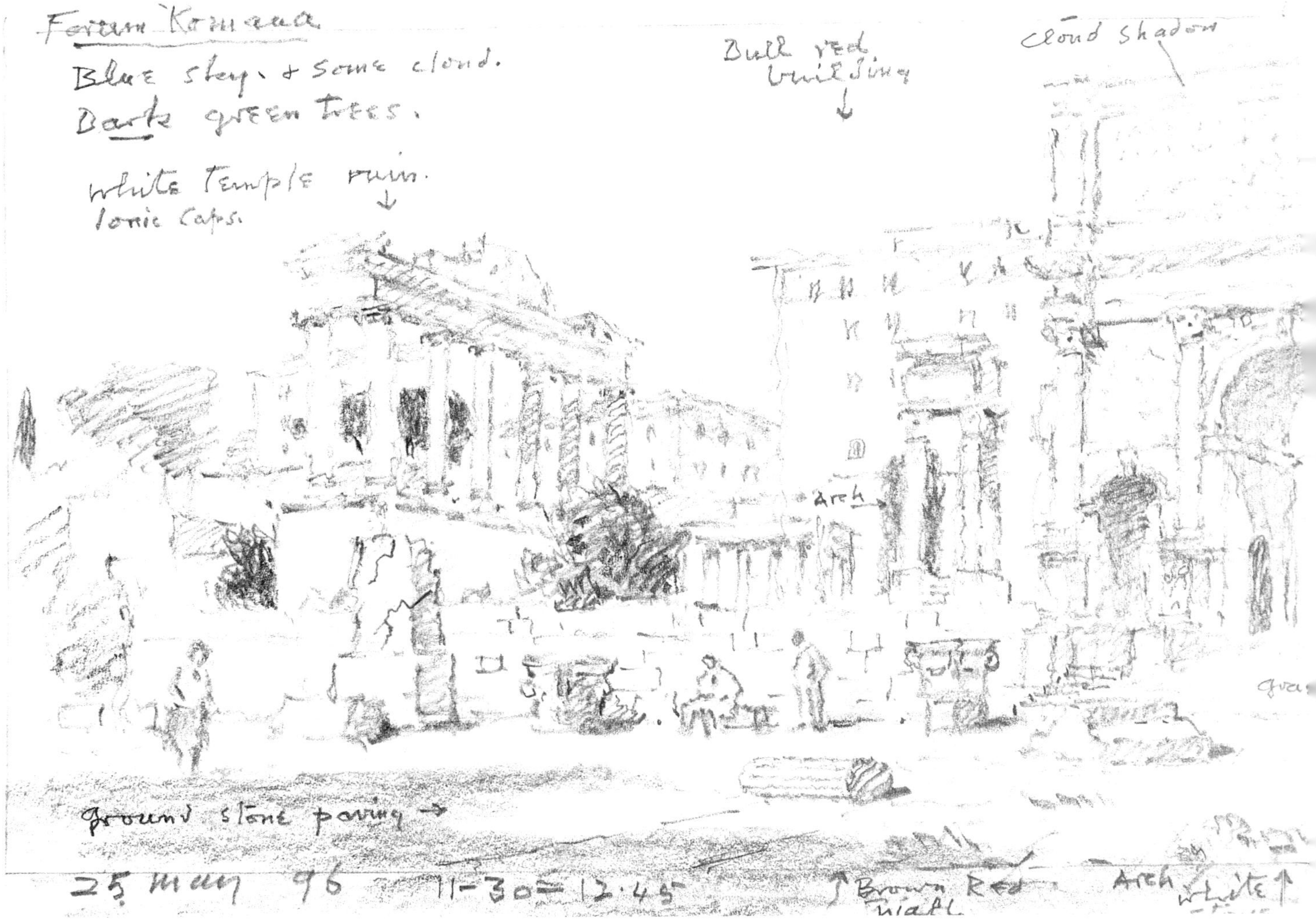

Figure 83
Pencil drawing done on the spot.

Figure 83 shows my pencil sketch, which was done on the spot. I felt that I could make a much better job of a watercolour if I painted it in my studio at home, and I made a note or two on the sketch about colours, etc. It took about one-and-a-quarter hours to draw *in situ*. The actual watercolour at home took two hours to draw and about three hours to paint. If you look closely at the sketch, you will see that the architectural details of cornices, capitals and columns are not at all precisely executed, but just painted quickly and suggestively. I did not use a very small brush, but a No. 8 with a really good point.

I used Cobalt Blue for the sky; Raw Sienna, Burnt Sienna, Burnt Umber and Cobalt Blue for the buildings and shadows; and Winsor Blue and Burnt Sienna for the trees.

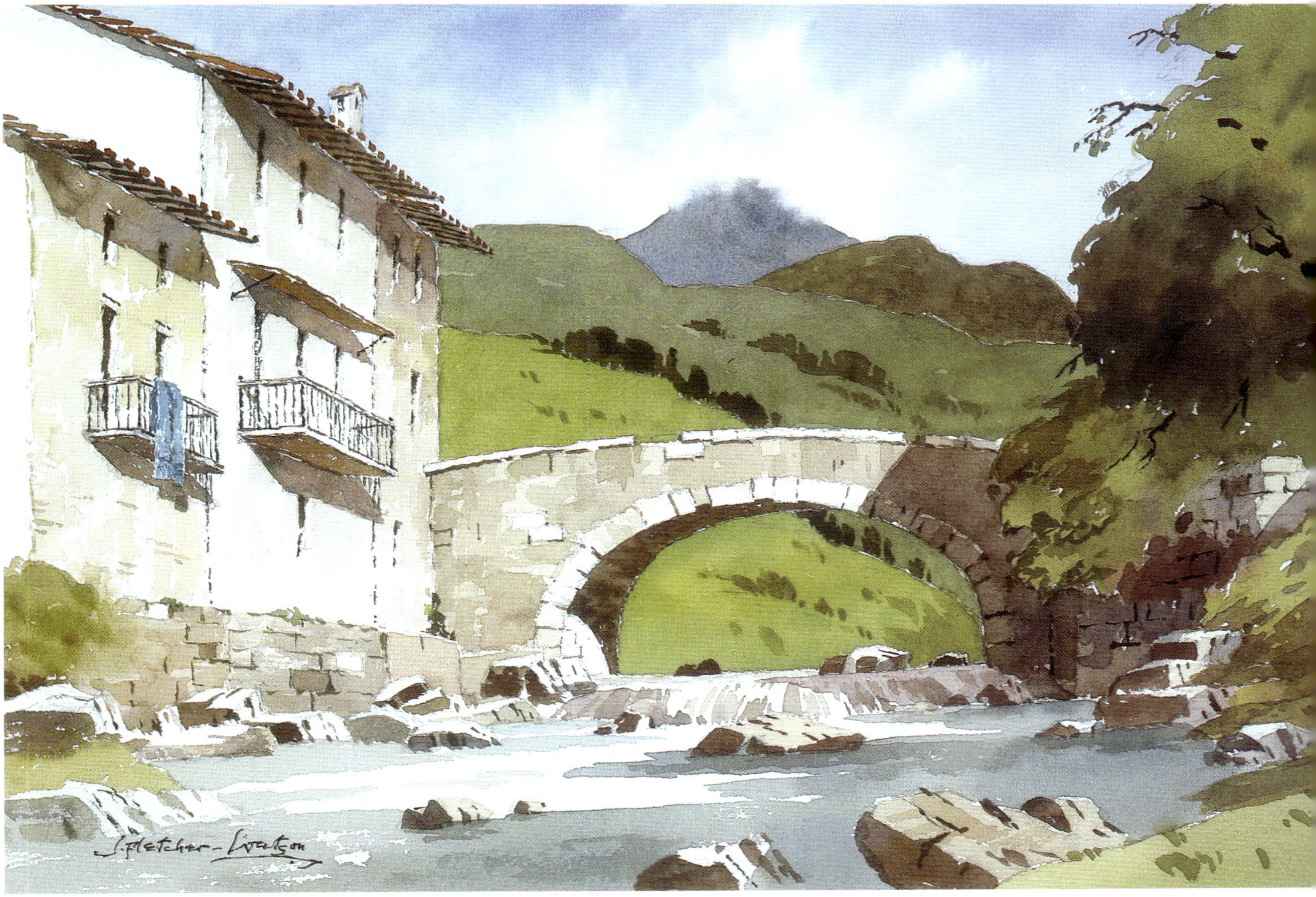

Figure 84
Regello, Tuscany.
318 × 476mm (12½ × 18¾in)

Figure 84, *Regello, Tuscany*, is a painting of a delightful little hill village where Gill and I stayed for a week, discovering many good subjects. I had to scramble down a narrow track and over some rocks to find this view. What makes this such a good subject? Well, the angle of the sun for one thing, though I had to wait for it to move where I wanted it. The glancing shadow from the trees onto the bridge was worth waiting for and also the shadows on the water. The rocks in the stream were valuable features, although I did need to adjust their positions slightly. The houses had good deep shadows under their eaves and balconies. This perfect composition with a mountain background made the whole scene a dream picture. I will not elaborate further, as the composition really speaks for itself.

The view of the historic town of *Lugo, Spain* in **figure 85** caught my eye directly I saw it, and I squatted down in the middle of the square with all my paints and got to work. The sun was at the right angle to give ideal shadows to the various buildings and I noted these fairly early on in my drawing work. Although the drawing in an architectural picture of this kind can take some time, I did manage to complete the picture on the spot, which is always an advantage. You will notice the value of paving stones with their joints in perspective, which helped give the necessary depth to the picture. I will explain perspective more fully at the end of this chapter.

Deia, Majorca (**figure 86**) is another extra-special subject. The village, with its characteristic stone buildings, nestles under the massive mountains behind. Having a small bridge over a mountain stream as the central focus of the painting added a lot to the architectural interest.

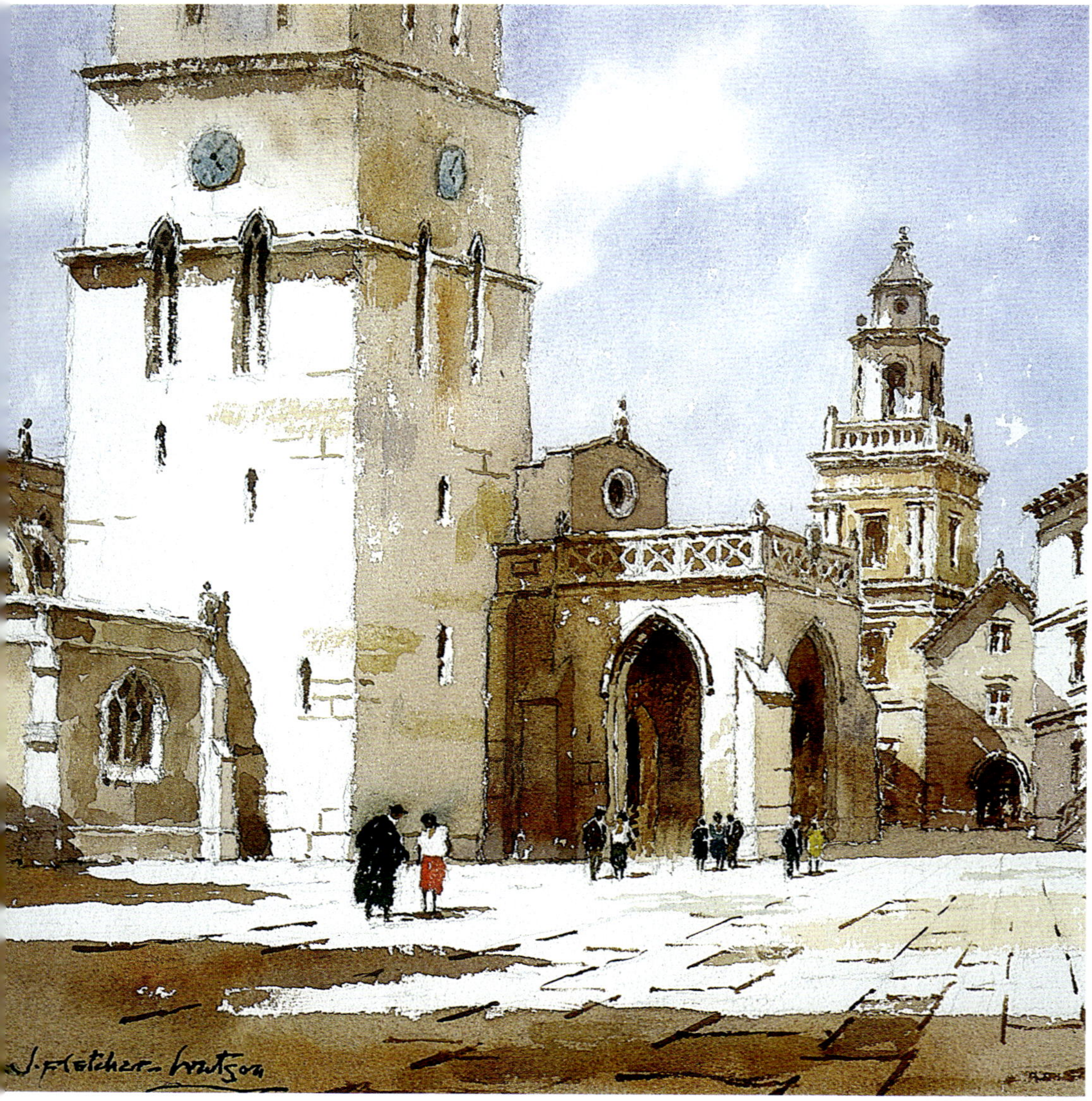

Figure 85 (left)
Lugo, Spain.
362 × 311mm (14½ × 12¼in)

Figure 86 (right)
Deia, Majorca.
362 × 311mm (14½ × 12¼in)

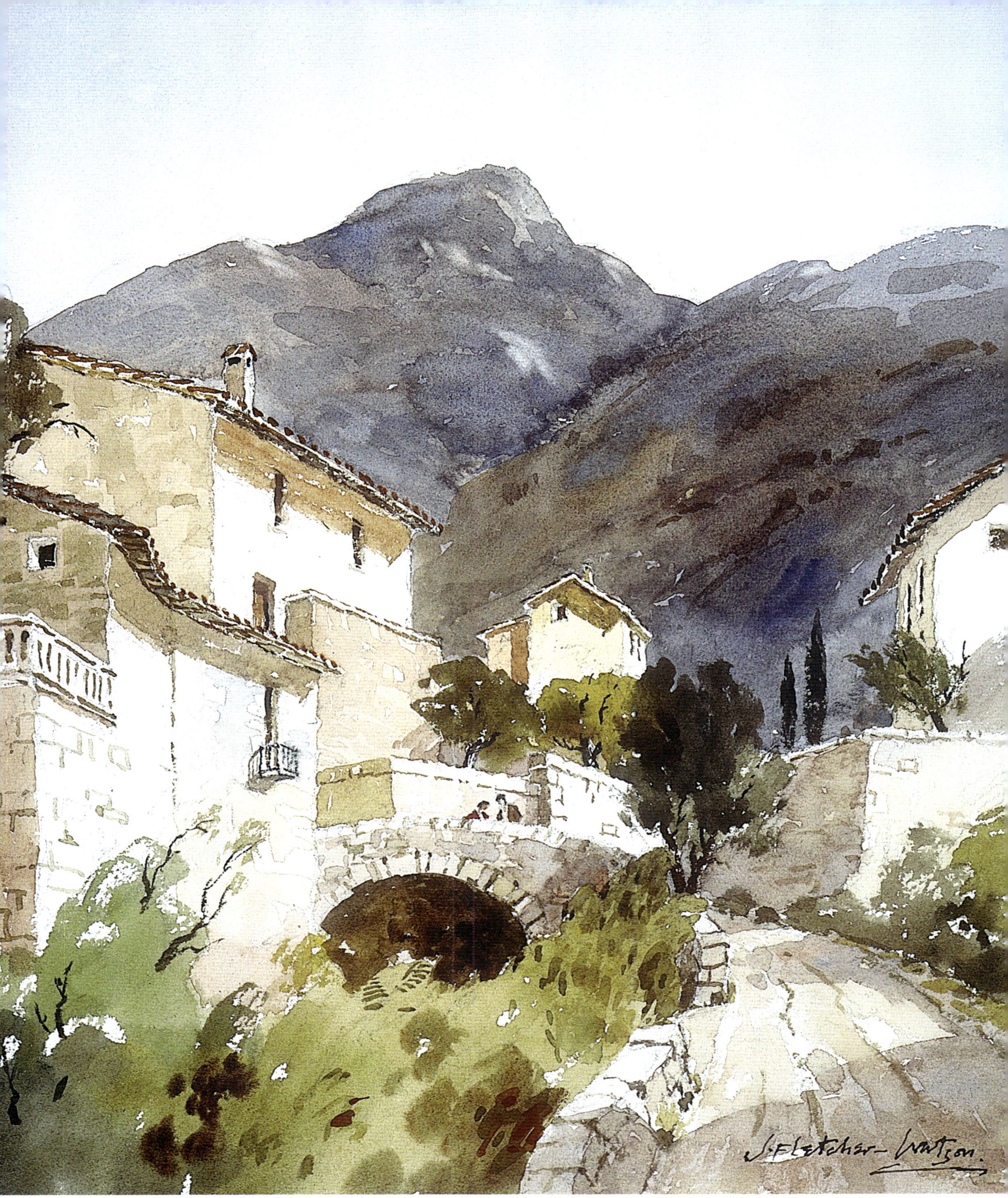
J. Fletcher-Watson.

Interiors can be great fun to paint and I show you another in **figure 87**, *Taynton church, Oxfordshire*. This view was taken from the south aisle, looking east towards the chancel arch by the pulpit. The walls are all whitewashed, hence the bright interior. I include this to show what delightful subjects country churches can be, so the next time you go sketching and it turns to rain, you could try something like this.

Figure 87a and **figure 87b** show two further examples of quite different church interiors.

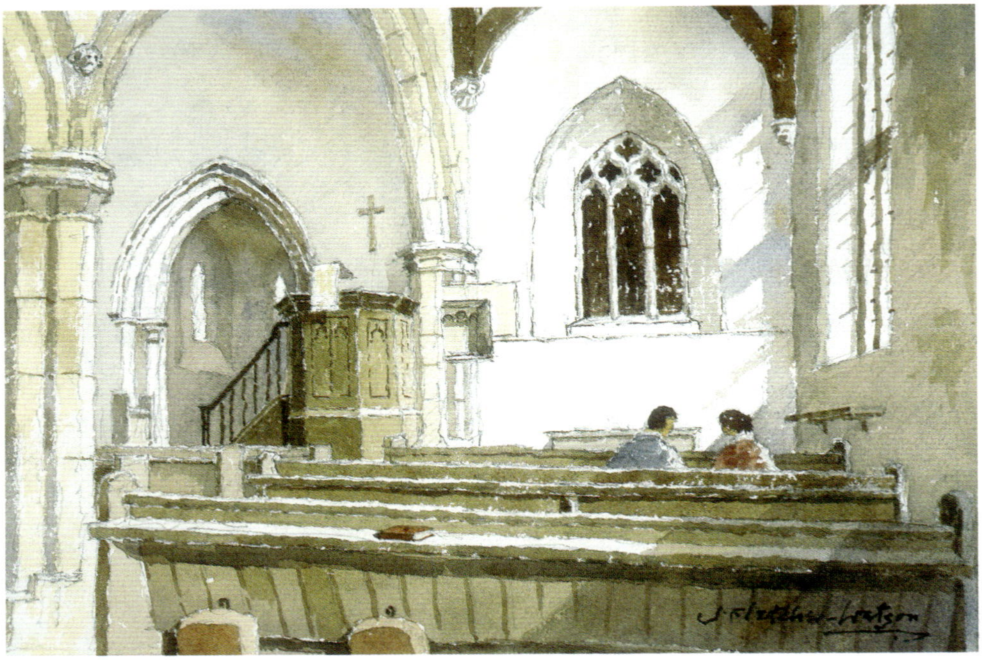

Figure 87 (left)
Taynton church, Oxfordshire, England.
248 × 368mm (9¾ × 14½in)

Figure 87a (right)
Windrush church, England.
318 × 470mm (9¾ × 14½in)

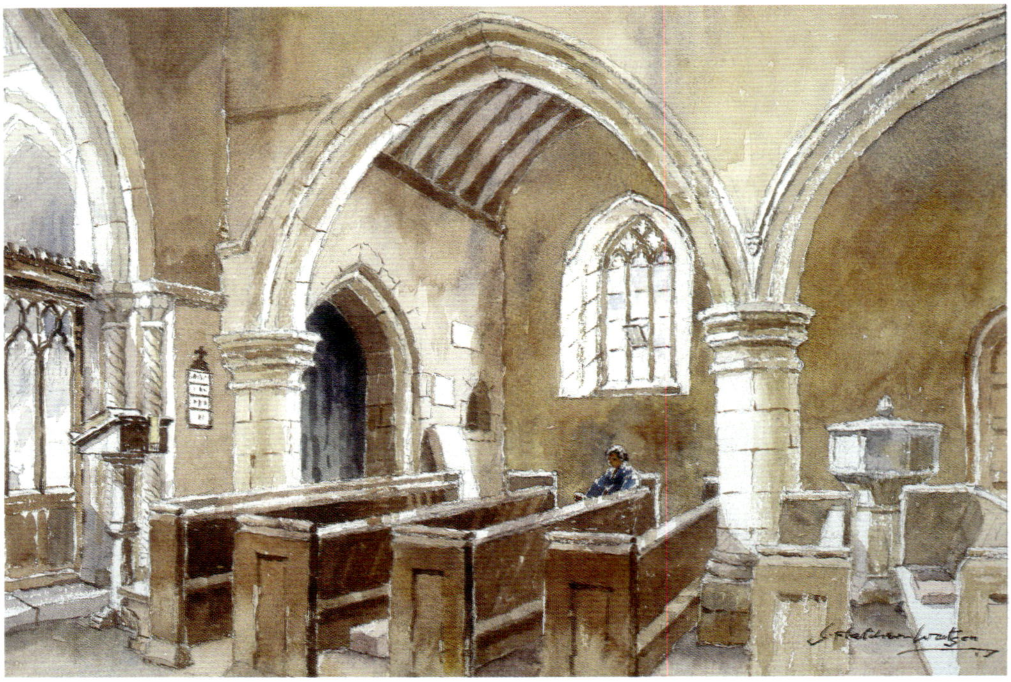

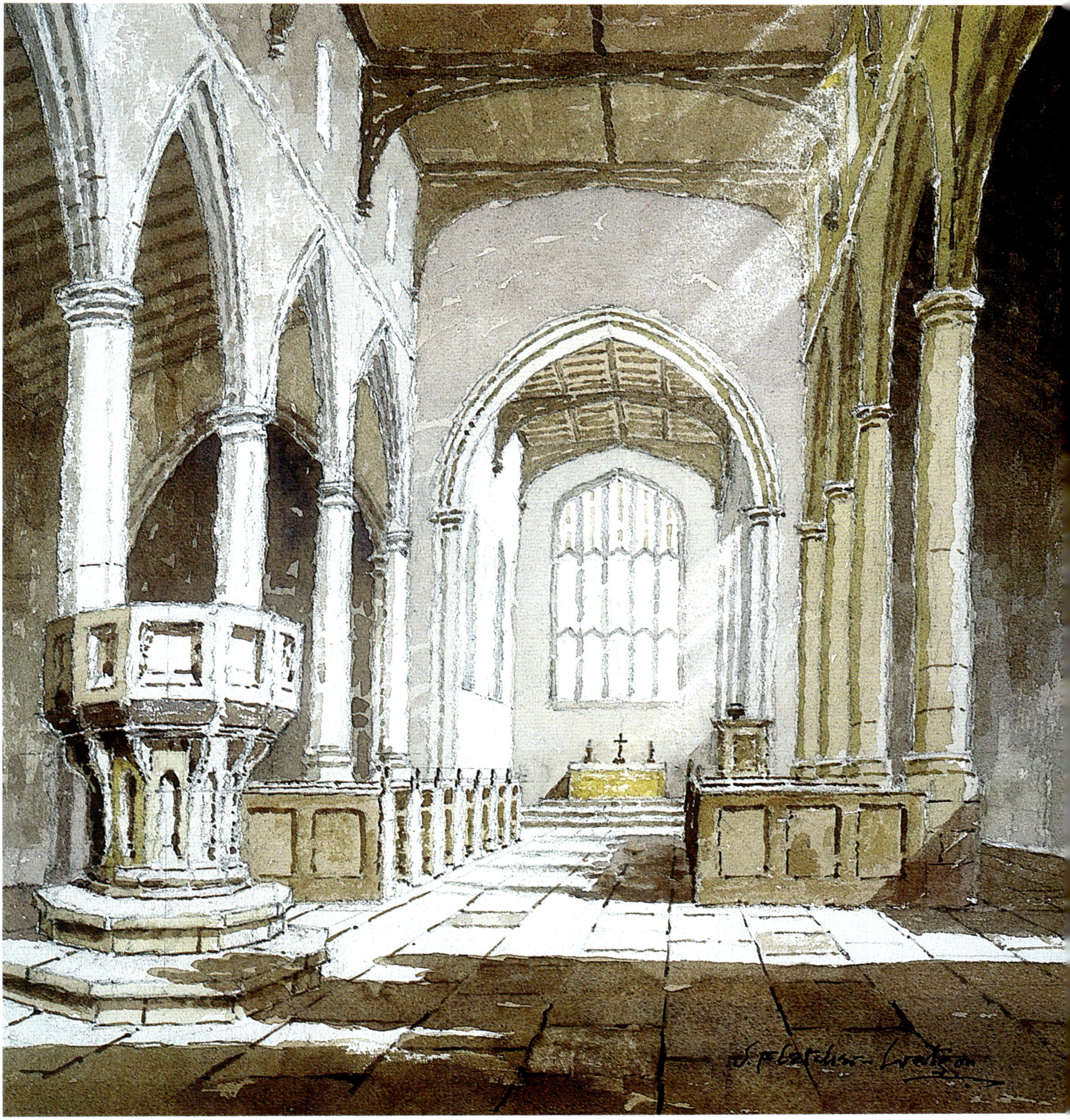

Figure 87b
Stoke by Nayland Church, Suffolk, England.
362 × 311mm (14½ × 12¼in)

The painting shown in **figure 88**, *Cordoba, Spain*, used toned paper, because I felt this was suited to the subject, which had an abundance of grey-brown stonework on the paving, the walls of the buildings and the monument. I highlighted some of the walls and the monument and paving by using touches of white paint (from a Titanium White watercolour tube by Winsor & Newton). The general effect of using white body colour is quite striking. I also used this white paint for a single female figure among the group of pedestrians on the right.

Various toned papers are available – Bockingford do three different tones and De Wint is another make that I use. Turner often used toned paper and sometimes colour washed a sheet of white paper himself using a light grey colour wash.

My picture received a single wash of Cobalt Blue on the sky. The walls of the cathedral on the left and walls of the other buildings were washes of Cobalt Blue, Light Red and Raw Sienna. When mixed, these three can give various tones of stone colour. A little Burnt Sienna was added for some areas.

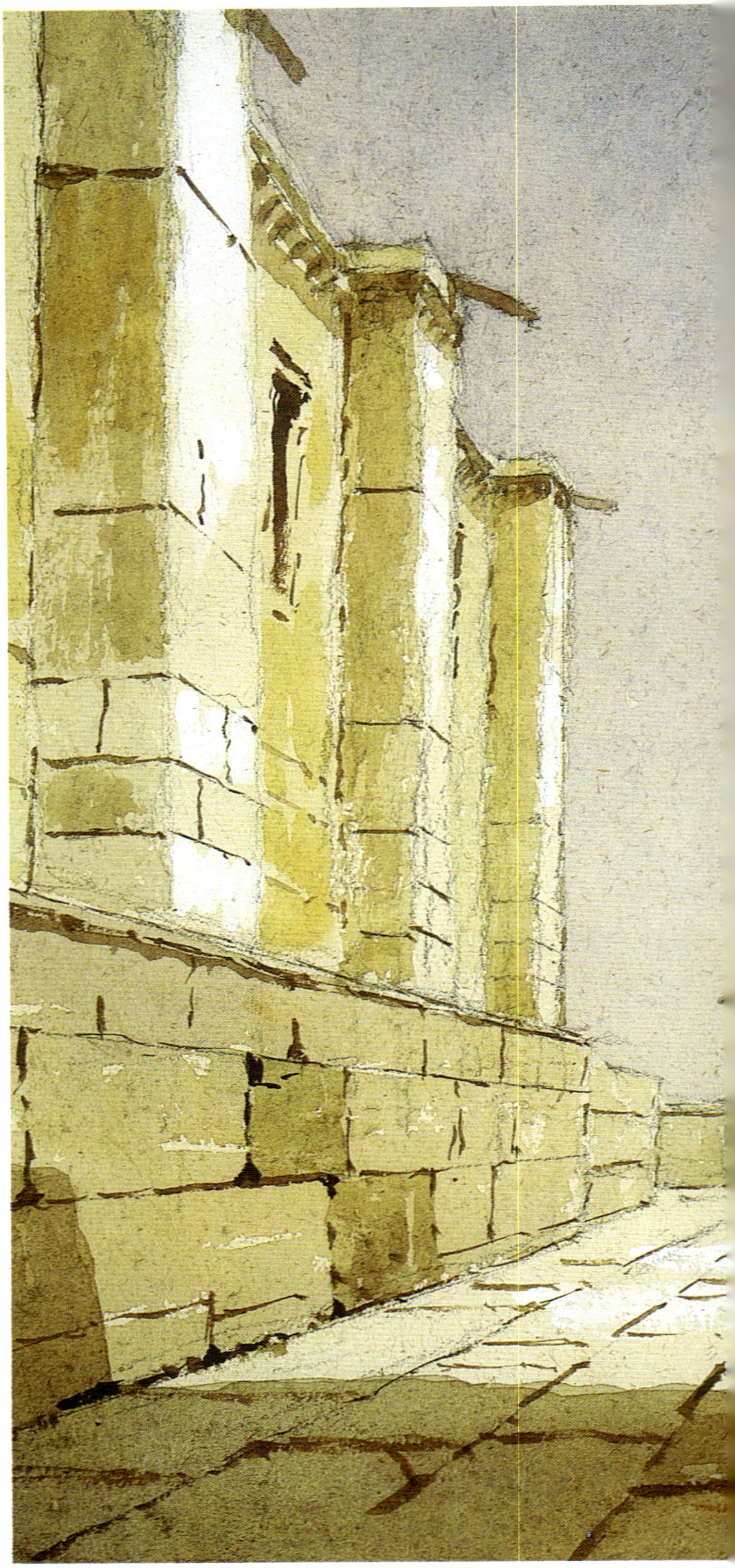

Figure 88
Cordoba, Spain.
318 × 476mm (12½ × 18¾in)

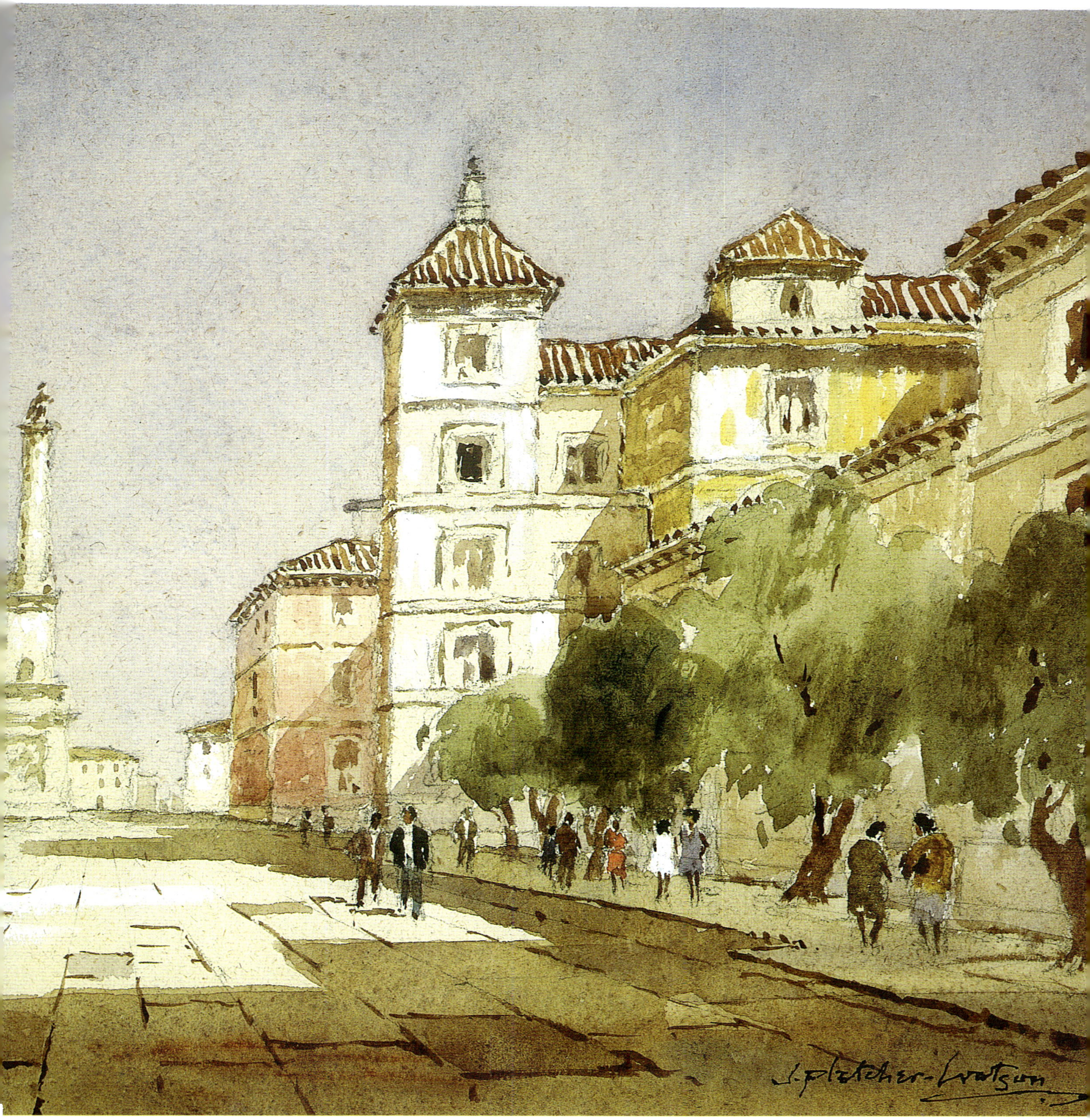
J. Fletcher-Watson

Perspective

At **figure 89a** I show a diagrammatic illustration of parallel perspective, using the picture of Cordoba shown in **figure 88**. You will observe the vanishing point at the base of the monument in the centre of the picture.

Figure 89b shows a diagrammatic illustration of angular perspective. The subject is a country cottage and the eye level when standing is a little below the top of the front door. You can see how helpful it is to have in mind the approximate vanishing point positions.

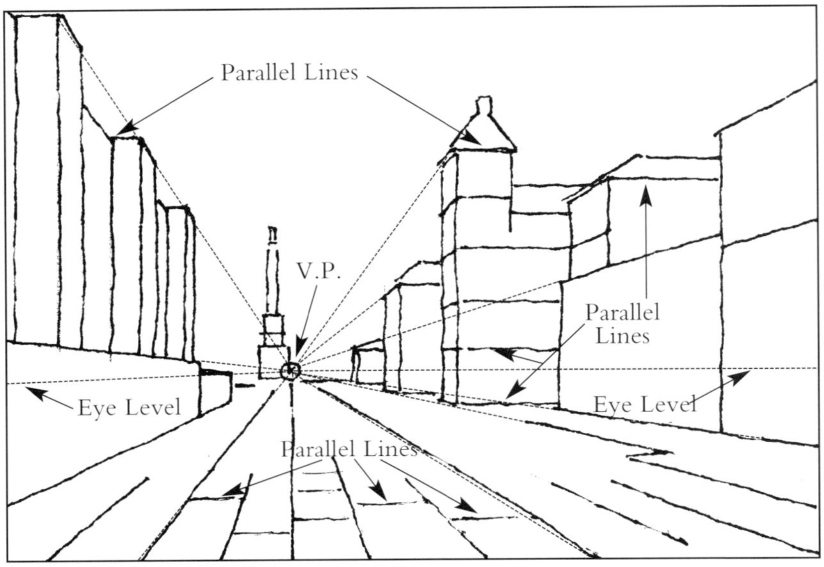

Figure 89a
Parallel perspective: one vanishing point.

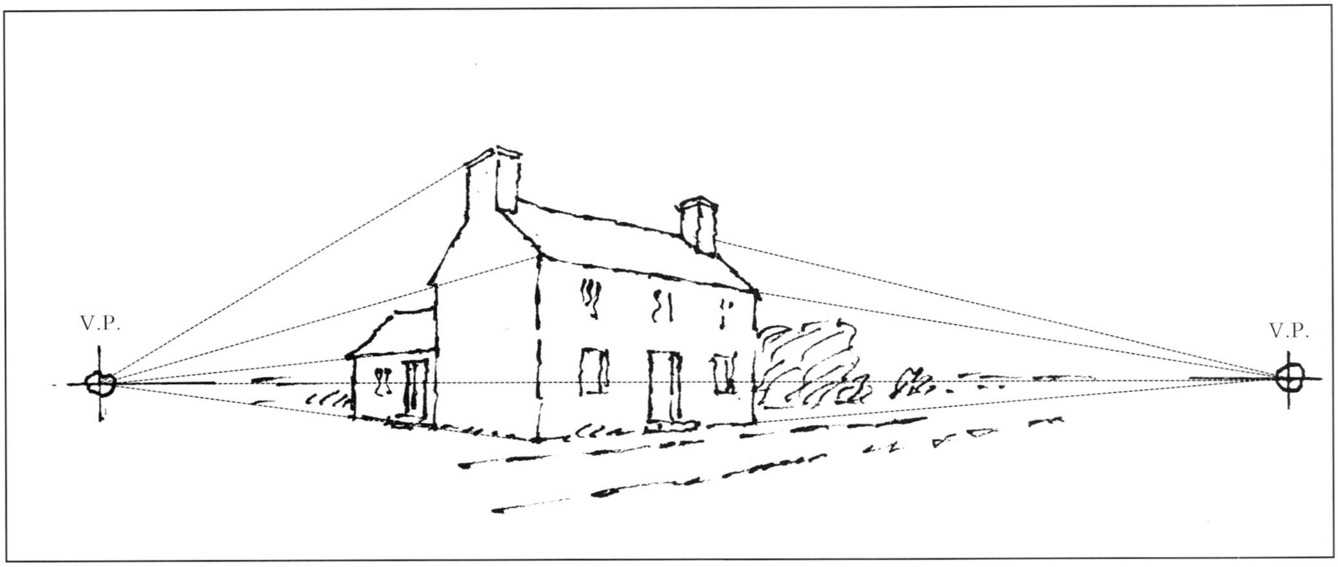

Figure 89b
Angular perspective: two vanishing points.

The picture featured on this page shows an interesting corner of the old part of Norwich. It is another good example of perspective in a scene with buildings.

Figure 90
Tombland Alley, Norwich, England.
241 × 368mm (9½ × 14½in)

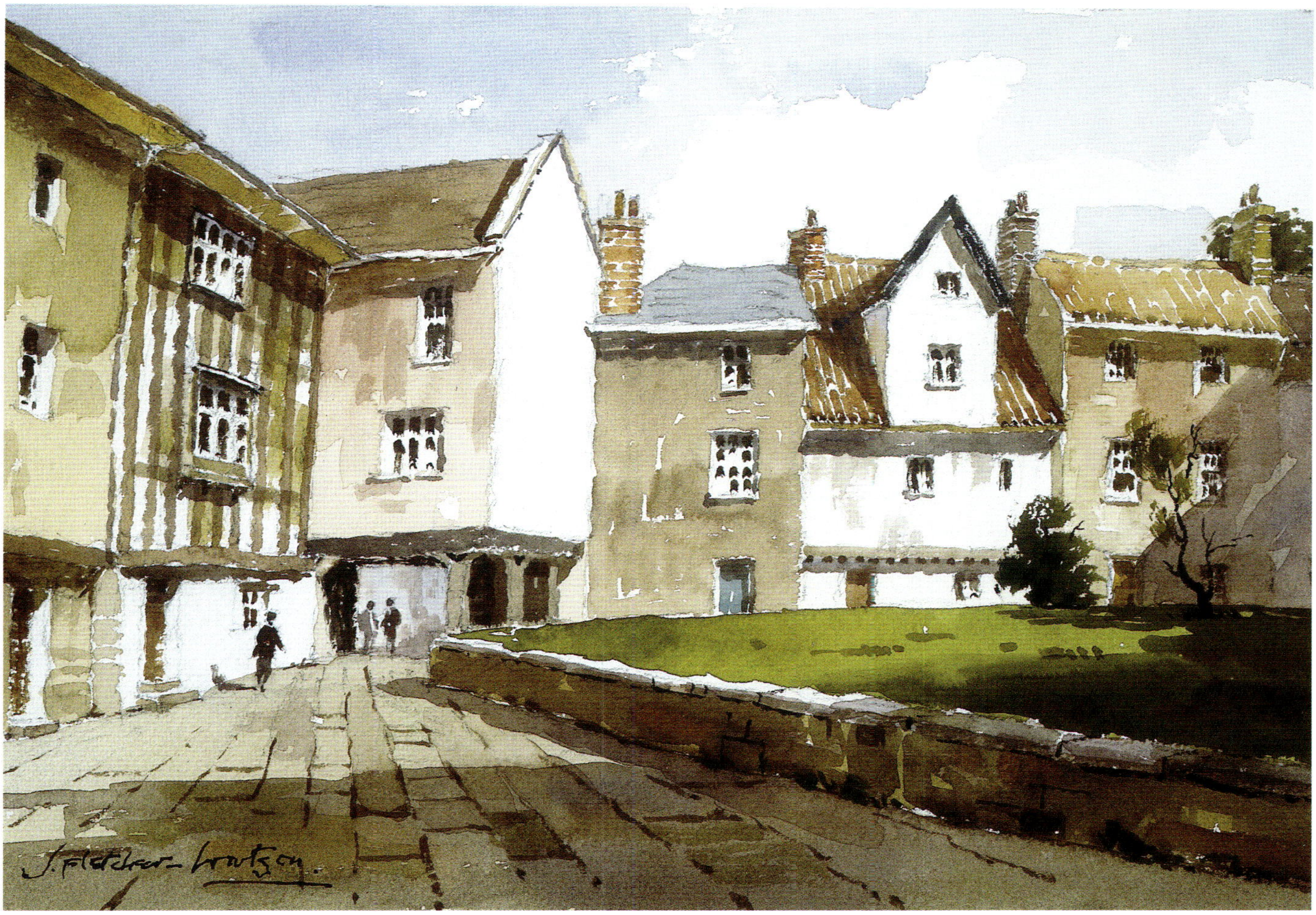

TIPS AND TECHNIQUES

- Architectural details need not be accurately captured, but can be painted quickly, just capturing an impression
- When painting more complicated subjects, I will often draw my chosen composition on the spot, making notes about the colour and tone. I then do the final painting in my studio, where there are fewer distractions
- It will always benefit you to establish the vanishing point when working on an interior architectural subject
- Toned paper can suit certain subjects, and touches of white paint can then be used to provide highlights

Chapter 11

ATTENTION TO DETAIL

Figures; cattle; boats; garden detail

In this chapter, I would like to begin with the subject of figures in a landscape setting. All painters should try to include in their training a little life drawing of the nude figure. In a sketchbook they should also practise making a range of studies of people talking to each other, sitting and especially walking (page 116).

Gavinana (**figure 91**) is a charming hill village in Tuscany and provides plenty of opportunity to include figures walking, talking or sitting outside their houses. It is important to include figures in small village scenes as well as in townscapes to bring the whole subject to life.

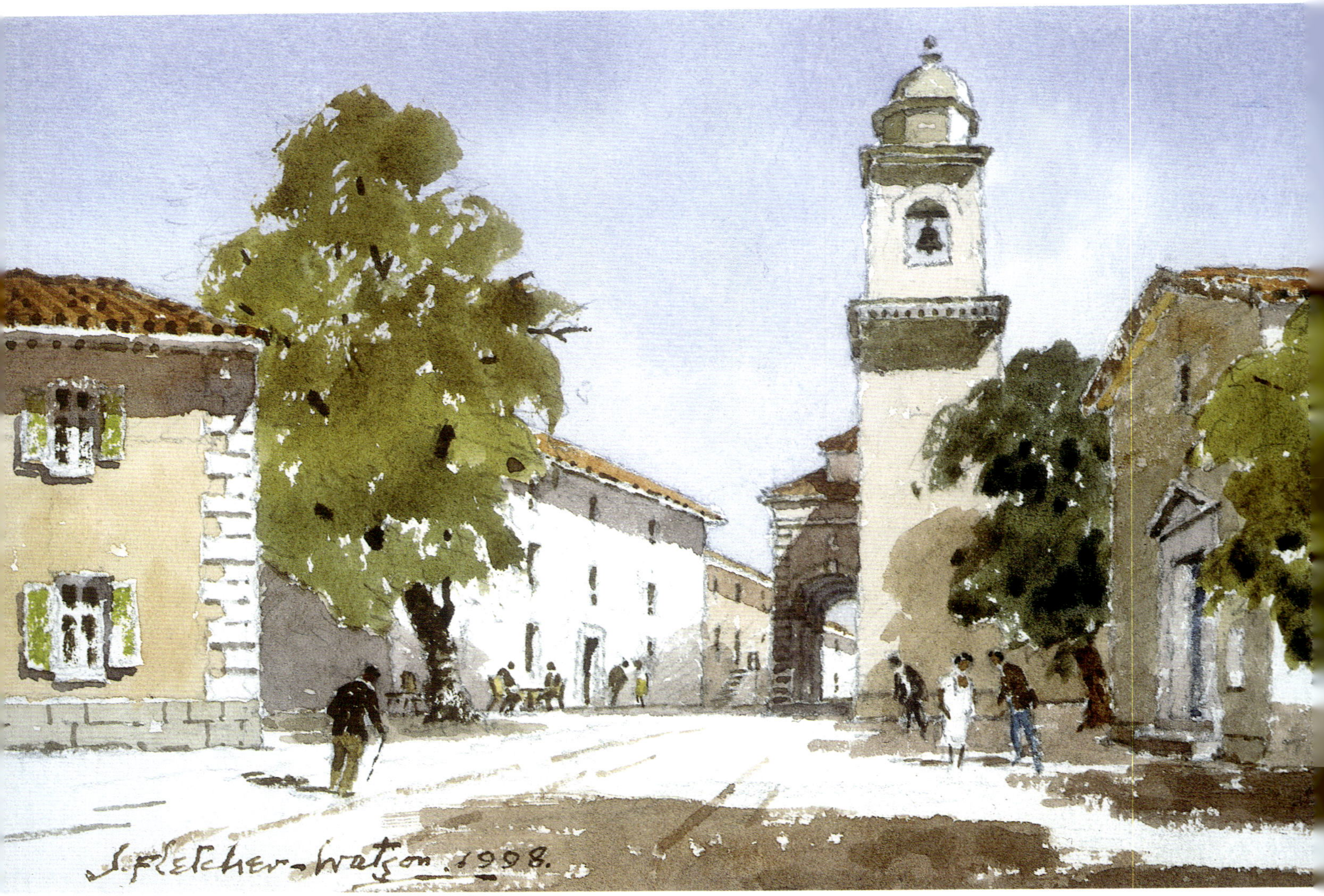

Figure 91
Gavinana, Tuscany.
318 × 476mm (12½ × 18¾in)

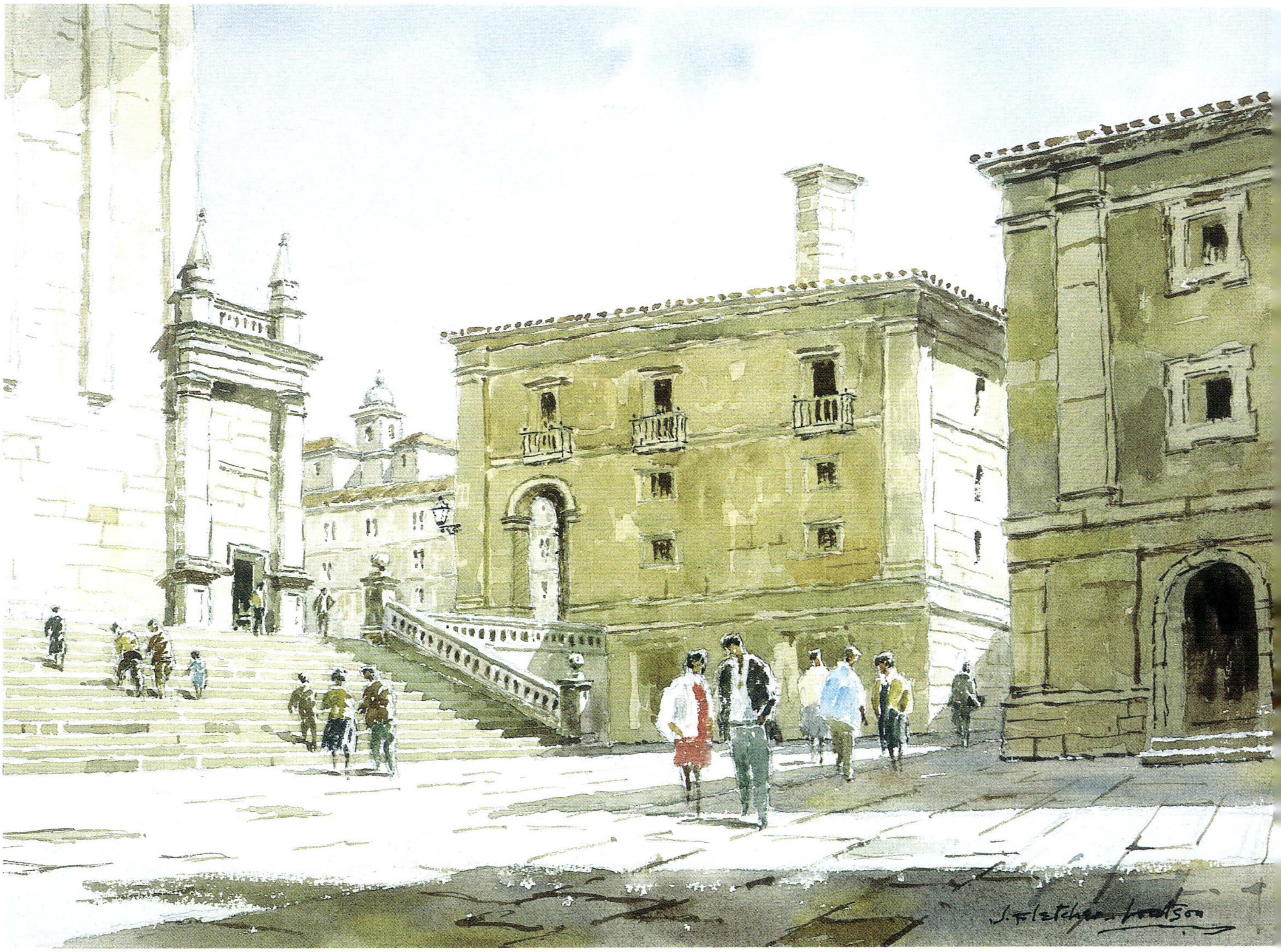

Figure 92
Santiago de Compostela, Spain.
318 × 476mm (12½ × 18¾in)

Figure 92, *Santiago de Compostela, Spain*, is a painting of a beautiful city, which we have already looked at in Chapter 6. The square shown here has a wonderful flight of steps leading up to the cathedral, and there were many people walking about when I painted this picture.

I am showing the picture purely to demonstrate the use of figures. The square varied from being quite crowded to having only a few people in it. I decided not to have too many and, after careful thought, placed them mostly walking within the square. The smaller groups of figures going up the steps were essential to break up the monotony of the lines of steps and to emphasize the distance in the scene. The two near figures in the foreground were important, giving colour and scale to the whole picture.

Tower Bridge, London (**figure 93**) is a very challenging subject and this is an example of how to simplify a very detailed architectural view. Many tall buildings were visible but, by keeping the painting of them fairly simple and concentrating on the bridge as the focal point, I was able to convey the impression of the City of London without painting individual buildings. Key buildings are recognizable, such as the Dome of St. Paul's Cathedral, but those to the west of the City, beyond the bridge, are painted in a very pale grey colour to suggest distance. The barges in the foreground are carefully positioned to balance with the central towers of the bridge.

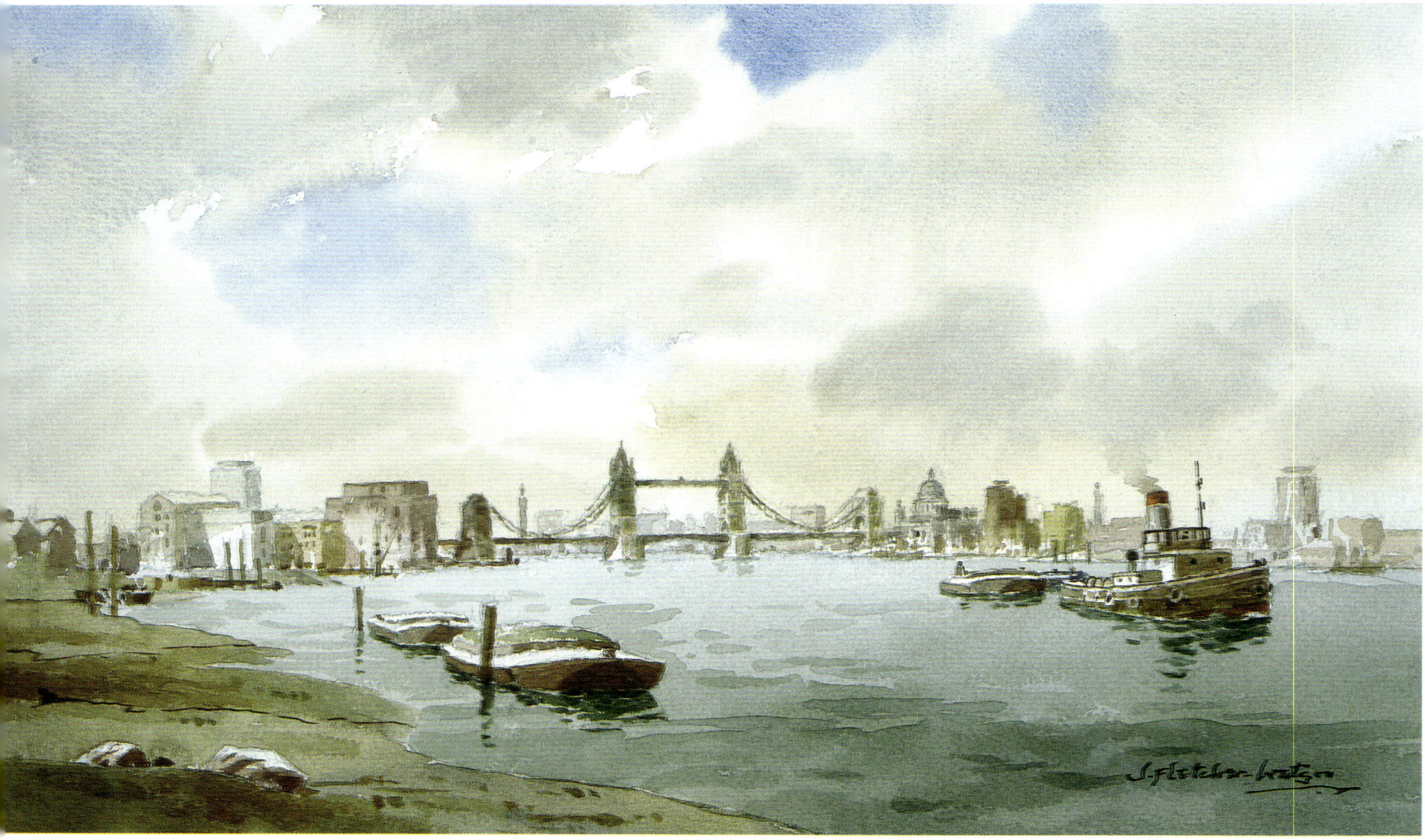

Figure 93
Tower Bridge, London.
318 × 476mm (12½ × 18¾in)

Figure 94, *Santa Maria della Salute, Venice,* is another picture of an ambitious subject, where figures and boats play a most important part. The buildings have been played down and treated in a fluid impressionistic way. The central arch feature is painted strongly with some detail, and the buildings at each side are painted with simplified brushwork. The centre gondola with the gondolier in the yellow shirt gives great scale to the whole scene, and as the other boats and figures recede into the background, getting smaller, they add perspective and depth to the picture as well as a nice sense of movement.

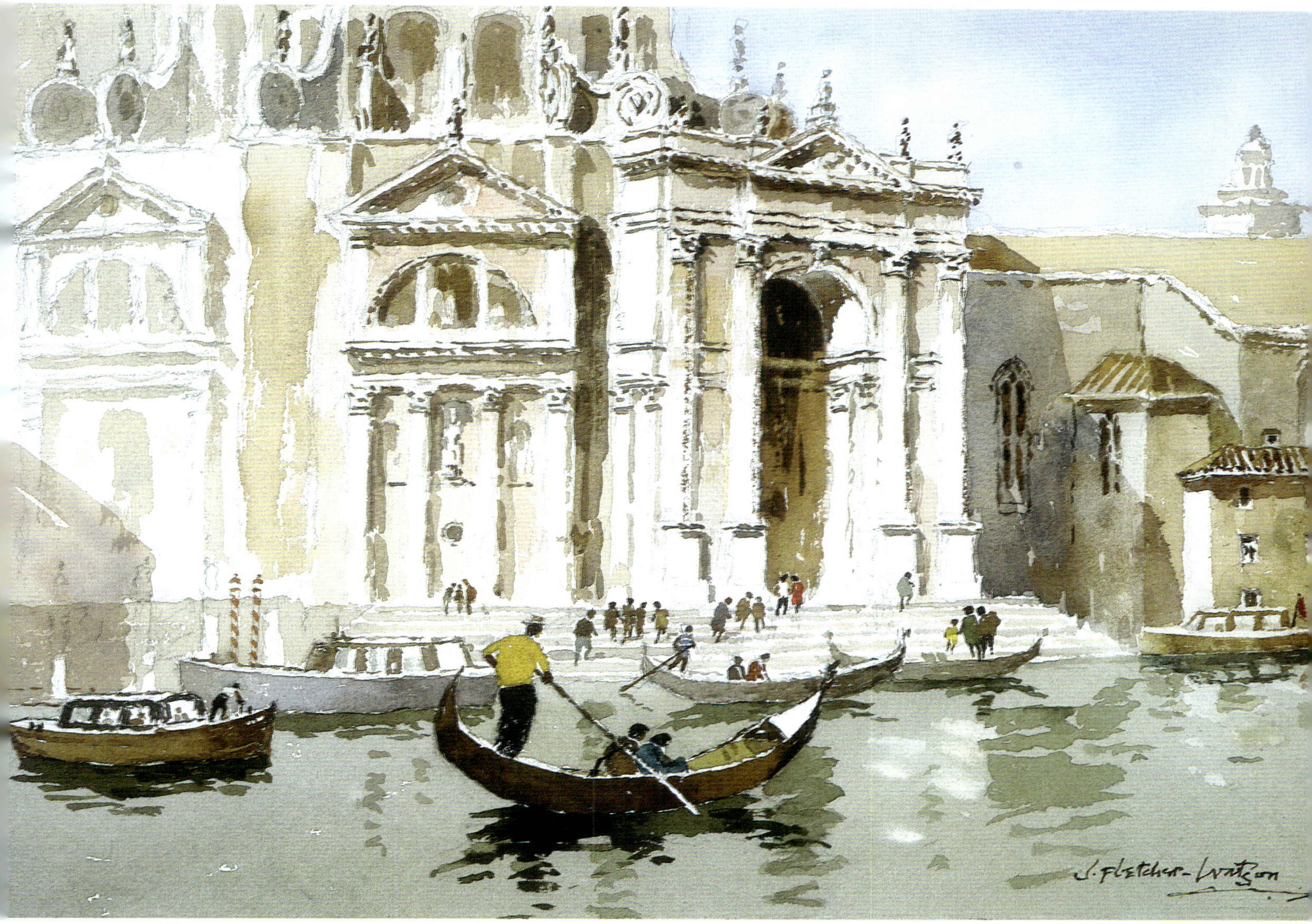

Figure 94
Santa Maria della Salute, Venice.
318 × 476mm (12½ × 18¾in)

Figure 96, *Burgos, Spain* (opposite), shows one more example of figures in a townscape. The far group is much smaller than the near group, which helps create distance and depth. Note that the heads of the figures in the far group are very slightly below the level of the heads of the near group. This is because I was sitting down. The heads of both groups would have been level if I had been standing.

With this picture, I used very few pencil guide lines and drew it almost entirely with the brush. You can see this clearly if you look at the stone paving and wall jointing. This method obviates fuss and the over-detailing of architectural subjects.

Figure 95
Sketchbook studies.

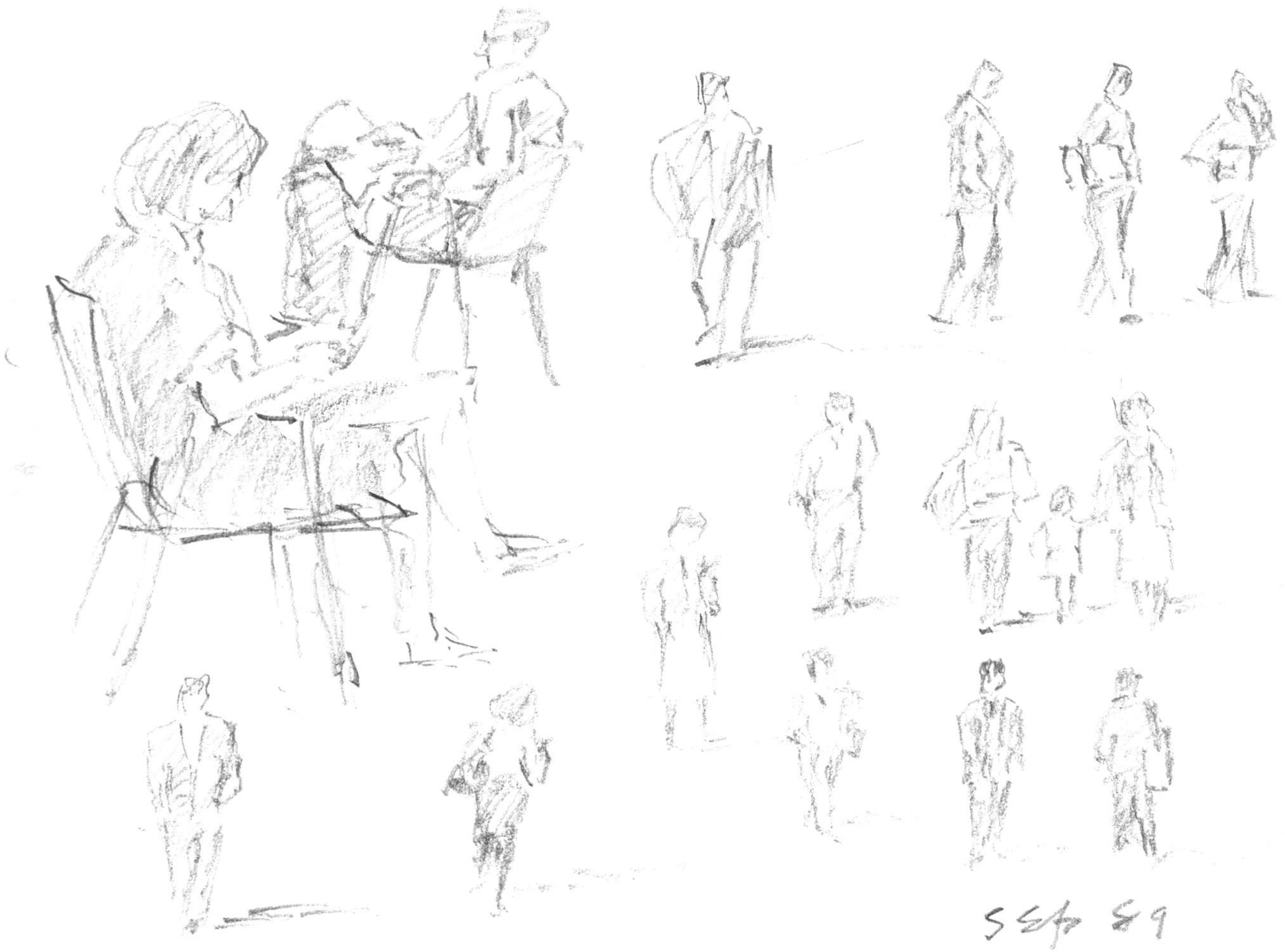

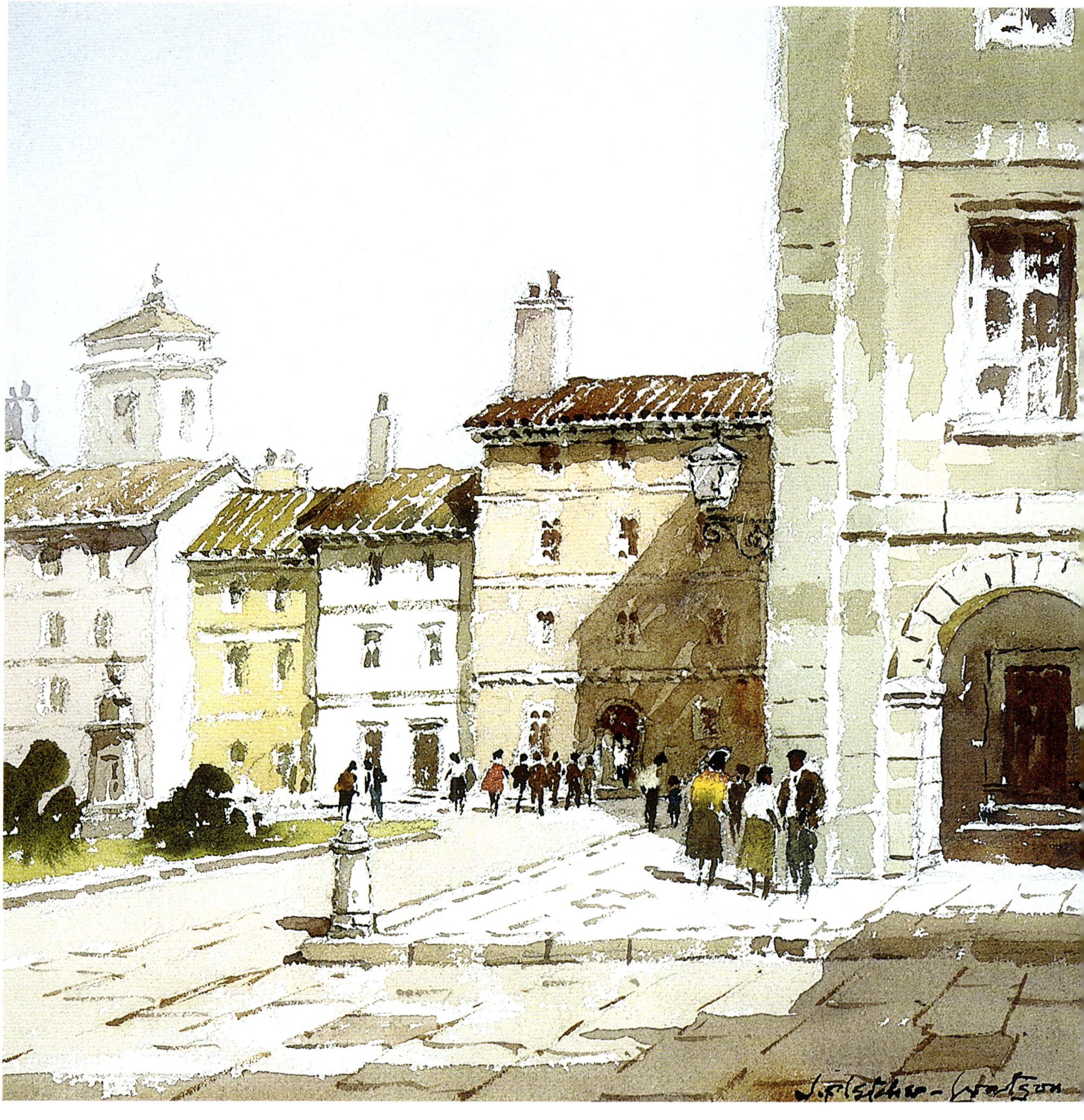

Figure 96
Burgos, Spain.
337 × 311mm (13¼ × 12¼in)

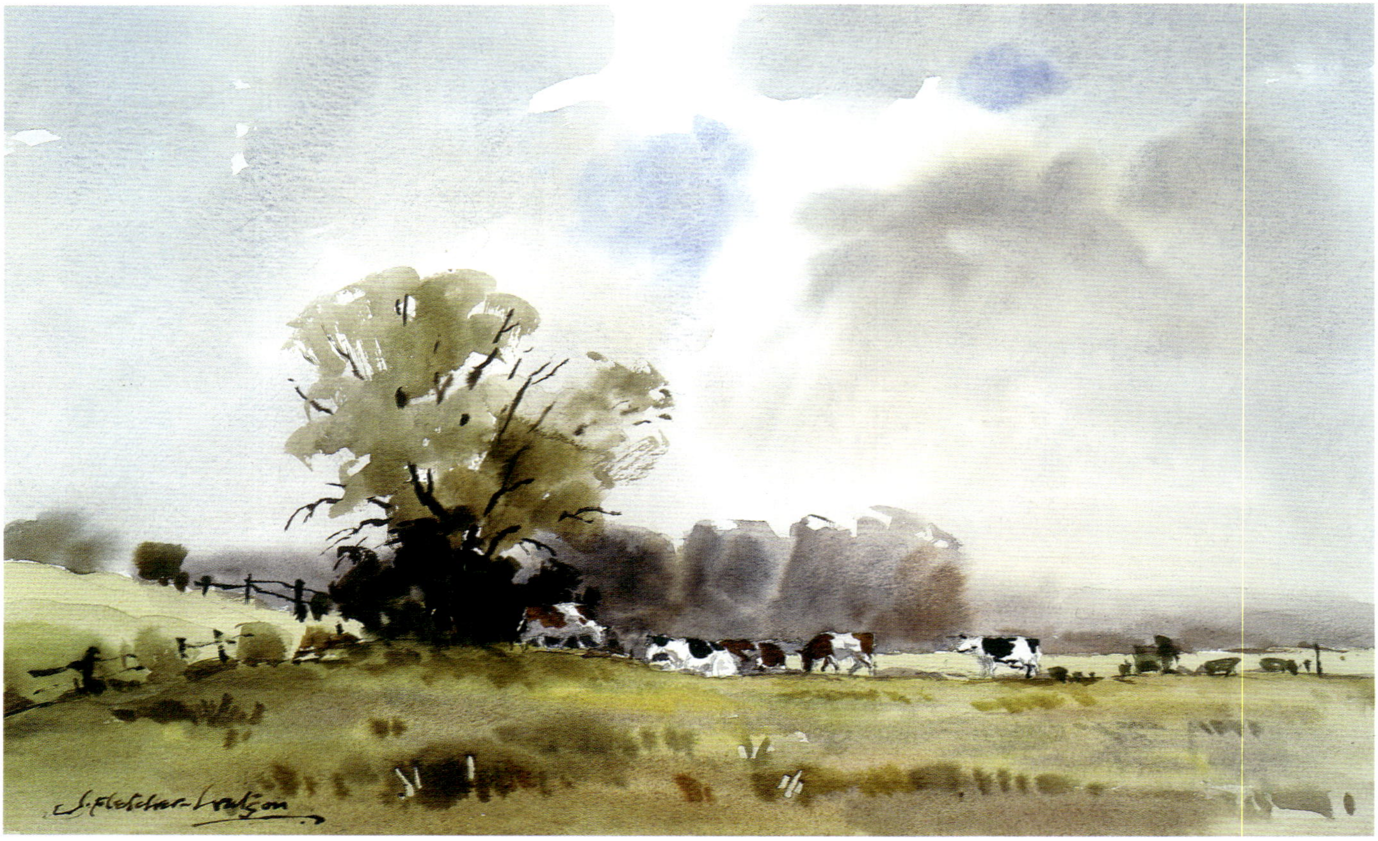

Figure 97
Cows on Windrush water meadows, England.
318 × 476mm (12½ × 18¾in)

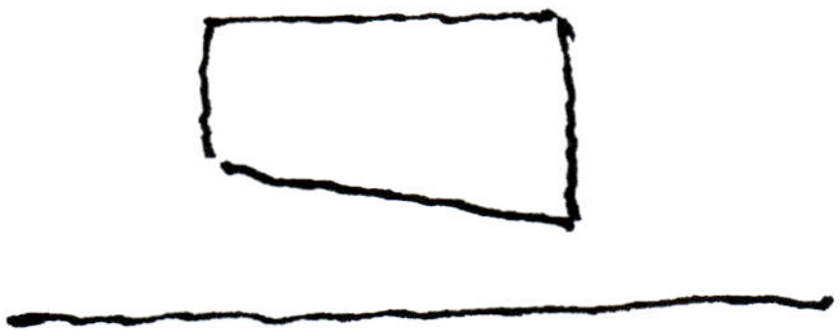

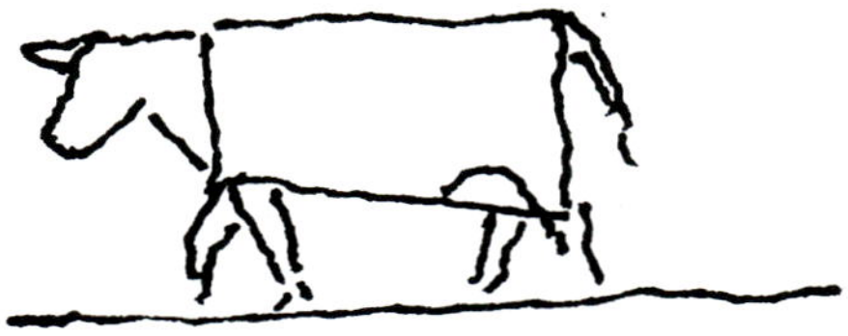

Figure 98a
Sketching cattle, stage one.

Figure 98b
Sketching cattle, stage two.

Figure 97, *Cows on Windrush water meadows*, shows a picture with rough foreground grass and trees. It makes a very pleasing subject, especially with an interesting sky. Cows are lovely animals to have in a country landscape. They are very angular beasts, as **figure 98** illustrates. To help you in drawing a cow, first draw a wedge-shaped rectangle (**A**), then simply add the head, legs and tail (**B**) to arrive at the basic shape. I rather like painting the breed shown in this painting, which has brown or black markings on white.

Walking down a narrow street in Florence, I turned through an arch and discovered the intriguing little courtyard shown in **figure 99**, *Small courtyard, Florence*. The figures were helpful in giving life and scale to the scene, but what really made it was the washing hanging out. There must be a wonderful understanding in Italy that you are allowed to use your neighbour's window for your washing line!

In this very small picture I left the washing till last and then put it in using white paint. It certainly gave a nice domestic touch, standing out from the rather large dark shadow that falls across the left-hand side.

Figure 99
Small courtyard, Florence, Italy.
127 × 165mm (5 × 6½in)

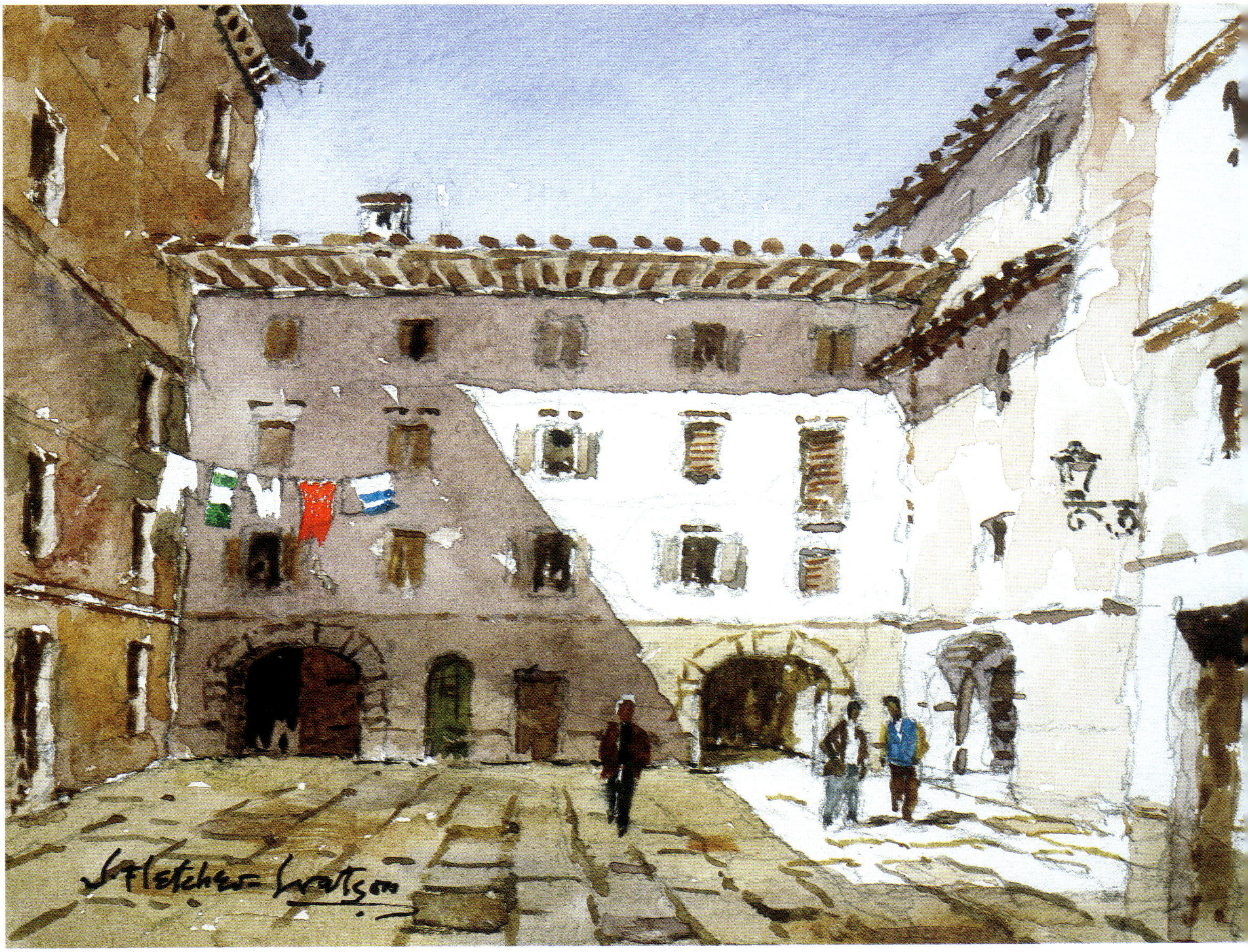

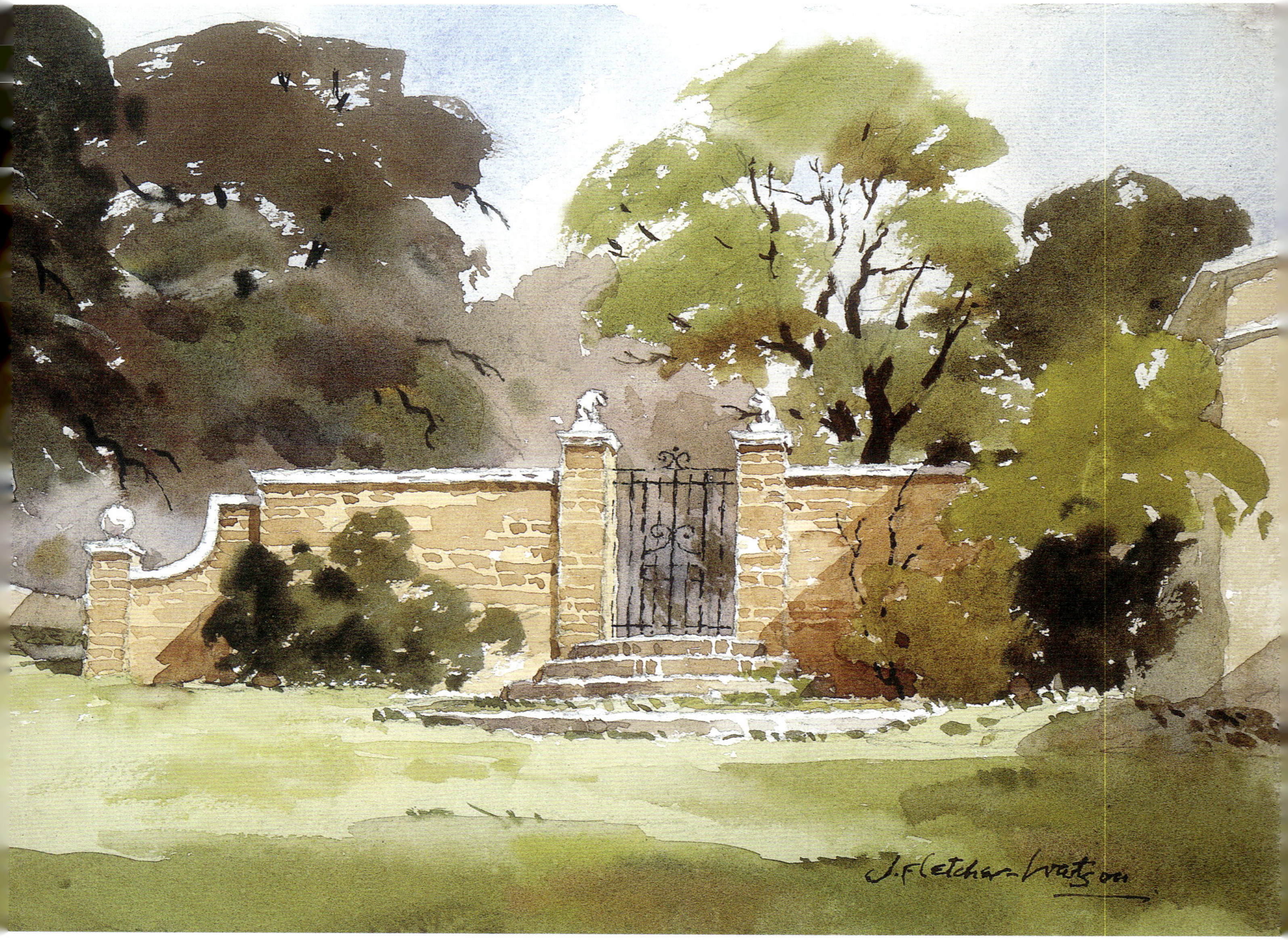

Figure 100
Architectural detail in a Suffolk garden, England.
248 × 368mm (9¾ × 14½in)

Figure 100 was done as a demonstration for a group of painters. It shows what delightful subjects gardens can be, especially when there is an architectural feature playing a prominent part.

The brick wall had turned a lovely mellow colour with age, and the wrought-iron gate and piers with stone finials made a splendid focal point. The tree groups behind the wall formed a beautiful backdrop of lovely autumnal colours. The copper beech to the left of centre greatly enriched the general colour scheme.

I was using a Saunders Waterford paper 250lb NOT surface. The order of painting was as follows.

1 The cloudy sky was washed in with Cobalt Blue and a little Burnt Umber added for the areas of grey cloud. I carried this wash over all the trees, down to the wall and into the gate area and allowed it to dry completely.

2 I then felt I wanted to get the brick wall painted, so that I could gauge the tonal strength of the tree background against it, which threw it into the sunlight. So I mixed Burnt Sienna with a touch of Cobalt Blue and applied it to all of the wall areas. When dry, I went over the walls with a second coat of a darker hue of the same mixture, indicating the brick jointing and the texture. The curved steps were also painted using some Burnt Umber added to the brick mixture, as they were a slightly darker brick colour.

3 I then moved on to the mown grass area of the foreground using Raw Sienna and not too much Winsor Blue. This wash completed, I left it to dry and laid the shadows on much later. By this stage I had eliminated all the white paper areas and could safely decide how dark a tone to make the trees in the background in relation to the rest of the picture – a very important matter.

The central grey tree area in the distance was dropped in after slightly damping the paper with clear water to give a distant blurred effect to these trees. I mixed Cobalt Blue and Light Red for this. Next I used Cobalt Blue and Raw Umber for the shapely tree to the right of centre and sketched in the trunk and branches with a small brush with a Burnt Umber and French Ultramarine mixture. Then the copper beech was painted to the left of centre using Cadmium Yellow, Winsor Blue and Indian Red, giving a dark reddish-green colour. Finally the left-hand tree was put in with Cadmium Yellow, Winsor Blue and Burnt Umber, making sure the result was a dark green. All these tree mixtures were painted quickly with a No. 8 brush and were allowed to run into each other slightly.

4 The distant wall on the left was next dealt with using Cobalt Blue and Light Red, and then I was ready to paint the various shrubs against the wall. The colour mixtures were mainly Raw Sienna and French Ultramarine, but for the very dark places I dropped in Payne's Gray to give real strength and punch.

5 The foreground shadows were washed across the grass with the same original mixture of Raw Sienna and Winsor Blue, adding a little Burnt Umber. The shadows were cast by trees just out of the picture to the right.

6 Finally the slanting shadows on the brick wall cast by the shrubs (which bring the whole picture to life) were painted with a stronger mix of the original brick colour and this was followed by the shadow lines under the stone copings. The iron gate was drawn in with a black pen, using an Edding 1800 with a 0.7 nib, which was ideal for the job.

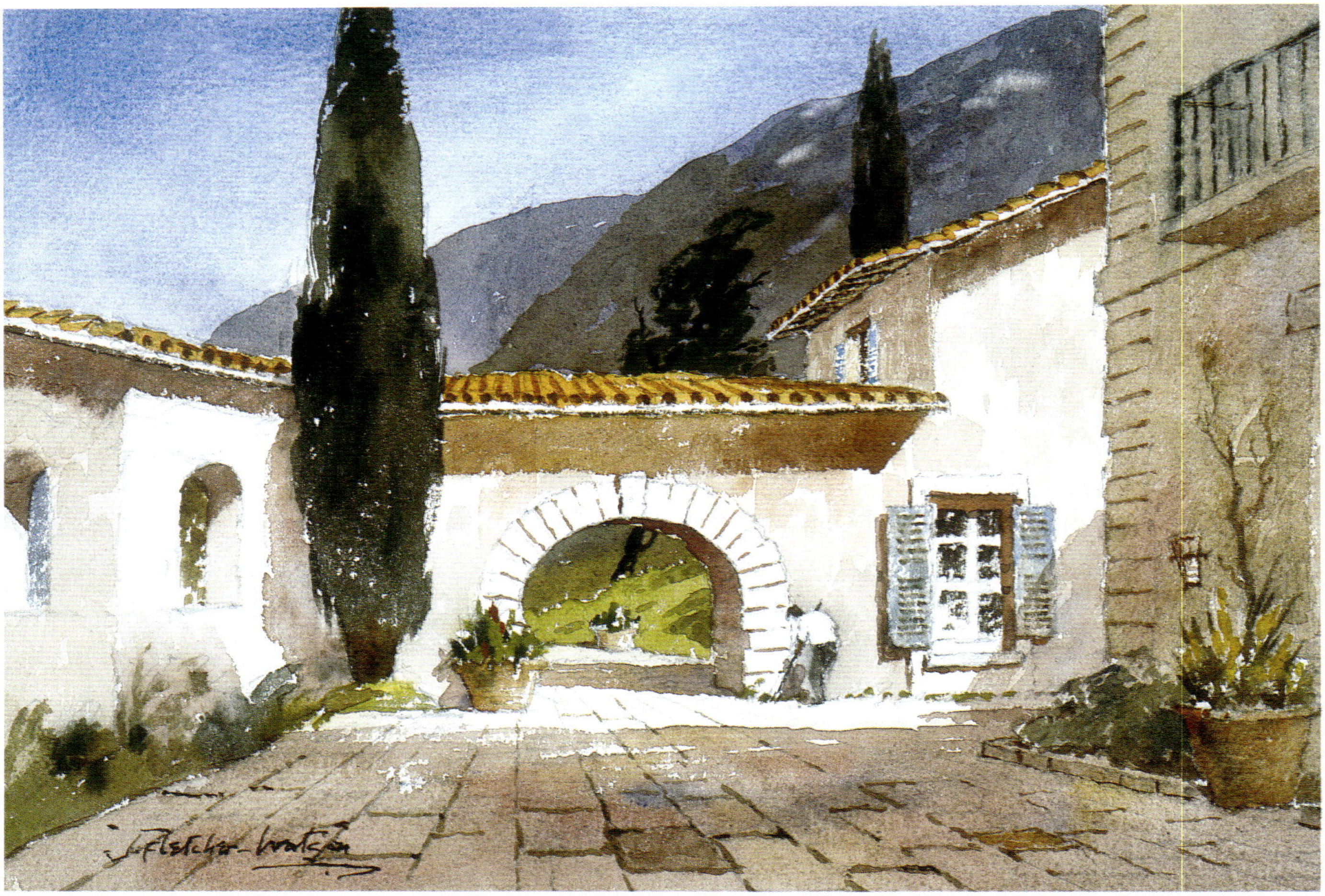

Figure 101
Spanish Courtyard.
248 × 368mm (9¾ × 14½in)

I have chosen this simple subject of a *Spanish Courtyard* in **figure 101** to demonstrate the effective use of detail within a simple subject. The terracotta pots, the small Mediterranean-style windows set deep into the walls, the vertical cypress trees, and the figure sweeping, all combine to make a pleasing composition.

Figure 102 is an example of the importance of technique. It is loosely painted, drawn mainly with the brush and hardly any pencilwork. This picture also demonstrates the skills used for water reflections, boats and figures. Thus it has gained in quality and impressionism, and the loose treatment of the architectural detail gives a nice feel to the work.

The water reflections of boats and buildings are quite dark in tone, and this is a point you should watch out for.

Several figures are necessary in most town subjects as they give the required life and scale to the buildings. There are good reasons therefore forstudying and improving your figure drawing, especially in relation to moving figures.

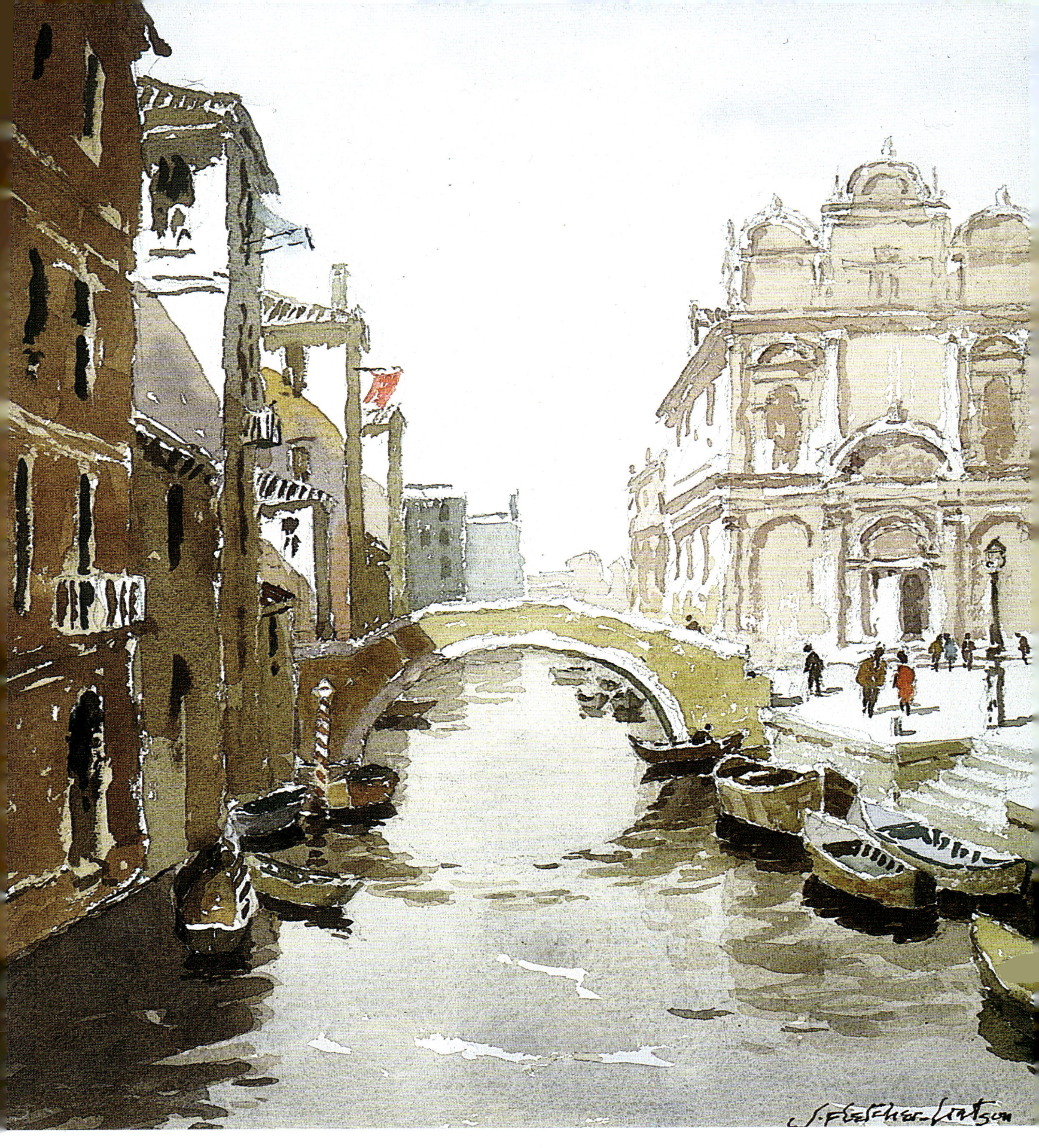

Figure 102
Rio dei Mendicanti, Venice.
365 × 311mm (14¼ × 12¼in)

Florence abounds in attractive little side streets and the one seen in **figure 103**, *Side street, Florence*, led into a small square, in which I could sit to get this excellent view. I took some small liberties with certain details to enhance the overall effect of the picture.

The sunblind on the left was not actually there. Instead, there was a café with a big umbrella and chairs and tables. However, I decided to include a sunblind because I felt it made a better picture. The big tower above the white house was in actual fact further to the left and almost merged with the foreground houses. Placing it in isolation like this improved the composition. The flag mast, sticking out on the right-hand building, was there but without a flag. I decided to add a dull red flag, blowing lightly in the breeze, which gave the picture a useful touch of colour as well as a sense of movement. Finally, the white house in the centre with green shutters was in reality a strong orange colour, which did not at all suit my preferred colour scheme, so this, too, was changed accordingly.

These are examples of quite legitimate artist's licence, but I do not often alter a scene as much as this. I only mention it to help you with your own painting work in towns. Remember that Turner was noted for altering views to suit his mood!

The picture is an excellent example of street perspective, showing buildings getting smaller in the distance and the slanting of lines of footpaths, roof eaves, and windows, which all help to convey the depth of the subject. Moving figures help enormously, becoming smaller as they get further away and giving life and colour. The cloud shadow over the tower also gives a sense of recession.

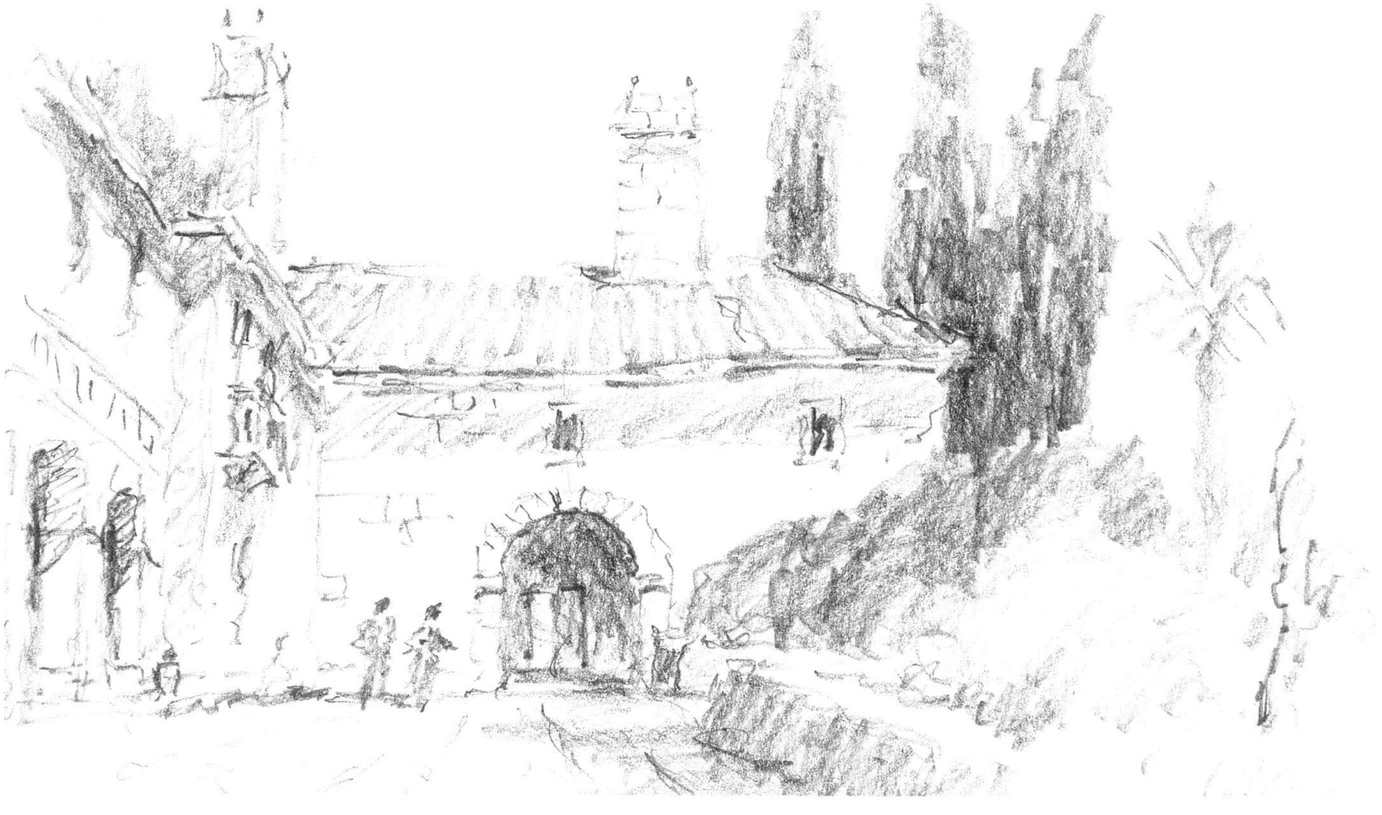

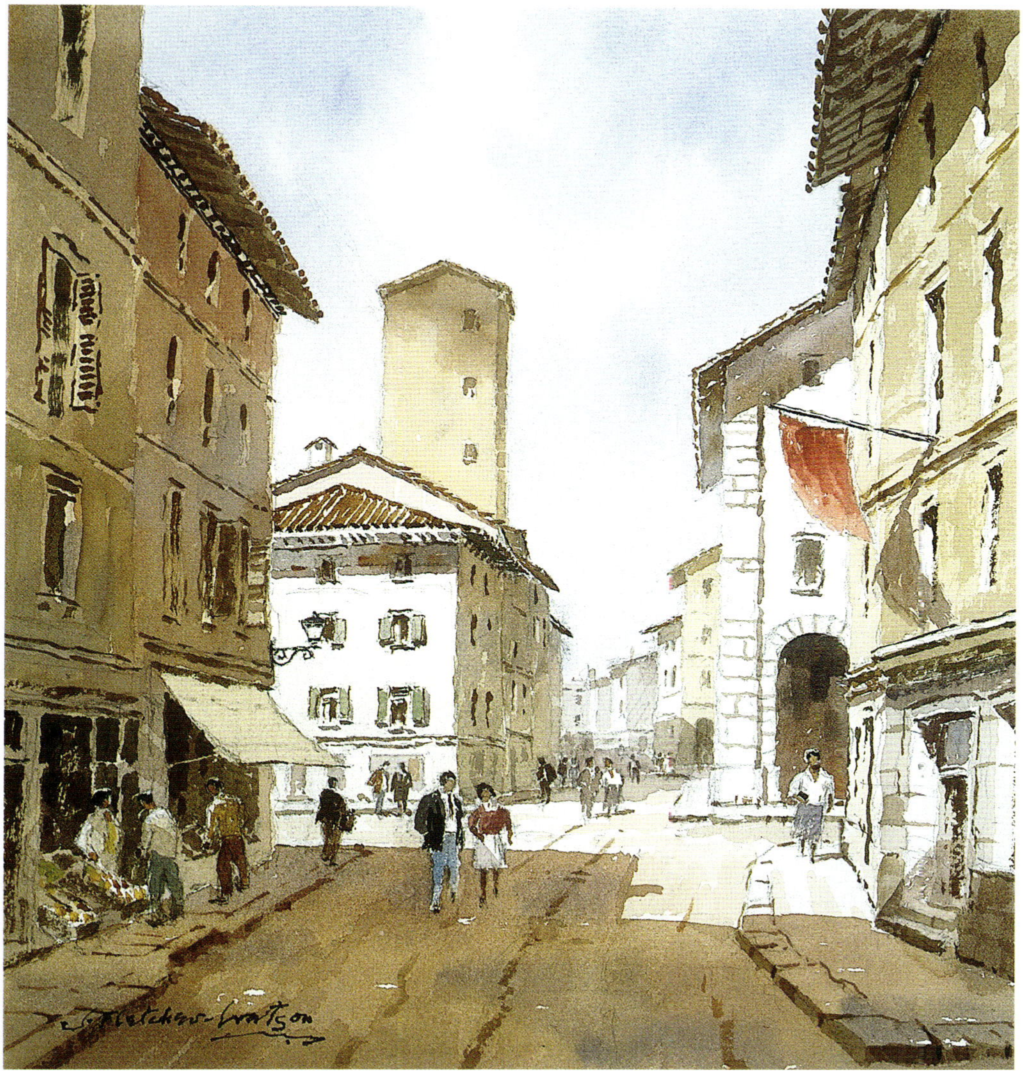

Figure 103
Side street, Florence, Italy.
343 × 317mm
(13¼ × 12¼in)

TIPS AND TECHNIQUES

- Look for special details that might give an otherwise ordinary scene a magic quality
- It is very useful to have had experience of life drawing when incorporating figures in any composition. You can also practise by keeping a sketchbook for making quick studies of people
- Plan carefully how you want to incorporate figures into a picture and don't be afraid to embellish or alter the balance of figures that you actually observe to improve the overall effect of the composition
- Be careful to keep the perspective in the graduated sizes of figures as you move into the picture
- Within reason, you can take liberties with certain details to enhance the overall effect of a picture

CONCLUSION

This book has covered a wide range of landscape subjects and I hope I have managed to be of help to many painters. I have included various types of architecture as well as a good mixture of pure landscapes such as farmland with trees, hedges, rivers, mountains and lakes. When you have mastered the techniques required for the individual features, you can begin to paint in an impressionistic manner, so that your pictures take on a magical, even mysterious, quality that the camera cannot capture.

This is the real secret of watercolour landscape painting. The key is to make a harmonious whole of your picture, subduing some areas and bringing others into prominence. It is just as important to know when to make small adjustments to the general pattern of light and shade where necessary. You will then have the confidence to produce watercolours of real quality.

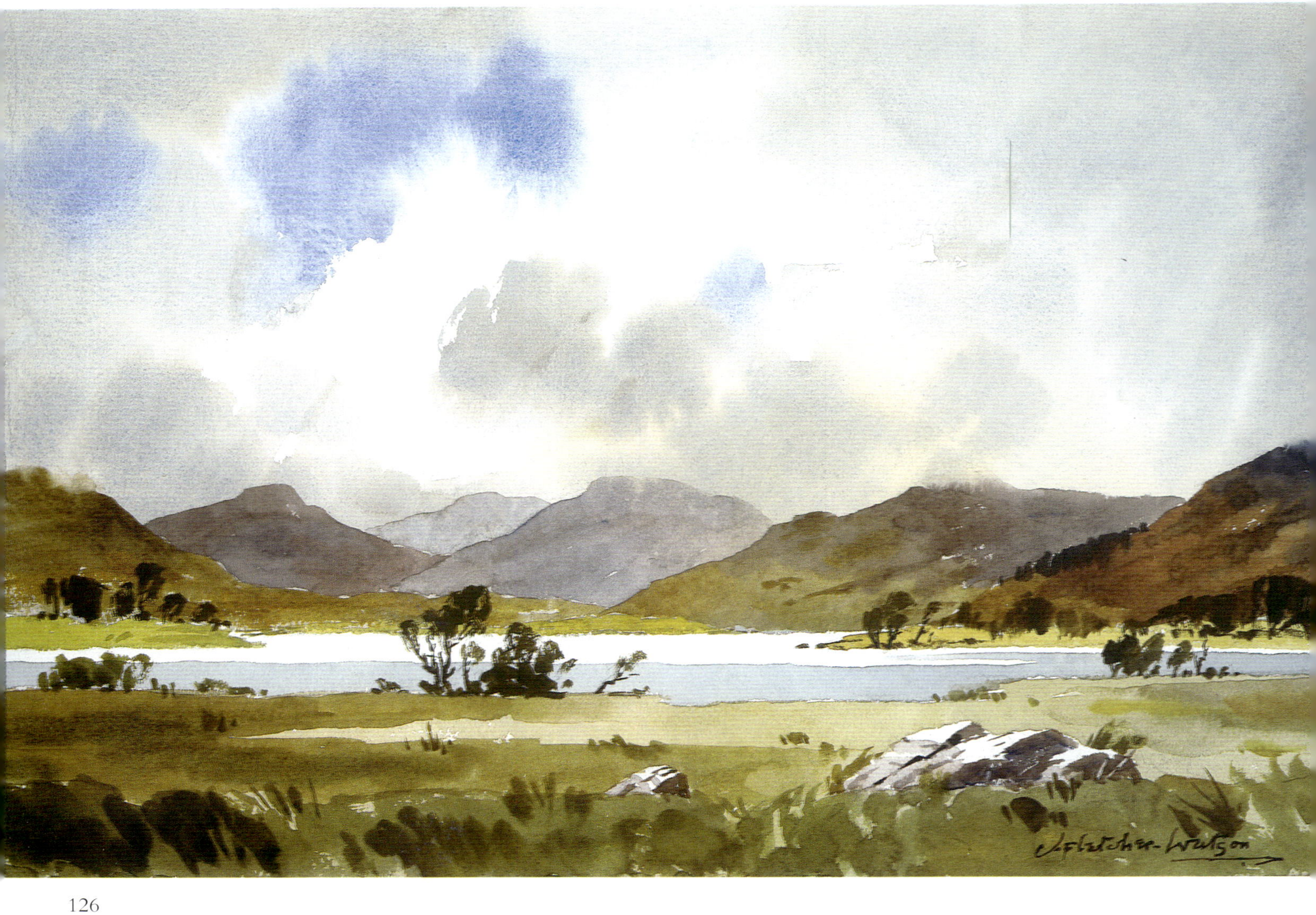

Watercolour Painting Videos

Three sixty-minute videos are available, *Outdoor Painting*, *The Magic of Watercolour* and *Painting from Sketches,* in which James Fletcher-Watson can be seen painting a range of landscape scenes. Produced by APV films, the videos are priced at £26 each, including postage from Country Heritage at the address below.

Soldier Artist in Wartime India is a fascinating account of James Fletcher-Watson's wartime experience with the Royal Engineers. This beautifully-produced hardback book is illustrated throughout with full-colour watercolours, painted by the artist between 1941 and 1945, from all over India and Burma. This book is available from Country Heritage, priced £19.95, plus £2 towards postage.

Country Heritage
Windrush House
Windrush
Near Burford
Oxon OX18 4TU

Tel. 01451 844425

INDEX